Centre for Sri Aurobindo Studies Publication

Understanding Thoughts of Sri Aurobindo

Centre for Sri Aurobindo Studies Publication

Understanding Thoughts of Sri Aurobindo

Edited by
Indrani Sanyal
Krishna Roy

PRINTWORLD
Publishers of Indian Traditions

in Association with

Jadavpur University
Kolkata

Cataloging in Publication Data — DK

[Courtesy: D.K. Agencies (P) Ltd. <docinfo@dkagencies.com>]

Understanding thoughts of Sri Aurobindo / edited by Indrani Sanyal, Krishna Roy.

pages cm. – (Centre for Sri Aurobindo Studies publication)

Includes passages in Sanskrit (roman).

Reprint. Originally published: 2007.

Papers presented in two seminars organized by Centre for Sri Aurobindo Studies, during 2004 and 2005, held at Kolkata, India; on the philosophy and thoughts of Aurobindo Ghose, 1872-1950, philosopher and writer from India.

Includes bibliographical references and index.

ISBN 9788124604021 (HB)

1. Ghose, Aurobindo, 1872-1950 – Congresses. 2. Philosophy, Indic – Congresses. I. Sanyal, Indrani, editor. II. Roy, Krishna, editor. III. Jadavpur University. Centre for Sri Aurobindo Studies, organizer. IV. Title: Sri Aurobindo. V. Series: Centre for Sri Aurobindo Studies publication.

LCC B5134.G424U53 2025 | DDC 181.4 23

ISBN 978-81-246-0402-1

First published in India in 2007

Second impression published in 2025

Editors: Indrani Sanyal (b.1950), Krishna Roy (b.1941)

Published by:

D.K. Printworld (P) Ltd.

Regd. Office: "Vedaśrī", F-395, Sudarshan Park

ESI Hospital Metro Station, New Delhi - 110015

Phones: (011) 4172 2626, 98713 94815

e-mail: indology@dkprintworld.com

Website: www.dkprintworld.com

in collaboration with

Jadavpur University

Kolkata (West Bengal)

Printed by: D.K. Printworld (P) Ltd., New Delhi

Contents

III. On Education

IV. On Poetry and Art

V. On Man and Relation

VI. On State and Politics

VII. On Yoga and Psychology

VIII. Sri Aurobindo — A Century in Perspective

Key to Transliteration

VOWELS

अ *a*	आ *ā*	इ *i*	ई *ī*	उ *u*	ऊ *ū*
(but)	(palm)	(it)	(beet)	(put)	(pool)
ऋ *ṛ*	ए *e*	ऐ *ai*	ओ *o*	औ *au*	
(rhythm)	(play)	(air)	(toe)	(loud)	

CONSONANTS

Guttural	क *ka*	ख* *kha*	ग *ga*	घ *gha*	ङ *ṅa*
	(skate)	(blockhead)	(gate)	(ghost)	(sing)
Palatal	च *ca*	छ* *cha*	ज *ja*	झ *jha*	ञ *ña*
	(chunk)	(catch him)	(john)	(hedgehog)	(bunch)
Cerebral	ट *ṭa*	ठ* *ṭha*	ड *ḍa*	ढ* *ḍha*	ण* *ṇa*
	(start)	(anthill)	(dart)	(godhead)	(under)
Dental	त *ta*	थ *tha*	द *da*	ध* *dha*	न *na*
	(path)	(thunder)	(that)	(breathe)	(numb)
Labial	प *pa*	फ* *pha*	ब *ba*	भ *bha*	म *ma*
	(spin)	(philosophy)	(bin)	(abhor)	(much)
Semi-	य *ya*	र *ra*	ल *la*	व *va*	
vowels	(young)	(drama)	(luck)	(vile)	
Sibilants	श *śa*	ष *ṣa*	स *sa*	ह *ha*	
	(shove)	(bushel)	(so)	(hum)	
Others	क्ष *kṣa*	त्र *tra*	ज्ञ *jña*	ळ* ḷ	ॠ* *ṝ*
	(*kṣatriya*)	(*triśūla*)	(*jñānī*)	(*play*)	

अं (ं) *ṁ anusvāra* (nasalisation of preceding vowel) like *saṁskṛti*

अः *visarga* = *ḥ* (aspiration of preceding vowel) like (*prātaḥ*)

ऽ *Avagraha* consonant #'consonant (like:- *ime 'vasthitā*)

Anusvāra at the end of a line is presented by m (म्) and not ṁ

* No exact English equivalents for these letters.

Introduction

In the present anthology entitled *Understanding Thoughts of Sri Aurobindo* an attempt is being made to explore some of the facets of Sri Aurobindo's multi-dimensional thougths. Within the canvas of one anthology, it is not possible to deliberate on all the diverse ideas and activities of Sri Aurobindo, who is being revered as a patriot, nationalist, poet, social reformer, educationist, historian, litterateur, visionary, *yogī* and philosopher. Sri Aurobindo was a philosopher *par excellence* though he may not be considered to be a philosopher in the professional sense of the term. Sri Aurobindo was not an academic philosopher but in the deeper and broader sense of the term "philosophy," Sri Aurobindo was truly a lover of wisdom and visionary of truth — *satyadraṣṭā*. He was thoroughly conversant with the philosophical developments of the East and the West and has bequeathed to us a unique metaphysical theory. In his *magnum opus*, *The Life Divine*, we find a synthesis of idealism and materialism, a new theory of integrated reality, a perceptive account of the evolution of the world, and an imaginative vision about the future progress of mankind. In his voluminous writings we get analytic evaluation of the past and the then present conceptions as well as synthetic integration of all that are fruitful and significant. He gave us interpretative accounts of the messages contained in the Vedas, the Upaniṣads, and the *Bhagavad-Gītā*. Sri Aurobindo was fully conversant with all the Indian and Western philosophical systems and wanted to incorporate in his thought process all those ideas, which he considered fruitful and are in conformity with his own distinctive *Weltanschauung*.

It is not that Sri Aurobindo's only concern was with that which is supramental and supramundane. He was equally concerned with the issues related with our practical lives. Hence he discussed the development of society, role of the state-system, need for having proper education system and such others. He was interested in literature, poetry, art, language and many other related issues.

In general, Sri Aurobindo has given us an integral philosophy of human nature, the basic principle of which is to emphasize that being full of possibilities, man has an innate tendency towards self-exceeding. It is inherent in all human nature to exceed himself by conscious evolution and by conscious *yoga* to something supramental and suprahuman. Having discussed the multiple dimensions of life and culture, Sri Aurobindo's primary objective was to transform the present life and society into a divine life and divinized society. Thus, in his integral philosophy of man Sri Aurobindo integrates not only the East and the West, tradition with modernity, materialism and idealism, but also theory and practice, practical lived world with spirituality.

The authors, who have contributed to this present anthology, *Understanding Thoughts of Sri Aurobindo,* have thrown light on some of these major areas discussed by Sri Aurobindo. The first section of this volume on philosophy, begins with articles by Kireet Joshi entitled "Philosophy of Sri Aurobindo" and by Umesh Chandra Dubey entitled "Integralism: The Distinctive Feature of Sri Aurobindo's Philosophy." Kireet Joshi engages himself in delineating the basic features of Sri Aurobindo's thoughts. He holds that in his major work, *The Life Divine,* Sri Aurobindo has built an edifice of philosophical thought, which has provided a rational assurance of the inevitability of the divine life on earth. In *The Synthesis of Yoga* he has given a scientific analysis of the various levels of consciousness. Joshi holds that Sri Aurobindo's views on integral consciousness is the foundation of his integral philosophy and this conception of cosmic consciousness is gradually being accepted by modern psychologists.

U.C. Dubey discusses the Integral Advaitism of Sri Aurobindo, wherein it is maintained that the *Brahman* or the Absolute is one, without denying the reality of the world, for he regards the creative force as conscious in nature. In Sri Aurobindo's view the *prakṛti* or unconscious force is an extension of the Absolute or consciousness. The absolute in its transcendent state is *Saccidānanda* and it is supermind in space and time. Sri Aurobindo does not deny the reality of any aspect of existence and that is the secret of regarding his position as Integral Advaitism. Thus the absolute is conceived to be both being as well as becoming and at the same time as transcending both. Dubey gives an account of the reconciliation as achieved by Sri Aurobindo on the conflict between one and many, silence and dynamic, infinite and finite in the all-embracing Absolute by reference to a higher reason. He traces back Sri Aurobindo's Integralism to the logic of the Infinite. In this respect our attention is drawn to the failure of the finite reason and finite logic in grasping the real nature of the Absolute.

The second section of the volume is on evolution and contains four important articles on the theme. Krishna Roy in her article entitled "Sri Aurobindo on Heraclitus: A Hermeneutic Overview" makes an attempt to trace a plausible source of Sri Aurobindo's theory of evolution and thinks that Sri Aurobindo's hermeneutics of Heraclitus, along with some other Eastern and Western influences, may give us some clues. The Heraclitian dictum, "One out of all and all out of one" seems to be the anticipation of the processes of involution and evolution, whereas, the second Heraclitian principle, "All things becoming according to strife" as bringing forth harmony out of strife, are the two notions that have been gradually elaborated and enriched in Sri Aurobindo's theory of involution and evolution.

"Theories of Evolution and Sri Aurobindo" by Kireet Joshi covers the following three themes:

(1) Darwin and other proponents of evolutionary theories,

(2) The evolution in connection with the *yoga* and the future of evolution, and

(3) Sri Aurobindo's yogic experiments in relation to evolution.

In this article Kireet Joshi has compared and contrasted the concept of evolution, the pivotal concept in Sri Aurobindo's philosophy with other theories of evolution, particularly those derived from the work of Erasmus Darwin, Lamarck, Charles Darwin and his followers. Joshi draws our attention to two worth-noticing features of Charles Darwin's theory of evolution as expounded in *The Origin of Species*: (1) that evolution is gradual and (2) that the nature of change is dictated by the natural laws and not by divine selection. Hence in the Darwinian scheme the possibility of one species jumping to another species in the process of evolution is forbidden. But Joshi feels that there is a deeper question as to why do variations occur among species and Darwin's answer that it is a mere chance is actually an expression of his inability to answer that question. He refers, in this connection, to Bergson's notion of *elan vital*, Alexander's notion of nisus or thirst of the universe for higher levels. Sri Aurobindo's notion of evolution is essentially spiritual and with this elaboration he opens up the debate between the chance theory of evolution and the teleological theory of evolution.

In his article on "Sri Aurobindo's Doctrine of Evolution" Arabinda Basu gives an overview of the theory. Contrary to Darwin's naturalistic theory he shows how Sri Aurobindo's theory is influenced by the Vedāntic conception of consciousness, which is not only self-luminous but also power. The world is the self-manifestation of this consciousness power. Basu discusses the two levels of evolution: the outer and the inner. The outer evolution is that of physical, vital and mental nature whereas the inner is more psychic and spiritual. He further holds that in Sri Aurobindo's metaphysical concept of man he has as his true self in the world, what the mystic philosophers call the psychic being. He shows how the supramentalization will follow spiritualization of mind, life and matter, consequently, bringing about their intended perfection.

In "Sri Aurobindo's Integral Approach to the Concept of Evolution," Dilip Kumar Roy elaborates the different nuances of the theory. He argues that Sri Aurobindo's claim to bring about the divine life on earth is not Utopian, but is the outcome of his yogic realization. He thinks that Sri Aurobindo's integral approach to the evolution of nature includes two other concepts of reality and supermind and as such Roy discusses Sri Aurobindo's view on all these three concepts at some length.

The next section is on education which is one of the very important areas where we have application of Sri Aurobindo's metaphysical ideas. Indrani Sanyal begins with a frequently asked questions as to what it is to be educated and tries to provide a reply to the question from the point of view of Sri Aurobindo in her article "What It Is to Be Educated? : In the light of Sri Aurobindo's Philosophy." From the age of seven Sri Aurobindo was nurtured and brought up in the British system of education and he was in and out familiar with the European model of education, especially the British model. But his views on education bear the stamp of being predominantly Indian in its perspective. Sanyal draws our attention to the fact that education always occupied a very important place in India and it was never equated with learning anything by rote. She observes that in general a spiritualistic turn in the conception of education is found in the writings of Sri Aurobindo and some of his contemporary thinkers. Sri

Aurobindo was very much critical of the type of education that was provided to the students. He characterizes Indian University education under the colonial rule as "smattering of facts in each department of knowledge" and that led to degradation. Man according to Sri Aurobindo is a developing being and education is accordingly a developing process. Sanyal discusses some fundamental mistakes in educating as has been pointed out by Sri Aurobindo. Over-emphasis on memory, neglect of the power of reasoning, the power of expression, neglect of the subject as an active, organic being, insensitiveness about the type of mind that is receiving education are among major deficiencies to be rectified as quickly as possible. According to Sri Aurobindo any education to be regarded as complete must aim at developing five main types of human activities like the physical, the vital, the mental, the psychic and the spiritual. All these aspects of Sri Aurobindo's vision have been elaborately analysed to establish that for Sri Aurobindo true education is finally for transformation of the being in its entirety.

The theme of education comes once again in the paper by Priya M. Vaidya entitled, "Relevance of Sri Aurobindo's Thoughts on Education to Teacher Educators." In this article the author seeks to establish a Holistic Educational Learning Programme (HELP) for teacher educators based on Sri Aurobindo's thoughts on education. Sri Aurobindo's thoughts on education may help the teacher educators to understand the importance of the mind, the sense organs, the intellect, the essence of moral nature in man and realize the spiritual aspect of the body. Vaidya observes that if the Divine in man is realized with the help of education then our educational institutions may become really temples of knowledge. This would enable a man to transform and a society to develop as a whole. Sri Aurobindo's thoughts on education, as Vaidya optimistically points out, may help and guide us to accomplish this goal.

Reshmi Sethi in her paper, "Education: A Faithful Transcription" begins by pointing out the perils of "separative existence" and instead of it, she draws our attention to integralism and its merit. Integralism opposes separatism and regards it to be unreal. Integral education, as she discusses, restores the lost delight of man; and it can become a faithful transcription, as she explains, by enabling the individual to identify with itself and to translate this identity into his activities. She also discusses about the role of *yoga* and also about the adoption of the yogic method in the domain of education.

The fourth section of the anthology is on poetry and art. Like a poetic artist, Sri Aurobindo had woven in an ingenious, heart-rending style a literary edifice with a rhythmic cast. However, Sri Aurobindo was more than a poetic artist for poetry was a channel for him to transcend the domain of poetry to the beyond. The author Pabitrakumar Roy in his article, "The Word That Knows: Sri Aurobindo's Metaphysics of Poetry" seeks to situate Sri Aurobindo's concept of poetry as *mantra* in the light of Sri Aurobindo's hermeneutics of the Vedic language and some dominant trends in philosophy of language in India. Poetry is an instrument of evolution upsurge, it raises itself to a power beyond itself, moving towards an intimate self-experience, deepening into a greater subjectivity. The evolution of consciousness is an adventure for man, the mental being, and in his ascent to newer heights of consciousness, man creates newer modes of expression. There is a long tradition which connects consciousness with language and Roy believes that Sri Aurobindo inherits this tradition. Sri Aurobindo celebrates *paśyantī vāk* as the paradigm discourse and refers to it as the tantic view of language. On the ascending movement from the *vaikharī* to the *paśyantī* the poetry of the future is possible. The author goes on stating that the concept of *paśyantī vāk* implies that the poet is a seer; seerhood is the goal towards which poetry, going beyond the categories of the intellect, is on the move. Roy explains after Sri Aurobindo that if the evolution of consciousness implies newer expressive potential of language, then the poet, in possession of *paśyantī vāk* will seize the reality in a direct manner. At such a height poetry becomes a vehicle of knowledge by identity, and thus visionary of truth. The vision of a poet is incomparable since it is neither a critique of life nor an intellectual or philosophical view of life, but is a "soul-view," a capturing by the inner sense. *Mantra* remains the high possibility of the word.

Supriyo Bhattacharya in his paper, "Sri Aurobindo's Understanding of Indian Art," refers elaborately to Sri Aurobindo's views regarding art, though he observes recent scholarship to be oblivious of Sri Aurobindo's contribution to the understanding of basic aspects of Indian Art. In fact, it was William Archer's misconceptions and wrong judgements about Indian culture in his book *India and the Future* that provoked Sri Aurobindo to provide a suitable reply in defence of Indian culture. In the domain of art, Sri Aurobindo believed that the Indian tendency must dominate over other tendencies. Sri Aurobindo observes a spiritual and psychic vision is predominant in Indian Art. He often draws a comparison between the Indian tendency in art with the tendency which is peculiar to the West as making a sensuous appeal to life. In Indian tradition, even if there is a sensuous appeal, it is never predominant. Bhattacharya narrates Sri Aurobindo's interpretation of various drawing of lines, painting of shapes, application of colours in any painting as suggestive of "moments of soul, its living self-experience." The whole work of Ajantā caves and Rājpūt paintings illustrate the difference between the Indian art form and the European. In the province of sculpture also, Bhattacharya shows how Sri Aurobindo would argue for the same inner and spiritual vision. Sri Aurobindo interprets Greek sculpture, in spite of its sublime aesthetic appeal, as lacking in spiritual depth. In the domain of Indian architecture also Sri Aurobindo observes some uniqueness of Indian tradition. Sri Aurobindo's defence for "artistic representation, a rhythm of artistic truth and unity" has been discussed in this article by the author in the context of Indian art, sculpture and architecture as well.

Sāvitrī is the gigantic epic that Sri Aurobindo wrote with a sub-title "A Legend and a Symbol." *Sāvitrī* is based on a story in the *Mahābhārata,* which depicts the victory of love over death: Sāvitrī of the *Mahābhārata* fights with the God of Death, who had taken away her husband Satyavān, to bring him back to life. The Death symbolizes sorrows of material life; Life is regarded as the symbol of light, i.e. Divinity. Vladimir in his article, "The Myth of Sāvitrī and Satyavān: Four Boons" interprets the event of Sāvitrī and Satyavān in the context of the evolution of consciousness, which takes from non-being into being, from death to immortality. Sāvitrī is the symbol of the Saviour, the Divine Mother.

Sarnath Basu in his article, "Some Reflexions on Sri Aurobindo's Essays on the Gītā" begins with the narration of the historical event of 1908, when Sri Aurobindo was mainly spending time reading the Upaniṣads and the *Gītā* as an under-trial prisoner at Alipore jail. One of the very important Indian classics is the *Gītā* that has been variously interpreted by the scholars from time to time. The *Gītā* occurs as a chapter of the great epic *Mahābhārata* wherein we find that Arjuna and Śrī Kṛṣṇa are engaged in a dialogue and through this dialogue some very important questions are raised by a *dharmasmmurhaceta,* i.e. one who is confused about what is virtue, and answered by one who is considered to be fit for answering all those questions. Sri Aurobindo looks upon the *Gītā* as a guide book, as a book that leads us to a certain goal. "We approach it for help and light and our aim must be to distinguish its essential and living message, that in it on which humanity has to seize for its perfection and its highest spiritual welfare" (p. 8). Like many other scriptures the *Gītā* is not based on the life of a great personality like Christ, Mohammad or Buddha. Sri Aurobindo does not interpret the *Gītā* merely in the light of spiritual philosophy or ethical doctrine. The *Gītā* has been interpreted "as bearing upon a practical crisis in the application of ethics and spirituality to human life" (p. 9). The *Gītā,* as Sri Aurobindo interprets it, is a vindication of the relationship between spiritual life and human existence. Kṛṣṇa's relation with his human disciple Arjuna symbolizes the relation between a teacher, who is God, descending into a man. A teacher is a spiritual being and so also is a disciple, but the difference lies in that one is divine and the other is human. Thus, the divinity and humanity may be seen to represent two levels of consciousness. Sri Aurobindo does not support the view that regards the *Gītā* as wholly a book on action. Basu discusses Sri Aurobindo's ways of understanding the *sāṁkhya* of the *Gītā* and the *yoga* of the *Gītā* in contrast to the classical *sāṁkhya* or the *yoga* and also about the influence of the Vedānta philosophy as making synthesis between the *sāṁkhya* ways of thought and *yoga* ways of thought.

The section five of the anthology *Understanding Thoughts of Sri Aurobindo* deals with his thoughts of Man and Human Relation. In his article on "Sri Aurobindo's Concept of Man," Gokulchandra has given an overview of Sri Aurobindo's philosophy of man, which has three aspects: the outer, the inner and the Divine. The outer nature is related to our physical nature, while the inner being of man reveals the central aspect — the *ātman,* above all is the *jīvātmā,* which is a portion of the Divine self. Such conception of man as integral being, according to Gokulchandra, is relevant even in these days of crisis and disintegration. It may guide us to live in communion with others and to perfect ourselves and our societies.

Sushmita Bhattacharya in her article, "Towards a Theory of True Human Relation: Jean Paul Sartre *viś-à-viś* Sri Aurobindo" proposes to discuss views of two great minds — Sri Aurobindo and Jean Paul Sartre — both of whom distinctively visualized human reality in terms of its future prospect and inward journey. An individual has two aspects, one as an individual and the other as related to other individuals. Sartre at one time viewed individual all alone, alienated from his own self as well as from all human relations, for ultimately any such relation involves subject-object dichotomy, hence to endless conflicts. Sartre also maintains that an individual discovers himself in a world of inter-subjectivity; it is in this world that man tries to find out what he is and what others are. As a humanist, Sartre asserts, as pointed out by Bhattacharya, that the ultimate truth about human relation is not the conflict but the urge to go beyond all conflicts, for there must be "something" which he has to find out. Sartre talks of brotherhood as the realization that all men are the offsprings of the same mother earth. But what is the source of this brotherhood has not been addressed by Sartre. In her attempt to elaborate the doctrine of humanism from the perspective of the existentialist philosophers, particularly Sartre, she finds some such questions remain unanswered for ever. Bhattacharya claims that some answers, however, can be given for those seemingly unanswerable questions from Sri Aurobindo's perspective of the true individual. Referring mainly to works of Sri Aurobindo's like *The Essays on Gītā* and *The Human Cycle* she finds some answers. Even admitting the presence of the conflict between egoistic and altruistic tendencies, Sri Aurobindo suggests that by increasing altruistic tendencies the individual may make a preparation for the expansion of his own consciousness. This intermediary stage subsequently aids in perceiving an impersonal universal existence. This is the deeper brotherhood, this is the supramental manifestation upon earth.

Sushmita Bhowmik in her article, "Sri Aurobindo and the Uplift of Humanity" attempts to highlight the contribution of Sri Aurobindo in the direction of spirituality, towards the reconstruction of life and conditions of the entire human race. Sri Aurobindo's optimism lies in believing that human beings can overcome all conflicts and difficulties that lie within and permeate human life and existence and thus move towards a life of peace. Sri Aurobindo thus chalked out a constructive way to enable the entire mankind to eliminate selfish and egoistic tendencies that lie at the root of all strife, conflict, discord and disparity. The way according to him lies in the gradual evolution of consciousness. The ideas of Sri Aurobindo may help the present suffering humanity to move towards a life where the values of peace, unity, and fraternity would reign. But what is necessary, as Sri Aurobindo had pointed out, is an aspiration on our part to realize the need for regeneration of such values in our life and to work for its realization.

On the section on State and Politics we have two articles, one by Dasharathi Sen Gupta on "The Problem of State in Sri Aurobindo's Political Philosophy" and the other by Kittu Reddy entitled "Relevance of Sri Aurobindo in Modern India." Sen Gupta gives an outline of Sri Aurobindo's position with regard to the institution of state that has been developing since mid-seventeenth century. The present article discusses Sri Aurobindo's views about the state as natural and incomplete instrument for the realization of human society. He neither accepts the Hegelian idea that the state is the final embodiment of reason nor does he accept the Gandhian view that state depends on mechanical order and is a machinery for uses of violence. A comparison has been drawn between Sri Aurobindo's views on state and those of Gandhi and Rabindra Nath to situate Sri Aurobindo's critique of state within the framework of his theory of global political evolution. This evoluton, as Sri Aurobindo views it, is a succession of stages. Each stage, after its potentialities are exhausted, yields its place to the next. The modern state is one such stage. The paper concludes by drawing our attention to Sri Aurobindo's optimism for the future and to his conviction that only the spiritual man could and would be the final author of Human Unity.

Kittu Reddy in his article, "Relevance of Sri Aurobindo in Modern India" analyses the political philosophy of Sri Aurobindo by touching upon some of the following significant concepts and ideas derived from Sri Aurobindo, proper understanding of which, Reddy thinks, is of great political importance: the nation as a psychological entity, unification of India and Pakistan, conflict of religions, democracy and socialism, and the role of state. Indeed religion and secularism is a subject of great importance in the context of present India. That the partition of Bengal was no solution to the Hindu-Muslim problem was long ago realized by Sri Aurobindo for he straightforwardly rejected the thesis that the Hindu and Mohammedan are separate political units. Referring to the subject of Hindu-Muslim unity, Sri Aurobindo says, as quoted by Reddy, "It must be sought deeper down in the heart and in the mind, for where the causes of disunion are there the remedies must be sought." The great ideals of the French Revolution, ideals of liberty, equality and fraternity were embraced by Sri Aurobindo. He believed that the ideal of democracy provided dignity to each individual as a soul. Reddy quotes a passage from Sri Aurobindo, wherein he speaks for socialism: "The final aim of nature in human life cannot be the exploitation of the many by the few or even of the few by the many." However, Sri Aurobindo felt that the practice of democracy or the practice of socialism to be effective, need to invoke the third ideal of the French Revolution, i.e. fraternity. Reddy elaborates that Sri Aurobindo's interpretation of fraternity is to be understood in the sense of a deeper spiritual brotherhood.

On the section on Yoga and Psychology, we have three papers. In his article on "Sri Aurobindo's Conception of Integral Yoga" V.N. Seshagiri Rao gives a lucid description of Sri Aurobindo's conception of *yoga*. He discusses how the goal of evolution to attain divine life can be expedited with the practice of *yoga*. Rao discusses how Sri Aurobindo's *yoga* integrates meditation with action. Through meditation, it is believed that internal conflicts and tensions are reduced and spiritual insights are gained; through action, it is believed, the ideal of relating oneself to other fellow selves is practised. Rao explains very distinctively the primary features of Sri Aurobindo's sense of Yoga, as aiming at the realization of the divine unity, as being a new birth in nature, the integral *yogī* becomes more powerful and more perfect.

In his article entitled, "The Mother's Prayers and Meditations: Another Manifesto of Sri Aurobindo's Yoga," Gautam Ghosal opines that Mother's diary may be considered as the practical handbook of Sri Aurobindo's *yoga*. He delineates how Mother anticipated Sri Aurobindo in accepting the universal unity determining an absolute independence of all actions even before Sri Aurobindo explicitly formulated it. Ghosal discusses that while Sri Aurobindo presents us his rich experiential theory in his *Synthesis of Yoga,* Mother in her *Prayers and Meditations* urges us to awaken psychic being, pressing for the higher degrees of truth. Hence we notice that while Sri Aurobindo gave us the theoretical framework of integral *yoga,* Mother give us the practical guidelines for implementing them in our lives.

Soumitra Basu in his article, "Sri Aurobindo's view on Psychology: Can it Offer a Better Therapeutic Model than Psychoanalysis?" aims to explore, as is evident from the title, whether Sri Aurobindo's psychological thoughts can offer a better model than Freudian psychoanalysis for alleviating psychological distress. Sri Aurobindo was a critique of Freud, as Basu writes, on the grounds of placing undue emphasis on the role of the unconscious, in destroying contents of the unconscious, and in unjustifiably claiming that future is completely determined by the past.

Basu mentions three grounds on which Freud was criticized by Sri Aurobindo. On the other hand as Basu brings out the basic tenets of Sri Aurobindo's views on psychology as consisting of the claims that psychology is the science of consciousness; there is a spectrum of consciousness having Inconscient and Superconscient in the two poles; the outer being of an individual is constituted by three elements, namely physical, vital and mental; mind here stands for the cognitive power of the being; and finally, the inner being of the individual is constituted by an element which Sri Aurobindo calls "the psychic being," which accounts for our existence as an individual. In accounting for psychological distress, there are important points of difference between the Aurobindonian model and the Freudian model. For Sri Aurobindo, either by the activity of the subconscient in the vital and physical level or identification with some content of different levels mental problems are produced. Comparing the position of Sri Aurobindo with that of psychoanalysts, Basu further maintains the method adopted for the resolution of conflicts is different in the two models. There are good reasons, as Basu suggests, for considering Sri Aurobindo's model as providing a better explanation than the Freudian explanation of the same.

Astor Patel in her article, "Sri Aurobindo . . . A Century in Perspective" included in the last section of the volume, sounds very restrospective as she goes back to the great historical event of founding of the National College with Sri Aurobindo as its first Principal and goes forth to the contemporary millennium. Patel raises some significant questions to evoke enthusiasm among the present generation to enter into dialogues with Sri Aurobindo. She senses that the gradual process of assimilation and silent absorption of thoughts of Sri Aurobindo has taken place among the later generation. Patel identifies some areas for scientific research that may corroborate or support Sri Aurobindo's thoughts. Patel enumerates some questions as follows: Are dynamic organic wholes primary? Do we seek another method and another framework of epistemology with relation to the existence of wholes? Is matter engaged in the process of recovering some truth about itself? Patel believes that Sri Aurobindo offers to the world a new basis or foundation for scientific research.

Centre for Sri Aurobindo Studies, Department of Philosophy, Jadavpur University, as a part of its publication programme, has taken this initiative for the publication of this anthology. Most of the papers included in this anthology were contributed by the authors in either of the two seminars, viz. "Sri Aurobindo's Contribution to Education and Culture" and "Understanding Thoughts of Sri Aurobindo" organized by the Centre during 2004-05. We are very grateful to each and every contributor for without his or her contribution and cooperation it would have been impossible for us to bring out this anthology. We are grateful to the University Grants Commission for providing us assistance under the Epoch-making Social Thinkers of India Programme to set up this Centre and carry on related academic activities including publication of this anthology. We are also thankful to the authorities of Jadavpur University for providing us all sorts of assistance whenever required. Our special thanks are due to Susheel Kumar Mittal of D.K. Printworld (P) Ltd., New Delhi. Mr. Mittal's sincere effort in bringing out this publication on time is highly appreciated.

30th March, 2006 **Indrani Sanyal**
Kolkata **Krishna Roy**

Part I
Philosophy

1

Philosophy of Sri Aurobindo

Kireet Joshi

IF our quest of knowledge is free from pre-conceptions and dogmas, and if our search aims at discovering action that ensures the highest good of the entire world, then the study of Sri Aurobindo will be found inescapable. For such indeed was his own quest, and his voluminous works provide ample proof of that quest, and they also provide to us a vast body of knowledge that he came to acquire and master and into which we can dive deeply and swim vastly for purposes of our own programme of inquiry, questioning and verification. In his *The Synthesis of Yoga* he has, like a scientist, given a detailed and precise exposition of the realms of knowledge in which he has travelled, covering various levels of consciousness in the individual and the universal, and in the transcendental, particularly those of the mind and the supermind, as also of the methods by which those realms can be approached, traversed and mastered. In his *The Life Divine,* he has fashioned in minuteness, subtlety and complexity an edifice of philosophical thought of such vastness and intricate reasoning that can provide a rational assurance of the possibility and inevitability of the evolution of the divine life on the earth and invite an earnest seeker to a long, sustained and patient inquiry at the highest levels of critical and self-critical examination. In his *Sāvitrī,* he has presented a supreme poetic creation of multiple dimensions relating to a symbolic story of epical character that raises and answers the central issue of human life on the earth in which the riddle of the world is locked, and in the heart of which the secret of the highest good of humanity is shown to be discoverable and realizable. These three are his supreme works, but there are many others, more than 30, in which Sri Aurobindo has expounded his vision and work, and we can approach them for attaining the highest and the best.

Consciousness is, according to Sri Aurobindo, the greatest underlying fact; it is the universal witness; it is to that witness that the worlds and their objects appeal for their reality; we have no other evidence that they exist. It is argued that the material universe existed before life and mind made their appearances and it will survive after they have disappeared. But this argument assumes that consciousness, the universal witness, consists of the individual embodied mind born in the world. But when we extend our consciousness, we find the presence of cosmic consciousness embracing the universe and appearing as an immanent Intelligence in its entire works.

Sri Aurobindo points out that the possibility of a cosmic consciousness in humanity is coming slowly to be admitted in modern psychology, as also the possibility of more elastic instruments of knowledge. According to Sri Aurobindo, it is only when we follow the yogic process of quieting the mind itself that a profounder result of our self-observation becomes possible. At a certain point of this self-observation, we discover that that which observes all the activities of the mind is the mental being supporting the mind substance and mind energy. It is further found that that mental being is the upholder and source of sanctions, and without its sanction, mental operations could not exist or operate. This mental being or the mental *puruṣa* as it is called in Indian philosophy, first appears as a silent witness and subsequently it is discovered to be the giver of the command, the Knower. At this stage, a question arises as to whether the entire phenomenal creation is presented to the mental being or whether it is something pre-determined by dynamic truth of Self within and only manifested on the mind surface. As Sri Aurobindo points out, in order to know that we would have to touch or enter into a cosmic state of being and consciousness in which the totality of things and their integral principles would be better manifest than to our limited mind experience.

It is here that one can discover, according to Sri Aurobindo, Overmind-Consciousness which is beyond individual mind and which is beyond even universal mind that can be found in the realm of what is called ignorance in Indian philosophy. According to Sri Aurobindo, Overmind-Consciousness carries in itself a first direct and masterful cognition of cosmic truth. One thing becomes clear at this level of consciousness; it is self-evident here that both the Individual and the Cosmos come from a transcendent Reality which takes form in them. But still at the level of the Overmind-Knowledge the question set out for us by the phenomenon of the universe is not solved, and three alternative views of creation are presented, and the Overmind permits each one of them to formulate itself in its own individual right and realize its own existence in cognition, in dynamic self-presentation: in substantiating experience. These three alternative views are (a) whether the building of thought, experience, the world of perceptions of the mental Person, the mind *puruṣa*, is truly a self-expression, self-determination proceeding from some truth of his own spiritual being, a manifestation of that truth's dynamic possibilities, or (b) whether it is not rather a creation or construction presented to him by Nature, by *prakṛti*, or else (c) whether it might be a play of a cosmic imagination, a phantasia of the Infinite imposed on the blank indeterminable of his own eternal power of existence.

According to Sri Aurobindo, Overmind gives us no final or positive solution. But there is still a higher cognition beyond the Overmind, a Supramental cognition which is the highest level of cosmic consciousness, and we are left to seek for an answer in that cognition. Sri Aurobindo describes the supramental cognition as a Supramental Truth-Consciousness and points out that it is at once the self-awareness of the Infinite and Eternal and a power of self-determination inherent in that self-awareness; the first is its foundation and status, the second is its power of being, the dynamics of its Self-Existence. In the Supermind, it is found the Supreme is not a rigid Indeterminable and all-negating Absolute; an Infinite of being complete in itself in its own immutable purity of existence, and its sole power, a pure consciousness, able only to dwell on the being's changeless eternity on the immobile delight of its sheer Self-Existence, is not the whole Reality. The Infinite of Being is also an Infinite of Power.

Sri Aurobindo speaks of the triple status of the Supermind. The first poise or status of the Supermind is distinguishable from the pure unitarian Consciousness which is a timeless and spaceless concentration of the Supreme Reality. The first poise of the Supermind is an equal self-extension of the Supreme Reality, all-comprehending, all-possessing, and all-constituting. The first poise of the Supermind founds the inalienable unity of things. As the thoughts and images that occur in our mind are not separate existences to us, but forms taken by our consciousness, in a somewhat similar way are all names and forms of this primary Supermind. It is the pure divine ideation and formation in the Infinite. But these names and forms are not an unreal play of mental thought but a real play of Conscious being. The names and forms are not mere Ideas; they are Real Ideas.

In the second poise of the Supermind there is an operation of apprehending consciousness, which consists of differentiation in the unifying consciousness with unequal emphasis. Apprehending consciousness is differentiating consciousness with unequal concentration, in each name and form the apprehending consciousness would realize itself as the stable

Conscious-Self, the same in all, but also it would realize itself as a concentration of conscious-self following and supporting the individual play of movement and upholding its differentiation from other play of movement, the same everywhere in soul-essence but varying in soul-form. This concentration supporting the soul-form would be the individual Divine or *jīvātman* as distinguished from the universal Divine or the one all-constituting self. In the second poise, the One manifests the play of the One with the many that are still one.

In the third poise, the underlying unity of supramental existence would come to be dominated by the individuals not only apprehending names and forms but even by projecting themselves into the movement of names and forms and to be in a way involved in it.

These three poises are only different ways of dealing with the truth of existence. The secondary and tertiary Supermind only develop and apply in the terms of the Divine multiplicity what the primary Supermind holds in the terms of the Divine unity. It is because in Time, the Many seem not to be eternal but to manifest out of the One and return into it as their essence that their Reality comes to be denied: but as Sri Aurobindo points out, it might equally be reasoned that the eternal recurrence of the manifestation in Time is a proof that the Divine multiplicity is an eternal fact of the Supermind beyond Time no less than the Divine unity.

According to Sri Aurobindo, Infinite consciousness holds within itself endless truth of its own self-awareness. These, in action, would appear to our cognition as aspects of its being, to our spiritual sense as powers and movements of its dynamics, to our aesthesis as instruments and formulations of its delight of existence. Creation, as Sri Aurobindo points out, would then be a self-manifestation; it would be an orderly deployment of the infinite possibility of the Infinite. But every possibility implies a truth of being beyond it, a reality in the

Existence, for without that support in truth there could not be any possibility.

In the Supermind cognition, three aspects of Reality, viz. an Infinite and Eternal Existence, an Infinite and Eternal Consciousness, and an Infinite and Eternal Delight of Existence, are always an inseparable Trinity, even though one can stand in front of the others and manifest its own spiritual determinates as its primal aspects or its inherent self-formulations, but all these together are original to the triune Absolute.

According to Sri Aurobindo, all deploying of powers and possibilities and their inherent consequence is held together by Supermind cognition in an intimate Oneness, it keeps them founded consciously on the original Truth and maintains the harmony of the truths they manifest. There is no imposition of imagination, no arbitrary creation, neither is there any division, fragmentation, irrecoverable contrariety or disparateness.

In the supramental consciousness, the objectivity of the objective universe attains certainty, for it is that very consciousness that puts forth the objective universe. Similarly, it is in the supramental consciousness that there is attained the certainty of the truth of the One that has inherent in it the Many, even though unmanifested, as also of the One and its relationship with the Many in various terms of identity and difference. As Sri Aurobindo points out, it is only when our human mentality lays an exclusive emphasis on one side of spiritual experience, affirms that to be the sole eternal truth and states it in the terms of our all-dividing mental logic that the necessity for mutually destructive schools of philosophy arises. Sri Aurobindo explains the situation as follows:

> Thus, emphasizing the sole truth of the Unitarian consciousness, we observe the play of the divine unity, erroneously rendered by our mentality into the terms of real

> difference, but, not satisfied with correcting this error of the mind by the truth of a higher principle, we assert that the play itself is an illusion. Or, emphasizing the play of the One in the Many, we declare a qualified unity and regard the individual soul as a soul-form of the Supreme, but would assert the eternity of this qualified existence and deny altogether the experience of a pure consciousness in an unqualified oneness. Or, again, emphasizing the play of difference, we assert that the Supreme and the human soul are eternally different and reject the validity of an experience which exceeds and seems to abolish that difference. But the position that we have now firmly taken absolves us from the necessity of these negations and exclusions: we see that there is a truth behind all these affirmations, but at the same time an excess which leads to an ill-founded negation. Affirming, as we have done, the absolute absoluteness of That, not limited by our ideas of unity, not limited by our ideas of multiplicity, affirming the unity as a basis for the manifestation of the multiplicity and the multiplicity as the basis for the return to oneness and the enjoyment of unity in the divine manifestation, we need not burden our present statement with these discussions or undertake the vain labour of enslaving to our mental distinctions and definitions the absolute freedom of the Divine Infinite.

It is because in the supramental consciousness, truths of various experiences are seen and comprehended in their true status and level, that supramental consciousness can be considered to be integral consciousness. A philosophy founded on integral consciousness can rightly be termed as integral philosophy. What is stated above is a brief and inadequate statement of a possible starting-point of the integral philosophy as expounded by Sri Aurobindo. In this brief statement no attempt has been made to argue or to establish or to demolish any particular standpoint. But if we are to understand the philosophy of Sri Aurobindo, the brief statement made here may prove to be of some initial use.

2

Integralism
The Distinctive Feature of Sri Aurobindo's Philosophy

U.C. Dubey

IT is very difficult to evaluate properly Sri Aurobindo's contribution to philosophy in a short paper, because any such effort must take into account his fundamental contributions to metaphysics, epistemology and his theory of evolution. In this paper an attempt has been made to discuss some issues concerning integralism in connection with his metaphysics in the light of the Logic of the Infinite. But before taking up integralism, it is pertinent to point out very briefly his notable contributions to metaphysics for a proper evaluation of the conception of integralism. Sri Aurobindo's foremost contribution to philosophy is his integral view of Reality. He establishes the oneness of the Absolute or *Brahman* without denying the reality of the world and it is possible because he regards the creative force as conscious in nature. The creative force or *cit-śakti* is regarded by him as one with the Absolute. Thus there is no opposition between the Absolute and its creative force in his system. The conscious force or *cit-śakti* assumes the garb of unconscious *prakṛti* by process of self-concentration in order to create or manifest the spatio-temporal world. Thus unconscious *prakṛti* is merely an extension of the Absolute or the consciousness-force. Matter is the last stage in the descending process of the Absolute. That is why Sri Aurobindo and the highest terms of the same existence. His conception of creative force as conscious in nature enables him to propound integral non-dualism. It is the conscious force of *Brahman* that manifests itself in the forms of mind, life and matter. Thus it is an important contribution of Sri Aurobindo's integral Advaitism to regard creative force as conscious in nature.

Sri Aurobindo's next and most fundamental contribution in connection with the theory of the Absolute is his conception of the supermind. It is the link, the mediatory principle between the Absolute and the finite world, and Sri Aurobindo accepts it as a logical necessity in order to explain the transition of the world of spatio-temporal limitations from the spaceless and timeless *Brahman*. It is the fourth — the creative, the dynamic, and the God aspect of *saccidānanda.* It is self-extension of spaceless and timeless *Brahman* in the realm of space and time. The Absolute in its transcendent poise is *saccidānanda* and it is supermind in space and time. It is truth-consciousness. It is divine law and through it the Absolute manifests itself in space and time. It contains the secret of creation within itself. It is because of this intermediate position that Sri Aurobindo calls supermind the child of *saccidānanda* and the parent of mind.

Sri Aurobindo characterizes this mediatory principle as "the beginning and end of all creation and arrangement, the alpha and the omega, the starting point of all differentiation, the instrument of all unification, originative, executive and consummative of all realized or realizable harmonies."[1] But the supermind is not, in fact, the whole of the Absolute reality. It is only the dynamic and creative aspect of the Absolute. As Sri Aurobindo observes, "We have to regard therefore this all-containing, all-orginating, all-consummating supermind as

1. *The Life Divine,* 1982, Sri Aurobindo Ashram Pondicherry, Book 1 & Book 2, Book I, p. 126.

the nature of the Divine-Being, not indeed in its absolute self-existence, but in its action as the Lord and Creator of its own worlds. This is the truth of that which we call God."[2] The supermind has the knowledge of the One but it is able to draw out of the One its hidden multitudes; it manifests the many, but does not lose itself in their differentiations. Thus Sri Aurobindo's conception of the supermind enables his system to reconcile in a harmonious vision the so-called opposite and contradictory aspects of the Supreme Being and it is because of this end in view that S.K. Maitra observes that "the conception of the supermind is the pivot round which the whole of Sri Aurobindo's philosophy moves."[3]

Integralism is the most distinctive feature of Sri Aurobindo's philosophy. Śaṅkara and Śaṅkarites have accepted the reality of the world from empirical standpoint but they deny its reality from transcendental standpoint. The denial of the reality of the world is the essential prerequisite for Advaitic standpoint. But Sri Aurobindo does not propound Absolutism at the cost of the world. Sri Aurobindo holds that Advaitism can be propounded even without denying the reality of the world. The contradictions that appear to exist between *Brahman* and the world are irreconcilable only to our finite or abstract reason because it takes a very narrow view of the different terms and categories.

According to Sri Aurobindo the so-called contradictions between the *Brahman* and the world do not exist in reality but they appear only due to our finite reasoning. He does not deny the reality of any aspect of existence and this is why his system has been rightly designated as Integral Advaitism. His Absolutism is integral and all-inclusive. He argues that "if *Brahman* alone exists" (एकमेवाद्वितीयम्) and "All this is the *Brahman*"

2. *The Life Divine*, Book I, p. 132.
3. *An Introduction to the Philosophy of Sri Aurobindo*, 1965, p. 29.

(सर्वं खल्विदं ब्रह्म) then there is no validity in the denial of the world. "The real Monism, the true Advaita," observes Sri Aurobindo, "is that which admits all things as the one *Brahman* and does not seek to bisect its existence into two incompatible entities, an eternal truth and an erternal falsehood, *Brahman* and non-*Brahman*, self and no-self, a real self and an unreal yet perpetual *māyā*. If it be true that the self alone exists, it must be also true that all is the self."[4]

The Absolute is being as well as becoming and at the same time it transcends both. It cannot be known and determined by finite reason. Our finite reason functions only in the framework of space, time and causality. It cannot transcend these categories. So with the help of this finite reason we are bound to determine the nature of reality as one or many, being or becoming. But Sri Aurobindo's Integral Advaitism reconciles all apparently different aspects of Existence in an all-embracing unity of the Absolute. There is no real opposition between different aspects of existence. Real opposition lies in our finite consciousness. Being and the becoming, *nirguṇa* and *saguṇa* are not opposed to each other, rather they are complementary aspects of the Absolute. If we concentrate on the static aspect of the reality we will miss the dynamic truth of the infinite. If we see only the dynamic truth we will miss the eternal status and the infinte silence, become aware of only dynamic being, dynamic consciousness, dynamic delight of being, but miss the pure existence, pure consciousness, pure bliss of being. "To deny one or the other is easy; to recognize the facts of consciousness and find out their relation is the true and truthful wisdom."[5]

So we must not concentrate only on one side of the truth and conclude from it. As Sri Aurobindo observes, "An experience of some one aspect of the infinte is valid in itself;

---

4. *The Life Divine*, Book I, p. 31.
5. Ibid., Book I, p. 78.

but we cannot generalize from it that the infinite is that alone. . . . The infinite is at once an essentiality, a boundless totality and a multitude; all these have to be known in order to know truly the infinite."[6] Thus it is evident that Sri Aurobindo propounds integrality of the Absolute. He reconciles one any many, silence and dynamis, infinite and finite in the all-embracing unity of the Absolute by a higher reason, i.e. the logic of the infinite. Let me discuss the nature of the logic of the infinite in nutshell as Sri Aurobindo's integralism is rooted in the logic of the infinite.

The logic of the infinite, as the name suggests, is the logic of the Divine. It is inherent in the consciousness of the divine being. The Absolute acts in accordance with its own established laws. "The Self-existent," observes Sri Aurobindo, "is the infinite and its way of being and of action must be the way of the infinite, but our consciousness is limited, our reason built upon things finite: it is irrational to suppose that a finite consciousness and reason can be a measure of the infinite; this smallness cannot judge that immensity."[7] Our reason cannot claim to understand even the mystery of matter and life. Material universe functions in accordance with its own laws. Life also acts in accordance with its own laws. "There are different orders of reality, and the conceptions, measures, standards suitable to one need not be applicable to another order."[8] So the material law is not applicable to life, and vital law is not applicable to mind. It is not only so but even our reason feels difficulty when it explains the nature of matter and life. Then how can reason measure or assess the nature of the Absolute which is suprarational. It is only the logic of the infinite which can enable us to know the nature of the Absolute. Infinite consciousness does not work arbitrarily. Its ways of

6. *The Life Divine*, Book 2, Pt. I, p. 331.
7. Ibid., Book II, Pt. I, p. 327.
8. Ibid., p. 328.

thought and action have their own definite and well-established laws. There is a reason in the entire working and operation of the infinite consciousness but that reason is much higher and greater than our normal reason. It is not intellectual or mental reason but a spiritual and supramental reason and this higher reason can be realized by man only if he attains the supramental consciousness. To our reason the working of the logic of the infinite appears as magic. So we should not conclude that there is no logic in the Absolute. Sri Aurobindo remarks that, "what is magic to our finite reason is the logic of the infinite. It is a greater reason, a greater logic because it is more vast, subtle, complex in its operation: it comprehends all the data which our observation fails to seize, it deduces from them results which neither our deduction nor induction can anticipate."[9] No earthly law, whether it is material, vital or mental can be accepted as ultimately valid, because of its inability to reveal the integral nature of reality. Since reality transcends nature, how can its nature be determined by natural laws?

But if we insist on applying a finite logic to the Absolute, we shall grasp only its shadow and a dead form. But "our way of knowing must be appropriate to that which is to be known; otherwise we achieve only a distant speculation, a figure of knowledge and not veritable knowledge."[10] Thus our mind being limited and because of its very constitution it cannot say anything conclusively about reality. However, even though Sri Aurobindo does not accept reason as the ultimate means of knowledge, he does not minimize the role of reason within its own sphere. He is of the view that so long as we are in the domain of mind, reason is the highest means of knowledge and we must not give preference to any other

---

9. *The Life Divine*, p. 329.

10. Ibid., p. 323.

means of knowledge in its place. Sri Aurobindo is not against the use of reason as such to understand the nature of reality but he is against the unconditional use of abstract and formal reason which cuts the integral reality into fragments. In fact, he suggests that our "reason must become plastic enough to look at all sides, all aspects and seek through them for that in which they are one."[11]

If we look from the point of view of the logic of the infinite at the difficulties which meet our reason when it tries to understand the Absolute, we shall see that the problem is verbal and conceptual and not real. We can reconcile the so-called opposition that seems to exist between the indeterminable aspect of reality and the world of determinations in the light of the higher reason. To our finite reason Absolute is indeterminable and the world of determinations is the creation of *māyā* and as such it can have no connection with the Absolute. But Sri Aurobindo says that all these determinations are nothing else except this indeterminable Absolute. The Absolute is illimitably free. It is "free to determine itself infinitely, free from all restraining effect of its own creations."[12] We can appreciate this self-determination and limitation if we take into consideration the characteristic of infinte self-limitation of the consciousness force of the Absolute. If freedom means to remain free from all limitations then it is also equally a freedom to indulge in the infinite cosmic play without being in any way bound by it. The indeterminate and determinate or *nirguṇa* and *saguṇa* are thus the complementary aspects of the Absolute. It is "only the dual statement of a single inescapable fact by human reason in human language."[13]

---

11. *The Life Divine*, pp. 331-32.
12. Ibid., p 333.
13. Ibid., p. 334.

We can also solve the so-called contradictory problems such as one and many, silence and dynamis, infinite and finite by applying the logic of the Infinite. We will discuss them one by one.

The Absolute has been described in Upaniṣads as one. It manifests itself as many. But how can the limited and the relative be Absolute? To our finite reason there is contradiction between one and many. But this contradiction is due to the failure of finite reason to understand the real meaning of the two terms. Our finite mind considers this oneness on mathematical basis, "which is sole in limitation, the one which is less than two and can become two only by . . . addition and multiplication; but this is an infinite oneness which can contain the hundred and the thousand and the million and billion and trillion. . . . It can be said of it that it would not be infinite oneness if it were not capable of an infinite multiplicity; but that does not mean that one is plural or can be limited or described as the sum of the many."[14] It transcends all limitations of multiplicity. Therefore, "in the logic of the infinite there is no such opposition and the eternity of the many in the one is a thing that is perfectly natural and possible."[15]

Some philosophers accept reality as static, immobile and immutable. But on the other hand there are some philosophers who perceive infinite movement in reality. Thus being and becoming are considered as contradictory to each other and the affirmation of the one implies the denial of the other. But according to Sri Aurobindo there can be no such opposition to the higher logic. "A solely silent and static infinite, an infinite without an infinite power and dynamis and energy is inadmissible except as the perception of an aspect; a powerless Absolute, an impotent spirit is unthinkable . . . an all-power

14. *The Life Divine*, pp. 335-36.

15. Ibid., p. 336.

must be the potency of the Absolute, an illimitable force must be the force of the Spirit."[16] But Sri Aurobindo says that this immobility is the basis of infinite movement. Thus, this opposition is conceptual and the silence of the spirit and the dynamis of spirit are complementary truths and inseparable.

> The immutable, silent spirit may hold its infinite energy silent and immobile within it, for it is not bound by its own force, . . . but it does possess them, does release them, is capable of an eternal and infinite action, does not weary or need not stop, and yet all the time its silent immobility inherent in its action and movement is not for a moment shaken or disturbed or altered by its action and movement; the witness silence of the spirit is there in the very grain of all the voices and workings of nature.[17]

In the same way Sri Aurobindo also reconciles the opposition of the infinite and the finite by applying the higher reason. According to him the finite is the self-determination of the infinite in space and time. It is a frontal aspect of the infinite and no finite can exist in itself and by itself. It exists by the infinite. The finite is considered as a division of the indivisible, but there is no real division. This division is only apparent because Absolute is immanent in the manifold objects.

Thus Sri Aurobindo reconciles the so-called contradictory aspect of reality and propounds integral Advaitism by alluding to higher reason. This integralism propounds matter and spirit as the lowest and the highest terms of the same existence. But this integrality is beyond the realm of formal reason. It moves only in fragments. It views the reality from its limited and fragmentary perspective. That is why there appears to be opposition of one and many, being and becoming. But from the point of view of higher reason there is no opposition between the different aspects of existence.

---

16. *The Life Divine*, p. 336.
17. Ibid., p. 337.

Sri Aurobindo accepts the importance of formal reason in its sphere but he does not accept it as unconditionally valid. The final enlightenment, according to him, "must come from the supramental truth-consciousness, from a supramental vision and knowledge." So, the insistence of formal reason to comprehend the Absolute and its relation with the world in real perspective is not acceptable to Sri Aurobindo. Śaṅkara and his followers determine the relation of the Absolute and the world with the help of the law of contradiction. They apply it unconditionally. But the law of contradiction and excluded middle cannot be applied unconditionally in the realm of experience. These laws can operate freely and unconditionally only in the realm of pure thought, i.e. in the field of geometry and formal logic.

According to the law of excluded middle, the two contradictory terms cannot both be false at the same time for the same individual thing. But Śaṅkara and his followers are fully conscious of the limitations of the law of excluded middle as it is evident from their conception of *māyā* as neither real nor unreal but indescribable. So this law according to Śaṅkara and his followers cannot be freely applied for determining the nature of experience. Its application depends upon the nature of the subject. If the subject is non-existent or illusory, then both the alternatives are denied of it. Sometimes it is not applicable even if the subject is existent. A dog is neither civilized nor uncivilized. But in the case of a man these two alternatives cannot be rejected.[18]

The law of contradiction cannot be applied also unconditionally in the realm of experience. But Śaṅkara and his followers apply the law of contradiction unconditionally and that is why they perceive an opposition between the Absolute and the world. And it is only because of this way of thinking, they reject the reality of the world. But this dialectical

18. R.S. Misra, *The Integral Advaitism of Sri Aurobindo*, 1957, p. 378.

intellect cannot be the adequate judge of the different levels of human experience. According to Sri Aurobindo, "the dialectical intellect is to be used only so far as it helps to clarify our arrangement and justify our expression of the vision and the knowledge, but it cannot be allowed to govern our conceptions and exclude truth that does not fall within the rigid frame of its logic."[19]

The law of contradiction merely states that a thing cannot possess contradictory attributes simultaneously. But it does not clarify, what qualities are really contradictory.[20] This can be known only in the light of experience. Experience can enable us to ascertain whether the two qualities predicated of a thing are contradictory or not.[21] This law is applicable in the case of an individual thing but not in the case of a class. Rāma is either honest or dishonest. But in the case of the class of men the two qualities "honest and dishonest" may be simultaneously accepted. So the two terms "honest" and "dishonest" can act as contradictories in the case of an individual, but they cannot act as contradictories in the case of a class. So it is evident that the more we take a subject in a narrow sense, the more it is liable to be involved in contradictions. As Bradley remarks, "standing contradictions appear where the subject is narrowed artificially, and where diversity in the identity is taken as excluded. . . . And, to speak in general, the more narrowly we take the subject, and the less internal ground for diversity it contains, the more it threatens us with standing or insoluble contradictions."[22]

By now it should be clear that the law of contradiction can be applied only in the light of experience, like the law of

---

19. *The Life Divine*, Book 2, Pt. I, p. 493.
20. Bradley, *The Principles of Logic*, 1963, vol. I, p. 146.
21. R.S. Misra, *The Integral Advaitism of Sri Aurobindo*, p. 376.
22. *Appearance and Reality*, Oxford Paper Back, 1968, pp. 505-06.

excluded middle. The validity and application of these laws depend upon the nature of the subject. These laws can be applied only if the nature of the subject is known. But the nature of the Absolute is not known. So the application of the law of contradiction to the Absolute is not justified. But Sri Aurobindo tackles the problem of the Absolute and its relation with the world from an entirely different angle, i.e. from the point of view of higher reason. Sri Aurobindo proposes a more plastic reason which can explain the real nature of different experiences and their relation in the light of higher experience. Thus this logic enables him to propound integralism. But at this juncture it can be mentioned that Sri Aurobindo does not explain sufficiently the nature of the logic of the infinite. He only recommends this logic in connection with the ultimate reality and as such it can be said that it is the logic of the Upaniṣads because we can see the operation of this logic in Upaniṣadic tradition. But the way the proposes this logic is undoubtedly his unique contribution in the field of Absolutism. This higher reason according to Sri Aurobindo can be attained only after supramental transformation.

Part II
On Evolution

3

Sri Aurobindo on Heraclitus
A Hermeneutic Overview

Krishna Roy

WE are all astounded by the depth and profundity of Sri Aurobindo's thoughts. The more we become impressed by the originality and creativity of his ideas, the more we become interested in exploring the plausible sources of those ideas. Being a *yogī* and visionary, his ideas undoubtedly were of an extraordinary character. Yet as we delve deeper into his thoughts and writings we notice some of the clues which may be considered as the plausible sources of Sri Aurobindo's ideas. While looking for such possible sources, I became fascinated by Sri Aurobindo's monograph on *Heraclitus,*[1] which, I presume, is the only major article written by Sri Aurobindo on any single Western philospher. S.K. Maitra in his thought-provoking book entitled *The Meeting of the East and the West in Sri Aurobindo's Philosophy*[2] has discussed the relation of Sri Aurobindo's thought with that of many Western thinkers like Plotinus, Plato, Nicholai, Hartmann Goethe, Hegel, Bergson and Whitehead. It is surprising that in spite of this monograph on Heraclitus

1. Sri Aurobindo, *Heraclitus,* The Series of Articles on Heraclitus first appeared in *Arya* between December 1916 and June 1917. It was first published as a monograph in 1941.

2. S.K. Maitra, *The Meeting of the East and the West in Sri Aurobindo's Philosophy,* Sri Aurobindo Ashram, Pondicherry, 1st Indian edn., 1956.

written by Sri Aurobindo himself Maitra has not discussed Heraclitus and his impact on Sri Aurobindo's thought-process. In the present article I would try to delineate on Heraclitus' ideas, as has been expounded by Sri Aurobindo and also to explore how these ideas may have influenced Sri Aurobindo's *Weltanschauung.*

Sri Aurobindo's monograph on Heraclitus is both stimulative and thought-provoking, "stimulative" for here we find not only a detailed, penetrating, interpretative account of the thought-process of Heraclitus, but also an interesting comparison with many of the Indian philosophical conceptions. The article is "thought-provoking" for here we notice Sri Aurobindo's hermeneutics of Heraclitus, which in association with many other influences, has helped the genesis and enrichment of Sri Aurobindo's ideas.

Heraclitus, we know, is one of the most important Greek philosophers of the ancient period. He has made significant contributions in the realms of cosmology and metaphysics. Though it may appear to some that Heraclitus used the style of the mystics, as his messages were mainly expressed in the form of aphorisms, yet Sri Aurobindo notices certain interrelation between those aphorisms and is much impressed by the "trend of rationalism" and believes that Heraclitus' philosophy started logically from his fundamental views of existence and their constant justification. Being a perceptive thinker, Heraclitus was concerned in solving a major ontological issue regarding the relation between the One and the Many. In our lived-world we experience numerous things and beings and the inevitable question that arises in our mind is whether they are real or phenomenal? This is a question that has puzzled most of the philosophers, who have offered diverse suggestions from diverse perspectives.

Among the noted pre-Socratic philosphers we find Anaximander who denied true reality to the many, and

Empedocles who considered the All to be alternately one and many. Unlike both these pre-Socratic philosophers, Heraclitus urged that both unity and multiplicity were real and co-existent. With his "strong concrete intuition of things," Heraclitus supported their co-existence as in our everyday life such eternal and inalienable co-existence can be experienced. It is undeniable that we experience one Matter but many atoms, one Energy but many forces, one Mind but many mental beings. Heraclitus wanted to base his philosophical thoughts on such principle of "eternal oneness and eternal multiplicity."

To Heraclitus Being is an eternal becoming and yet the Becoming resolves itself into eternal Being. Since both Being and Becoming were important to Heraclitus, Hegel's characterization of the Heraclitean philosophy only as a philosophy of Becoming can hardly be accepted. Regarding the ontological status of the "Eternal one Being," Heraclitus was of the opinion that this was the "Everliving Fire." One should not think that Heraclitus' selection of Fire as the ultimate reality was motivated by a negative factor of offering a distinct account of reality from that of Thales and Anaximenes. There is, rather, a positive reason of being in consonance with the general trend of his philosophy. We all know that fire consumes and transforms; it is always in a state of flux and tension. Fire is both Being and Becoming. Everyday we see a new sun rising, yet it is the eternal Fire that rises in the form of the Sun. This supports the Heraclitean dictum: "One out of all and all out of One." The eternal Fire takes different forms and names, changes itself into all that is and yet remains itself; Fire changes and is yet immutable. There are, moreover, two processes — the upward and the downward — through which the cosmos comes into being. "Out of Fire, the radiant and energetic principle, air, water and earth proceed, that is the procession of energy on its downward road; there is equally in the very tension of this process a force of potential return which would lead things backward to their source in the reverse order. In the balance of these two upward and downward forces resides the whole cosmic action."[3]

Sri Aurobindo considers that such Heraclitean account of the cosmos is of great consequence and he regards this as "an evolution and involution" out of the eternal principle of Fire, "so the All by upward change may resort completely to the One and yet essentially exist, since it can again return into various being, by the repetition of the downward movement. All difficulty disappears if we remember that what is implied is a process of evolution and involution, so too the Indian word for creation, *sṛṣṭi*, means a release or bringing forth of what is latent — and that the conflagration destroys existing forms, but not the principle of multiplicity."[4] Such law of change that determines the evolution and involution prevails all along the path, through all its stages and returns. Sri Aurobindo thinks that this Heraclitean principle is in conformity with science, which shows how the human body preserves its apparent identity in spite of constant change. The principle of conservation of energy states that even though the energy dissipates, it is not destroyed.

In his monograph on Heraclitus Sri Aurobindo makes a very thought-provoking comparison of Heraclitus' thought with that of Nietzsche. Sri Aurobindo regards Nietzsche to be "the most vivid, concrete and suggestive of modern thinkers." He holds that like Heraclitus, Nietzsche too emphasized on the vast will-to-become and the world as the play of Forces. Though Sri Aurobindo is impressed by the insightful remarks by Nietzsche, yet he was not quite satisfied with the outcome of his thought-process, as Nietzsche affirmed

---

3. Sri Aurobindo, essay entitled "Heraclitus" in *The Supramental Manifestation and Other Writings*, Sri Aurobindo Ashram, Pondicherry, 1997, p. 384.

4. Ibid., p. 386.

only on Becoming and has excluded Being from his ontological discourse. Hence, Sri Aurobindo holds that Nietzsche's philosophy is "in the end unsatisfactory, insufficient, lopsided."[5] Here Sri Aurobindo considers Heraclitus to be more dynamic as he has given importance to both Being and Becoming. In his account of the cosmos Heraclitus gave importance to change and Becoming yet his cosmos has an "eternal basis, a unique original principle." Though there is identity in things, in all existences, yet there is a constant change, there is a Being as well as a Becoming. Besides being impressed by this ontological account, Sri Aurobindo considers Heraclitean account as "profound and full of suggestive truth" because of his striking comments regarding war and justice, tension and the furies. "He is the first thinker to see the world entirely in the terms of power."[6]

Such statements exemplify Sri Aurobindo's high appreciation for Heraclitus. But Sri Aurobindo's perceptive mind has not overlooked the deficiencies of Heraclitus' thought and Sri Aurobindo was not fully satisfied with the views of Heraclitus, as it cannot clearly explain why the energy remains unaltered even after change. Here he prefers the views offered in the Indian system, where *śakti* is consciousness, which preserves by its energy its original scheme of ideas and corresponding forms of things. The upward and downward movement of Heraclitus reminds Sri Aurobindo of the Indian concepts of *pravṛtti* and *nivṛtti.*

> The Indian thinkers were preoccupied with this double principle in so far as it touches the action of the individual soul entering into the procession of Nature and drawing back from it; but still they saw a similar periodic movement forward and back of Nature itself which leads to an ever-

5. Sri Aurobindo, "Heraclitus" in *The Supramental Manifestation and Other Writings*, 1997, p. 376.
6. Ibid., p. 388.

> repeated cycle of creation and dissolution; they held the idea of a periodic *pralaya*. Heraclitus' theory would seem to demand a similar conclusion.[7]

Moreover, Sri Aurobindo does not approve of the abstract, metaphysical principles of Heraclitus as they were lacking in practical efficacy. Sri Aurobindo thinks that not only Heraclitus but many of the Western philosophers have not paid much attention to the practical effects on human lives. Among the Western thinkers, Nietzsche, according to Sri Aurobindo, is the one who brought back dynamism and practical force in philosophy. Such emphasis on practical utility and divine joy is the main foundation of the Indian tradition and Sri Aurobindo wants to imbibe this spirit in his own thought process.

Thus, we notice that in formulating his innovative interpretation of the theory of evolution. Sri Aurobindo is open to both Indian and Western influences. While developing his theory of evolution, Sri Aurobindo has been undoubtedly influenced by the world-views of both the East and the West. In his article on "Evolution" he has given us a critical assessment of the Darwinian theory and detects certain paradoxes in the theory. The "first paradox" according to him is that the Darwinian theory could not offer any satisfactory rationale of the transformation from one stage to the other, for example, from matter to life and from life to consciousness. The "second paradox" of the mechanistic theory is to suppose a rigid chain of material necessity. Sri Aurobindo thinks that if matter, life and consciousness are thoroughly distinct from one another, it is not proper to explain the higher manifestations on the basis of the principle of a lower order. Without denying the importance of the mechanistic theory, Sri Aurobindo wants to give us his "conscious, supple, flexible, intensely surprising and constantly dramatic evolution by a

7. Sri Aurobindo, "Heraclitus" in *The Supramental Manifestation and Other Writings*, 1997, pp. 385-86.

super conscient knowledge which reveals things in Matter, Life and Mind out of the unfathomable inconsequent from which they rise."[8] The conscious spirit is tacitly present in the inconscient. Sri Aurobindo is strongly suggesting that without the descent of the spirit into the world there cannot be any ascent of the world into the Spirit. The distinctiveness of Sri Aurobindo's theory is that his evolution is preceded by involution, where the higher descends into the lower. It is not intended in the present paper to give a detailed account of Sri Aurobindo's theory of evolution. In the present paper I have only tried to suggest that Heraclitus' account of cosmology might have given Sri Aurobindo the clues to develop the notions of evolution and involution further. Sri Aurobindo admits that the Heraclitean dictum "One out of all and all out of one" seems to be the anticipation of the processes of ascent and descent, evolution and involution, alienation and dealienation. The second Heraclitean principle "All things becoming according to strife" must have influenced both Hegel and Sri Aurobindo. It is well known that in Hegelian dialectic contradiction and opposition are inalienably involved, there strife is a sign of marching towards greater harmony. Regarding the plausible impact of Hegel on Sri Aurobindo's thought I have discussed my view in an article entitled "Interpretations of Evolution by Sri Aurobindo and Hegel."[9] Here, in the present article I have tried to show that in the Heraclitean principles, Sri Aurobindo recognizes the very significant message that within each there is an eternal opposition, a tension of contraries and it is this tension that brings forth the balance that is necessary for harmony. We can notice the similar spirit in Sri Aurobindo, where he acknowledges that man's highest aspiration, his seeking for

8. Sri Aurobindo, "Heraclitus" in *The Supramental Manifestation and Other Writings*, 1997, p. 321.

9. Krishna Roy, "Interpretations of Evolution by Sri Aurobindo and Hegel" in *Sandhan*, vol. IV. no. 2, July-December 2004.

perfection, his search for truth and bliss is in constant opposition to his physical existence and normal experience.

The facts that Sri Aurobindo has given so much importance to Heraclitus' philosophy as to write a separate monograph on him, interpreting the first Heraclitean dictum as emphasizing the process of evolution and involution, the second Heraclitean principle as bringing forth harmony out of strife and imbibing similar spirit in developing his own cosmological theory, exemplify that Sri Aurobindo has been influenced by Heraclitus' ideas, which he assimilates with many other Eastern and Western influences. Yet we have to remember with great regard that he has not accepted those prevalent ideas without criticisms. Rather, he evaluates them and with his profoundly creative, imaginative and innovative potentiality re-created them anew.

4

Theories of Evolution and Sri Aurobindo

Kireet Joshi

Darwin and Others

THE process of evolution was detected in ancient times. Both in India and in Greece, there were important ideas of evolution. In modern times, the theory of evolution is mainly the work of Linnaeus (1707–78), Buffon (1707–88), Erasums Darwin (1731–1802), Lamarck (1744–1829), Charles Darwin (1809–82) and his followers.

On the Origin of Species written by Charles Darwin (1859) gave details and demonstrations of his scientific theory of evolution, according to which, life on the earth evolved by a gradual and yet continuous process from the earliest forms of living organisms to the latest product, man. Natural selection, variation and heredity are said to be the factors through the operation of which new species arise out of existing ones. When new characters are produced by the variability of organisms, natural selection decides their survival or death. If the characters do not adapt to their environment, they are eliminated in the competition. If, on the other hand, they equip themselves better for the struggle, they tend to survive. The offsprings of the successful tend to resemble the parents in exhibiting the favoured variation to a greater degree than the parents, and a new type becomes established by a continuous piling up of small useful accretions through many generations.

The two original components of Darwin's theory were (i) that evolution is gradual, and (ii) that the nature of the change is dictated by natural, not divine, selection. Both of these are closely interlinked, and both are at the heart of controversy today, as they were in Darwin's time.

Many naturalists accepted Darwin's gradualism because it accorded well with what they saw in living species. But critics could not accept that all the world's marvellous species and their extraordinary structures, such as those of the eye, could have arisen only by chance. Some biologists accepted that minor changes might be the result of natural selection, but held that beyond extremes within a range of variation, a new species could not arise by natural selection alone. The only way in which the boundaries of species might be breached, they contended, would be through a sudden jump.

Paleontologists who dug up and classified the remains of extinct species raised another major objection to gradualism. They argued that if Darwin were right, they should be able to find a series of specimens that could be laid out in a gradual continuum from one major type of animal to another. If, for example, reptiles evolved into mammals, there should be fossils representing every gradation between these two groups. Instead, the paleontologists found more gaps than continua. Darwin conceded this, but he thought that further researches would reveal the intermediate links. As it turned out, only a few links have been found, and this issue is a part of today's controversy.

There are biologists today who maintain that the evolutionary process jumps from one species to another. Their theory is called "saltationism" (from Latin *saltare,* to leap).

The early geneticists maintained that plants and animals sometimes produce offsprings with unusual abnormalities or variations that could be considered well outside the normal range of variation. These odd offsprings were called sports. Hugo de Vries, an early Dutch geneticist, also observed that the sports undergo some kind of permanent, large-scale alteration of the hereditary units. He called the change a mutation. On the other hand, gradual changes or variations were called by him fluctuations.

In the early twentieth century, evolutionists were divided into two camps. There were geneticists, who saw only evidence for sudden discontinuous change or mutation. They supported the saltationist view. On the other hand, there were naturalists who supported Darwinian gradualism. By the 1930s, however, the rift between these two camps came to be healed by a new evolutionary theory that Julian Huxley named the "modern synthesis." As part of the new theory, Dobzhansky emphasized the need for what he called isolating mechanisms. He recognized that a new species could not emerge from an old one in the wild, if its early members continue to breed with the parent stock. The novel features would either be swamped by the parent stock, or they would be spread throughout the existing species, causing the entire species to evolve slightly. If part of the species population is to split from the parent stock, it must be isolated from the larger population of stock. A river, mountain range, or some other geographic feature must prevent the small variant group from breeding with its original stock. Eventually, the isolated population would become so different that biological differences would prevent inbreeding. In 1972, Stephen Jay Gould and Niles Eldredge asserted that evolutionists had become too rigid in insisting on gradualism. They put forth a new theory that reduced gradualism to a rare event and named the dominant phenomenon "punctuated equilibria." According to them, species are, for most of their existence, in evolutionary equilibrium or stasis. They change very little, if at all. But once in a while the stasis is punctuated by a sudden "speciation event," somehow, a small population of the parent species begins evolving rapidly and, within a relatively few generations, becomes a distinct species.

However, there are evolutionists who continue to stick to the gradualist view, and at the moment, there is no clear resolution in sight. The present debates point to the possibility of the emergence of a new scientific theory which might give a better understanding of the intrinsic "how" of the evolutionary process.

A Deeper Question

If we were to go back to the stage when life had just emerged on the earth, it could not have seemed possible to us that in this little life, a mental being would emerge and create all manner of utensils, erect cities, houses, temples, theatres, laboratories, factories, chisel from it statues and carve cave-cathedrals, invent architecture, sculpture, painting, poetry and a hundred arts and crafts, discover the mathematics and physics of the universe, and live for the sake of knowledge, develop into the thinker, the philosopher and scientist and become even the hunter after the invisible, the mystic and the spiritual seeker.

But if after several ages or cycles we had looked again and seen this miracle in full process, even then perhaps, we would still not have understood, it would still seem impossible to us that the hidden spirit could wholly emerge, complete in its consciousness, and dwell upon the earth as the self-known and world-knower, Nature's ruler and possessor.

We would have said: "Impossible! all that has happened is nothing much, a little bubbling of sensitive grey stuff of brain, a queer freak in a bit of inanimate Matter moving about on a small dot in the universe."

But if we were more deliberate, we might have probably concluded that man, the mental being, is sublimated by the endeavour of the Energy to evolve out of him as the spiritual man, the fully conscious being, man exceeding his first material self and discoverer of his true self and highest nature.

There is still a deeper question. Why do variations occur? Whether they are small or great, gradual or abrupt. We cannot trace them to the influence of the environment. For types without variations seem to be just as well adapted as those with them. Darwin's view of chance variations is virtually a confession of his inability to explain the source of variations.

Modifications and variations do not come singly but in complexes, involving many minor and consequential modifications and variations. Each single small variation is not independently selected. In other words, the organisms seem to "vary" as a whole.

Bergson pointed out that the molluscs in the order of evolution proceed by steady steps to develop an eye, which resembles very much the eye developed by the independent line of vertebrates. How does it happen, he asked, that similar effects appear in different lines of evolution brought about by different means? How could the same small variations occur in two independent lines of evolution if they were purely accidental? According to Bergson, the two series must have been governed by a common vital impulse to this useful end. There is something more in evolution than merely mechanical urge. He is inclined to attribute a "rudiment of choice" to the species which, travelling by "different paths, reach the same goal. Given a new situation, the "urge" (*élan vital*), common to all members, leads them to meet it by a new method. According to Bergson, it is the inner urge, or life force, or an upward drive, that incites the whole species in a definite direction. The striving of the organism is the creative effort to which evolution is due.

The biological theory of evolution assumes that life always came from life. Herbert Spencer questioned this assumption and attempted to give a philosophical account of the rise of the living from the non-living, the mental from the non-mental. According to him, the differences between these are due to the degree of the complexity of the organization. But still the question why life should occur at all? The theory of the survival of the fittest does not carry us far. Life has little survival value as compared with matter from which it is supposed to have sprung. A rock survives for hundreds of millions of years, while even the oldest tree is only a few thousand years old. If survival was the aim of nature, life would never have appeared.

Other significant philosophical theories have also come to be formulated. According to Samuel Alexander, the whole process of the universe is a historic growth from space-time. The original matrix is space-time. Time is the mind of space. In course of time, space-time breaks up into finites of ever-increasing complexity. At certain points in the history of things, finites assume new empirical qualities, which are distinctive levels of experience — primary qualities, matter; and secondary qualities, life and mind. As explained in his book, *Space, Time and Deity*, the cosmic process has now reached the human level, and man is looking forward to the next higher quality of deity. According to him, men of religious genius are preparing mankind for this next stage of development. The divine quality or deity is a stage in time beyond the human. The whole world is now engaged in the production of deity. As time is the very substance of reality, no being can exhaust the future. Even God is a creature of time.

Alexander's philosophy is called the philosophy of emergent evolution. According to him, when physical structure assumes a certain complexity, life "emerges" as something new. When the physical structure alters in complexity, as it does when it produces a central nervous system, "mind" emerges, and the gap between life and conscious behaviour is supposed to be covered. Alexander finds the explanation in a *nisus* or thirst of the universe for higher levels. It is the *nisus* that is creative, that satisfies the thirst.

But is *nisus* an unconscious drive coming by degrees to consciousness in man? Unless we assume the *nisus* to be a spiritual power ever drawing on its resources and ever expressing new forms, Alexander's whole account becomes unsatisfactory.

Lloyd Morgan, who comes very close to Alexander in his account of emergent evolution, acknowledges God as the *nisus* through whose activity emergents emerge, and the whole course of emergent evolution is directed. According to him, God is not the emergent deity, but an activity within which qualities emerge. God is the breath of the whole movement, the deep root which feeds the whole tree. The course of history is the gradual coming of God to Himself. Lloyd Morgan contends that emergent evolution is not predictable. But it is not in the strict sense undetermined like Bergson's creative evolution, not only unpredictable for human minds but, in principle, for all minds. Lloyd Morgan infers the coming of divinity from the purposeful direction of the universe, and he is inclined to make his God completely immanent. He maintains that the whole course of events subsumed under evolution is the expression of God's purpose.

Lloyd Morgan is basically an adherent of Spinoza, and although he speaks of "emergence" in the evolutionary process, one suspects that changes occur according to rule, and there is no spontaneity.

According to Pierre Teilhard de Chardin (1881-1955), the evolutionary process cannot be described or evaluated in terms of its origin. What comes later is more than what was there earlier. There is, according to him, a developing process marked by increasing complexity. It is true that the powers and properties of matter, life, mind, history and values are not entirely different. They interpenetrate and produce an increasing complexity and concentration. In man, evolution becomes conscious of itself. Tracing the story of evolution, he examines the phenomena, big and small, from subatomic particles and cells to stellar galaxies, biospheric and neospheric. There are, according to him, two complementary tendencies in the evolutionary process, *differentiation* and *integration*. In his paleontological studies, he found that evolution tends towards unification.

According to him, all energy is essentially psychic. In his book *The Phenomenon of Man*, he conceives for man a superhuman future and presents a transcendental vision of omega-workings. Evolution is pushing man towards a higher goal, an omega point, which can be described as collective divinity. A cosmic divine manifestation is in the making.

Whitehead, who recalls the Platonic view of the cosmic process, maintains that nothing can emerge in the evolutionary process of the universe if its constituents were not already in existence. The qualities which are said to emerge historically in the philosophy of Alexander are ingredients into events from the beginning, according to Whitehead. The ingredient of eternal objects into events is the explanation of the historical becoming. He admits that at every step there is the emergence of what is genuinely new. Every event, according to him, is a miracle, but it embodies an idea from beyond the developing series of events in the universe. Whitehead suggests an eternal order and a creative reality. The cosmic series has a *nisus* towards the eternal order which is beyond itself, though it is increasingly realized in the cosmic.

According to Whitehead, an actual event is the meeting point of a world of actualities, on the one side, and a world of ideal possibilities, on the other. Like Plato, Whitehead believes in eternal objects. He maintains that eternal objects in this interaction with creative passage issue in actuality, reckoning with space-time, limitation, causal push or drag of the past, and that ultimate irreducibility which we may only call God. It is God who envisages the realm of possibilities and the world of settled fact so as to focus them on each occasion for the creation of something new. It is He who determines the ideal plans of event by the imposition of His nature. In the words of Whitehead, "The universe exhibits a creativity with infinite freedom, and a realm of forms with infinite possibilities; but this creativity and these forms are together impotent to achieve actuality apart from the complete ideal harmony, which is God." God, according to Whitehead, is the home of the universals and the ideal harmony.

"Ingressive evolution" is a phrase that aptly describes Whitehead's theory. There is, according to Whitehead, a progressive ingression and incorporation into the cosmic series of the eternal order which God embraces in himself. The "primordial" nature of God is capable of harmonious concurrent realization. These possibilities are called by Whitehead "eternal objects." They are eternal forms or ideas, to use the Platonic expression, but unlike Plato's ideas, they are not substances, but possibilities, conceptuality realized in God. They are not imaginary or abstract. Some of them are apprehended as possibilities logically prior to their manifestation in existence, and others as symbols of values that we pursue. The relation of form to the temporal world is that of potentialities to actualities. In the view of Whitehead, the temporary actualities realize the possibilities surveyed in God's nature. The order and purpose we see in the world is the result of actuality fulfilling the highest possibilities it sees before itself, which is the vision of God as relevant for it.

According to Sri Aurobindo (1872-1950), evolution presupposes an involutionary process. If Life evolves in Matter and Mind in Life, it must be because Life is involved in Matter and Mind in Life. The material inconscience is the involved Super-conscience. Evolution is fundamentally a spiritual phenomenon. It is a phenomenon of an evolutionary self-building of Spirit on a base of Matter, which is itself a formation of spiritual reality. There is first an evolutionary foundation in which all that is to evolve is present although not yet manifested or not yet organized. An original inconscience without any previous deployment cannot evolve consciousness. In the evolutionary process, there is a development of a triple character. An evolution of forms of Matter, more and more subtly and intricately organized so as to admit the action of a growing, a more and more complex and subtle and capable organization of consciousness is the indispensable physical foundation. An upward evolutionary progress of the consciousness itself from grade to higher grade, an ascent, is the evident spiral line or emerging curve that, on this foundation, the evolution must describe. A taking up of what has already been evolved into each higher grade as it is reached and a transformation more or less complete so as to admit of a total changed working of the whole being and nature, an integration, must be also part of the process, if the evolution is to be effective.

The end of the evolutionary process would be to manifest the supramental consciousness-force in material body. Man is a transitional being, and the spiritual man is the sign of the new evolution. The intention of Nature in the evolution of the spiritual man is not merely to awaken him to the supreme Reality and release him from herself. There is a further intention — not only a revelation of the Spirit but a radical and integral transformation of Nature. The spiritual man has evolved, but not the supramental being who shall thenceforward be the leader of that nature. There is thus something that is not yet accomplished, and there becomes clear to view the much that has still to be done; "there is a height still to be reached, a wideness still to be covered by the eye of vision, the wing of the will, the self-affirmation of the Spirit in the material universe."

Evolution, Yoga and Future of Evolution

Many questions arise:

It may be contended that the only statement of which we are certain is that there are events, but there is no warrant to admit that events have any internal or causal connections among themselves or any plan or design behind them. There is, in other words, no teleology. It is, therefore, argued that every event is a "chance event," and that the quest of man to seek any meaning or purpose or any teleological or evolutionary goal may have some emotional significance but none in terms of objective truth. But if we examine this view, we find that it leaves us with some dissatisfying paradoxes. If everything were a chance, we may ask, how did the sense of meaning and design arise at all? It may, of course, be answered that that also was a matter of chance. But that precisely is the paradox, namely chance generating the sense of meaning and design. Again, if chance rules the world, then it is only a chance and not a certainty, that the chance theory may be valid. In other words, the chance theory has no obligatory force. On the other hand, if there is a secret consciousness in or behind the apparently inconscient Energy in Matter, then the chance theory cannot hold its ground. In the same way, the materialistic position, too, cannot maintain its validity. At the other extreme, it may be contended that if there is an ultimate Reality, which is infinite, perfect and absolute, then such a Reality cannot have any purpose in manifestation. It may, however, be conceded, as in the Indian theory of *līlā,* that the only purpose that the Absolute can have in manifestation would be the delight of manifestation, or the delight of a game would not carry within itself an object to be accomplished in a part movement of the universal totality. Indeed, it may be conceded that a drama without denouement may be an artistic possibility, existing only for the pleasure of watching the characters and the pleasure in problems posed without a solution or with a forever suspended, dubious balance of solution; the drama of the earth's evolution might conceivably be of that character, but an intended or inherently predetermined denouement is also, and more convincingly, possible. In that case, it may be said that Delight or *ānanda* is the secret principle of all being and support of all activity of being; but *ānanda* does not exclude a delight in the working out of a Truth inherent in being, immanent in the Force or Will of being, upheld in the hidden self-awareness of its consciousness-Force. There can then be no objection to the admission of a teleological factor, if the purpose is not a purpose in the human sense — the sense of the need to *acquire* what one does not possess, — but in the sense of the intention to *manifest* fully all the possibilities inherent in the total movement.

It may be admitted that science affirms today an evolutionary terrestrial existence and that there are, in recent trends of thinking, bold and plausible speculations on evolution and the evolutionary future of man, particularly among philosophers. But it may be argued that the scientific theory of evolution can be challenged on the ground that it is insufficiently founded and that it is superfluous as an explanation of the process of terrestrial Nature. If the facts with which science deals are reliable, the generalizations it hazards are short-lived; it holds them for some decades or some centuries, then passes to another generalization, another theory of things. No firm metaphysical building, it may be concluded, can be erected upon these shifting quicksands.

But Aurobindo's theory of spiritual evolution is not identical with the scientific theory of form-evolution and physical life-evolution. According to the theory of spiritual evolution, there are three stages in the process of becoming. An involution of the spirit in the inconscience is the beginning.

An evolution in the ignorance with its play of possibilities of a partial developing knowledge is the middle. A consummation in a deployment of the spirit's self-knowledge and the self-power of its divine being and consciousness is the culmination. It is admitted that the two stages that have already occurred seem at first sight to deny the possibility of the later consummating stage of the cycle, but it is stressed that logically they imply its emergence. For, it is argued, if the inconscience has evolved consciousness, the partial consciousness already reached must surely evolve into complete consciousness. It is contended that it is a supramentalized, perfected and divinized life for which the earth-nature is secretly seeking, and that a progressive manifestation of this kind can only have for its secret of significance the revelation of Being in a perfect Becoming.

Let us elucidate this view in fuller terms. An involution of the spiritual reality in the apparent inconscience of matter is the starting point of the evolution. Existence appears out of the inconscient in a first evolutionary form as substance of Matter created by an inconscient energy. Consciousness involvd and non-apparent in Matter, first emerges in the disguise of vital vibrations, animate but subconscient; then in imperfect formulations of a conscient life, it strives towards self-finding through successive forms of that material substance, forms more and more adapted to its own complete expression. Consciousness in life, throwing off the primal insensibility of a material inanimation and nescience, labours to find itself more and more entirely in the ignorance (a middle term between inconscience and plenary consciousness) which is its first inevitable formulation. But it achieves at first only a primary mental perception and a vital awareness of self and things, a life perception which in its first forms depends on an internal sensation responsive to the contacts of the other life and Matter. Consciousness labours to manifest, as best as it can through the inadequacy of sensation, its own inherent delight of being; but it can only formulate a partial pain and pleasure. But when we come to Man, we find that the energizing consciousness appears as Mind more clearly aware of itself and things. This is still partial and limited, not an integral power of itself; but a first conceptive potentiality and promise of integral emergence is visible. That integral emergence is the goal of evolving Nature.

The appearance of Man in the evolutionary movement is, according to this view, highly significant. It is true that Man's first and primary business is to affirm himself in the universe. But his chief business is to evolve and finally to exceed himself. He has to enlarge his partial being into a complete being, his partial consciousness into an integral consciousness. He has to achieve mastery of his environment, but also world union and world harmony. He has to realize his individuality, but also to enlarge into a cosmic self and undergo a process of a transformation, a chastening and correction of all that is obscure, erroneous and ignorant in his mentality, an ultimate arrival at a free and wide harmony and luminousness of knowledge and will and feeling and action and character. This can only be accomplished by his growing into a larger being and a larger consciousness: self-evolution from what he partially and temporarily is in his actual and apparent nature to what he completely is in his secret self and spirit. This hope is the justification of his work and struggle upon the earth amidst the phenomena of the cosmos.

It has been affirmed that, in fact, life, mind and supermind are present in the atom, are at work there, but invisible, occult and latent in a subconscious or apparently unconscious action of energy. The electron and the atom are in this view eternal somnambulists. In the plant the outer form-consciousness is still in a state of sleep, always on the point of waking, but never waking. Animal being is mentally aware of existence, its own and others, it has even a practical intelligence, founded on memory, association, stimulating need, observation, a power of device. It is not all a half-conscious instinct, the animal prepares human intelligence. But when we come to man, we see the whole thing becoming conscious. Man not only turns his gaze downward and around him, but also upward towards what is about him and inward towards what is occult within him. To climb to higher altitudes, to get a greater scope, to transform his lower nature, this is always a natural impulse of man as soon as he has made his place for himself in the physical and vital world of the earth and has a little leisure to consider his further possibilities. He is capable, unlike other terrestrial creatures, of becoming aware of what is deeper than mind, of the soul within him, and of what is above the mind, of supermind, of spirit, capable of opening to it, admitting it, rising towards it, taking hold of it. It is in his human nature, in all human nature, to exceed itself by conscious evolution, to climb beyond what he is. And where is the limit of effectuation in the evolutionary being's self-becoming by self-exceeding?

A spiritual evolution, it is affirmed, an evolution of consciousness in Matter, in a constant developing self-formulation till the form, even the physical body, can reveal the highest supramental knowledge and power and harmony, is the keynote, the central significant motive of terrestrial existence.

The theory of spiritual evolution may accept the scientific account of physical evolution as a support or an element, but the support is not indispensable. What is common between the theory of spiritual evolution and scientific theory is the account of certain outward aspects of evolution, namely, that there is in the scale of terrestrial existence a development of forms, of bodies, a progressively complex and competent organization of Matter, of Life in Matter, of consciousness in living Matter; in this scale the better organized the form, the more it is capable of housing a better organized, a more complex and capable, a more developed or evolved Life and consciousness. In regard to these common aspects, there does not seem to be a basis for dispute, once the evolutionary hypothesis is put forward and the facts supporting it are marshalled. The dispute arises in regard to those aspects which are not indispensable for the theory of spiritual evolution, namely, the precise machinery by which the evolutionary process is effected or the exact genealogy or chronological succession of types of being, the development of one form of life out of a preceding less-evolved form, natural selection, the struggle for life and the survival of acquired characteristics. These may or may not be accepted. What is of primary consequence is the fact of a successive creation with a developing plan in it. Another conclusion is that there is a graduated necessary succession in the evolution; first the evolution of Matter, next the evolution of Life in Matter, then the evolution of Mind in living Matter, and in this last stage an animal evolution followed by a human evolution. In particular, the essential point in the theory of spiritual evolution is the fact of the evolution of consciousness, a progression of spiritual manifestation in material existence.

But even if all this is accepted, it may still be doubted that Man would evolve so unimaginably as to develop into a superman or supramental species. It may be argued that Man is a type among many types so constructed and like others, so he, too, has his own native law, limits, special kind of existence, within whose limits he can extend and develop, but which he cannot transcend. To exceed himself, to grow into the superman, to put on the nature and capacities proper to the supermind, would be, it may be concluded, a contradiction of his self-law, impracticable and impossible.

In reply, it has been conceded that each type or pattern of consciousness and being in the body, once established, has to be faithful to the law of being of that type, to its design and rule of nature. But it has been pointed out that it may very well be that part of the law of the human type is its impulse towards self-exceeding, that the means for a conscious transition has been provided along with the spiritual powers of man, and that the possession of such a capacity may be a part of the plan on which the creative Energy has built him.

It has further been pointed out that there has been a tremendous human progress since man's appearance or even in his recent ascertainable history. It may, however, be argued that this process has not carried the human race beyond itself, into self-exceeding. In reply, it has been contended that that was not to be expected until a critical stage was reached and that it is only now that stage is being reached. The action of evolutionary nature in a type of being and consciousness is first to develop the type to its utmost capacity by subtilization and increasing complexity till it is ready for bursting the shell, the ripened decisive emergence, and the reverse turning over of consciousness on itself.

It has been pointed out that in the evolutionary process, at each stage of higher ascent from a lower stage, the higher does not abandon the lower, but its first occupation is to take up and assimilate the lower by intenser cultivation, sharpening, subtilizing and sublimation. As man ascends from the animal, he looks downward from his plane of will and intelligence and enlarges, subtilizes and elevates his use of those elements which are central to the animal — sensation, sense-emotion, vital desire and pleasure. He does not abandon the animal reactions and enjoyments, but more lucidly, finely and sensitively mentalizes them. But as he develops further, he puts his lower being to a severer test, to demand from it on pain of rejection something like a transformation that is the mind's way of preparing for a spiritual life still beyond it. As there are several lower and higher elements in man, the process of assimilation and sublimation becomes long and complex, and there appears to be not a straight line of progression, but development in a cycle. In reality, when the process is examined more closely, it turns out to be a process of spiral progression, in which a cycle of development ends at a higher point than the point which was earlier reached before entering into a period of a downward curve. Looked at from this point of view, it may be conceded that what man has until now principally done is to act within the circle of nature, on a spiral of nature-movement, sometimes descending, sometimes ascending. But what he has achieved — and this is important from the point of view of a preparation for a future secure ascent — is that he has sharpened, subtilized and made an increasingly complex and plastic use of his capacities. In that sense, it can be said that however great the ancients, however supreme some of their achievements and creations, however impressive their powers of spirituality, of intellect or of character, there has been in later developments an increasing subtlety, complexity and manifold development of knowledge and possibility in man's achievements, in his politics, society, life, science, metaphysics, knowledge of all kinds, art and literature. Even in his spiritual endeavour, it has been urged, there has been this increasing subtlety, plasticity, sounding of depths and extension of seeking, even though the heights reached were less surprisingly lofty and less massive in power than those reached by the ancients. It is not surprising that there have been falls from a high type of culture, a sharp temporary descent into a certain obscurantism, cessations of the spiritual urge, plunges into a barbaric natural materialism. Considering the total spiral of progress, these may be viewed as temporary phenomena, at worst a downward curve, preparing for a higher curve. It is thus true that this progress has not carried the race beyond itself, into a self-exceeding or a transformation of the mental being; but this was not to be expected. All that has developed so far can be regarded, it has been concluded, as a process of developing the human type to its utmost capacity, and it is only now that we are ready to feel that it has ripened to a point of a decisive emergence or mutation. And the present crisis of mankind is an indicator of the coming movement of that mutation.

It has been observed that the appearance of human mind and body on the earth marks a crucial step, a decisive change in the course and process of evolution. Up to the advent of man, evolution had been effected, not by the self-aware aspiration, intention, will or seeking of the living being, but subconsciously or subliminally or by the automatic operation of Nature. But in man the necessary change has been made in him, the self-aware participating individual will has emerged, and the being has become awake and aware of himself. Man has seen that there can be a higher status of consciousness than his own; the aspiration to exceed himself is delivered and articulate within him. He becomes conscious of a soul, he comes to discover the self and spirit. Until his emergence, evolution was subconscious; with him a conscious evolution becomes conceivable and practicable.

It has been further pointed out that if we observe closely the operations of Nature, we find that in the previous stages of the evolution, nature's first care and effort had to be directed towards a change in the physical organization. That change was a prerequisite of a change of consciousness. But in man a reversal is possible, indeed inevitable. It is through his consciousness, through its transmutation, and no longer through a new bodily organism as a first instrumentation, that the evolution can be effected. It may even be surmised that in the inner reality of things, a change of consciousness was always the major fact, that evolution has always had a spiritual significance and the physical change was only instrumental. This relation was concealed by the first abnormal balance of the two factors, the body of the external inconscience outweighing and obscuring in importance the spiritual element, the conscious being. But once the balance has been righted, it is no longer the change of body that must precede the change of consciousness; the consciousness itself by its mutation will necessitate and operate whatever mutation is needed for the body.

It may, however, be still argued that if an evolutionary culmination in the production of the spiritual and supramental being is intended and man is to be its medium, it will only be a few especially evolved human beings who will form the new type and move towards the new life; that once done the rest of humanity will sink back and remain quiescent in its normal status. In reply to this argument, it has been conceded that there is not the least probability or possibility of the whole human race rising *en masse* to the supramental level. What is suggested, it has been admitted, is nothing so revolutionary and astonishing, but only the capacity in the human mentality, when it has reached a certain level or a certain point of stress of the evolutionary impetus, to press towards a higher plane of consciousness and its embodiment in the being. It has further been explained that the being will necessarily undergo by this embodiment a change of the normal constitution of its nature, a change certainly of its mental and emotional and sensational constitution and also to a great extent of the body-consciousness and the physical conditioning of our life and energies; but the change of consciousness will be the chief factor, the initial movement; the physical modification will be a subordinate factor, a consequence. As to whether humanity will sink back after the mutation of the human species, it has been suggested that the urge of man towards self-exceeding is not likely ever to die out totally in the race, and that the human mental status will always be there, not only as a degree in the scale, but also as an open step towards the spiritual and supramental status.

Man as he is, it has been affirmed, cannot be the last term of an evolution, if a spiritual unfolding on the earth is the hidden truth of the emergence of consciousness that has been taking place in Nature. He is, it is stressed, too imperfect an expression of the Spirit, Mind itself a too limited form and instrumentation. Man, the mental being, can only be a transitional being. If man is incapable of exceeding his mentality, it has been suggested, he must be surpassed, and Supermind and superman must manifest and take the lead of the creation. But if his mind is capable of opening to what exceeds it, then there is no reason why man himself should not arrive at Supermind and supermanhood or at least lend his mentality, life and body to an evolution of that greater term of the Spirit manifesting in Nature.

Sri Aurobindo's Yogic Experiment in Evolution

A distinctive feature of Sri Aurobindo's philosophy of evolution is that it is not speculative; its premises and conclusions are tested on the anvil of experimentation. "The animal is a living laboratory in which nature has, it is said, worked out man. Man himself may well be a thinking and living laboratory in whom and with whose conscious cooperation she wills to work out the superman, the god. Or shall we not say, rather to manifest God?" Indeed, Sri Aurobindo made an experiment upon his entire integral being, using it as an evolutionary laboratory, so as to evolve and manifest higher and higher grades of consciousness reaching up to the supermind and to supramentalize the human body to the furthest extent possible. Even when he left his body, he assigned the task to his collaborator, whom he called The Mother (1878-1973), to continue the task of the supramentalization and integral transformation.

Sri Aurobindo discovered in the ancient systems of Yoga some of the basic clues for the experiment. He did not, however, find in any one of them *the secret* that would enable him to eventually bring about the mutation of the human species. He and The Mother, therefore, experimented, day after day, for years and decades, and they developed a synthesis of Yoga and laboured to perfect it.

The practical necessity of this experiment was not merely to advance knowledge, nor was this experiment directed towards seeking any personal gain, gratification or glory. But Sri Aurobindo and The Mother saw that the contemporary human crisis cannot truly be met without the evolutionary saltation or mutation. There are, according to them, only two alternatives before mankind today: either a revolutionary and evolutionary ascent towards the supramental manifestation on the earth or abyss.

An account of the momentous experiments undertaken by Sri Aurobindo and The Mother cannot truly be given; they can only be glimpsed from the records they have left. Sri Aurobindo's *The Life Divine, The Synthesis of Yoga, Letters on Yoga, The Mother, The Supramental Manifestation upon Earth,* and The Mother's own account of the supramental action on the earth, recorded by Satprem (born 1924) and published in 13 volumes as *L'Agenda de Mere,* give us some indications of both the secret and the fulfilment of their momentous experiments.

Indeed, if the human body were a functioning of Matter, and if Matter were merely chemical and nothing more, then it is obvious that any divinization or divine transformation of the body or of anything else would be nothing but an illusion, an imagination, a senseless and impossible chimera. But even if we suppose a soul or a conscious will at work in the body, it could not arrive at a given transformation if there were no radical change in the bodily instrument itself and in the organization of its material workings. As Sri Aurobindo points out, "A radical transformation of the functioning and, it may well be, of the structure and certainly of the too mechanical and material impulses and driving forces of the bodily system would be imperative. . . . A total transformation of the body would demand a sufficient change of the most material part of the organism, its constitution, its processes and its set-up of nature." Sri Aurobindo conceives of the possibility where all the physical life and its necessary activities could be maintained and operated by higher agencies and grades of consciousness in a freer and ampler way and by a less burdensome and restricting method. The evolutionary urge, he maintains, would proceed to a change of the organs themselves in their material working and use and diminish greatly the need of their use and even of their existence. According to Sri Aurobindo, this might well be part of a supreme total transformation of the body, though this too might not be final. He admits that to envisage such changes is to look far ahead and minds attached to the present form of things may be unable to give credence to their possibility.

At the same time, Sri Aurobindo acknowledges that all does not have to be fundamentally changed; on the contrary, all that is still needed in the totality has to be preserved, but all has to be perfected. "The human body has," says Sri Aurobindo, "in it parts and instruments that have been sufficiently evolved to serve the divine life; these have to survive in their form, though they must be still further perfected, their limitation of range and use removed, their liability to defect and malady and impairment eliminated, their capacities to cognition and dynamic action carried beyond the present limits." On the other hand, new powers have also to be acquired by the body which our present humanity could not hope to realize, could not even dream of or could only imagine. Sri Aurobindo's own words:

> The body itself might acquire new means and ranges of communication with other bodies, new processes of acquiring knowledge, a new aesthesis, new potencies of manipulation of itself and objects. It might not be impossible for it to possess or disclose means native to its own

constitution, substance or natural instrumentation for making the far near and annulling distance, cognising what is now beyond the body's cognizance, acting where action is now out of its reach or its domain, developing subtleties and plasticities which could not be permitted under present conditions to the needed fixity of a material frame. These and other numerous potentialities might appear and the body will become an instrument immeasurably superior to what we can now imagine as possible. There could be an evolution from a first apprehending truth-consciousness to the utmost heights of the ascending ranges of supermind and it may pass the borders of the supermind proper itself where it begins to shadow out, develop, delineate expressive forms of life touched by a supreme pure existence, consciousness and bliss which constitute the worlds of a highest truth of existence, dynamism of *tapas*, glory and sweetness of bliss, the absolute essence and pitch of the all-creating *ānanda*. The transformation of the physical being might follow this incessant line of progression and the divine body will reflect or reproduce here in a divine life on the earth something of this highest greatness and glory of the self-manifesting Spirit.

5

Sri Aurobindo's Doctrine of Evolution

Arabinda Basu

SRI Aurobindo is known as a philosopher of evolution. This is one aspect of his total philosophy and it is very original and comprehensive. The moment somebody hears or reads the word evolution he is immediately reminded of Darwin's theory of the emergence of new forms and species. It is a biological theory and naturalistic. Darwin was not a philosopher and he did not enquire into the why of the process of evolution. What he described was the how of the process. One of the main points of his theory is that what happens happens by "natural selection." There is apparently no work of reason or thought in the process unless we mean by reason the cause of an effect which follows. Sri Aurobindo is a Vedāntist and naturally for him the *Brahman*, the supreme Reality is *cit* (pron. chit), Consciousness. Consciousness has many meanings and there are many theories about it. Here Consciousness is for Sri Aurobindo self-luminous, meaning thereby that it is not revealed by anything other than itself. This Consciousness is also Power, it is dynamic and can act and put out things and forms out of itself. And the world is the self-manifestation of God as Consciousness-Force.

This is important to remember because Consciousness-Force, according to Sri Aurobindo, arranges itself on different planes which are eight. They are Existence, Consciousness Force, Ānanda, supermind, mind, psyche, life and matter. "We may," writes Sri Aurobindo, "if we will, pose eight principles — and then we perceive that our existence is a sort of refraction of the divine existence, in inverted order of ascent and descent, thus ranged —

Existence	Matter
Consciousness-Force	Life
Bliss	Pyche
Supermind	Mind

It is the world in which we live, move and have our being, in which evolution takes place. *Brahman,* Reality as such has no progression and therefore no evolution in it but since, according to Sri Aurobindo, *Brahman* is both transcendent of the world and immanent in it, it is the immanent God which evolves in the world.

Sri Aurobindo says that it is necessary to think of a process of involution before there is any possibility of evolution. This means that what is evolving in the world is Consciousness-Force which is present though unmanifest in matter also. It is from there that the Consciousness-Force begins to manifest itself more openly in planes of consciousness above matter. The other planes are also formations of the same Consciousness Force, though it is not completely open in them either, but more manifest than in matter.

There are basically two lines of evolution, one of forms and the other that of latent consciousness. The evolution of forms is really brought about to provide instruments for the function and manifestation of consciousness in a higher degree.

There is another aspect of evolution in which there is a progressive manifestation of consciousness which may be described as outer and inner. The outer evolution is that of physical, vital and mental Nature, and the inner is more psychic and spiritual. The latter may happen even though the outer may not keep step with it. But according to Sri Aurobindo evolution in a complete sense is both inner and outer. Here I put inner first because it is the stress of the inner evolution that brings about more open unfoldment of consciousness in its outer formations of physical, vital and mental planes.

It is clear from what has been said before that the main motive force of evolution is the urge of consciousness to manifest itself more overtly where it is hidden and wanting to unfold itself.

It will not be possible to go into the details of the "mechanics" of evolution which is, however, not mechanistic according to Sri Aurobindo as described by him in his writings on evolution. One may be mentioned here, viz. that organisms in which evolution takes place become more and more complex as the *nisus* of evolution presses forward. Needless to say that life can evolve itself out of and in matter because it is already inherently present in it. So also mind is present but unmanifest in living matter. We have till now the patent fact of the evolution of matter, life and mind brought together in man who seems to be the crown of the evolutionary effort of conscious force. Sri Aurobindo asks the pertinent question: has evolution ended with the manifestation of mind, of which man is the best example? His categorical answer is that mind is not the last term of the evolution of consciousness in the world. While mind has achieved amazing results, it is none the less an imperfect instrument. Perhaps it is not wrong to say that while it knows a great deal, there is a good deal more that it does not know. And because it does not know completely, most of its ventures yield mixed results.

Sri Aurobindo believes that there is a plane of consciousness where there is no trace of ignorance and therefore no possibility of mistakes and errors. He calls that plane, in the absence of a better term, the Supermind. Supermind is Consciousness as the Knowledge and Will of the Divine. It is the instrument which the Divine uses for self-manifestation as the world and all that is in it.

In point of fact Supermind is everywhere as a spiritual reality which is inherently present but unmanifest in mind, life and matter. Because it is not fully manifest, the three — body, life, and mind — though wonderful are yet imperfect instruments. Supermind, being Consciousness, complete Knowledge and infallible Will, can bring about a transformation of mind, life and matter in such a manner that Consciousness will be fully manifest in them. Consequently, they will be perfect on their own respective planes, within their own potentialities. Sri Aurobindo boldly declares that if the supramental transformation of Matter is complete, it will be capable of knowing its truth in relation to Consciousness, the Reality, and thus be liberated from its own present limitations. Life will shed off its limitations of incapacity and ebbing out which results in death. Mind, now an instrument of Ignorance, will be illumined by the Truth-Consciousness which is another name of the Supermind. This is what Sri Aurobindo means by the transformation of Nature.

It should also be at the same time mentioned that in Sri Aurobindo's metaphysical concept of man, he has as his true self in the world what the mystic philosopher calls the psychic being. This is a descent from *Brahman* into the world and is an individual form evolved from a more general reality called the psychic entity or psychic essence or the soul. It must be briefly mentioned that the word soul here does not at all mean either the animating principle of life or reason or high moral conscience. It is on the other hand a portion of the Divine in the world of evolution progressively taking form as an individual being which itself evolves towards its original Reality, the Divine. Here we see how evolution is outer and inner, though as mentioned before, the inner really pushes forward the evolution of the outer as evolution is of both nature and spirit, and is heading towards a state of equilibrium of Matter and Spirit and spiritual Nature.

I have spoken of descent of conscious force which is the means of God's self-manifestation as the world in which evolution occurs. Evolution is a product of the joint process of descent and ascent of consciousness. Actually for evolution ascent of consciousness is the first movement. This ascent in fact means what Sri Aurobindo calls an aspiration. Conscious Force involved in matter, lying dormant and hidden, aspires for an expression of itself which is not there in matter. This aspiration calls down a response from the immediate higher plane of consciousness, viz. Life, and the result is the emergence of life in matter. In the same way the conscious force in living matter aspires for still more unhampered expression to which there is a response from the plane of Mind and there is evolution of mind in living matter. There is a primary descent of Conscious Force through the supermind into its own lower planes, viz. mind, life and matter, but there are further descents of conscious force in response to its ascent from lower planes to higher planes. Mind itself is a transitional stage in which the involved supermind is seeking expression of itself in mentally living matter, or in other words, man.

Mind is a derivative reality, as I have suggested before, from the supermind, which is already present in it in an unmanifested manner. Sri Aurobindo is emphatic in his declaration that evolution is surging towards the manifestation of supermind in mentality life and matter, that is to say, in man.

Sri Aurobindo describes evolution as a manifestation of the Many from the One, an unfolding of involved Conscious Force to more and fuller expression, as the self-building of Spirit in Matter. Just as the Spirit is present everywhere and in everything as the essential Reality, so also spirituality is present in materiality, vitality and mentality waiting to assert itself as their inner essential quality, which when expressly manifested, will bring about the spiritualization of the categories of existence. Supramentalization will follow spiritualization of mind, life and matter and bring about their intended perfection. The world has a meaning, a significance and a value which is the unveiled manifestation of God in all existence.

6

Sri Aurobindo's Integral Approach to the Concept of Evolution

Dilip Kumar Roy

THE whole gamut of Sri Aurobindo's philosophy centres round one main theme — the theme of the divine life upon earth. The manifestation of the divine upon earth is not any utopia that will never be realized, nor is it any figment of imagination, since whatever Sri Aurobindo has said has a solid ground, the ground of his yogic realization. The future achievement of a divinised life in the earth's evolution is marked by "the intention of the inner Spirit and the logic of Nature's process."[1] The meaning of this phrase becomes manifest to us through three concepts — the concept of Reality, the concept of evolution and the concept of Supermind — the very concepts which Sri Aurobindo deals with integrally. In the light of these concepts we come to see how the divine life upon earth becomes inevitable.

Sri Aurobindo's integral approach to the evolutional process of Nature includes, and that indispensably, the other two concepts — the concept of Reality and the concept of Supermind. Hence a brief reference to those concepts becomes a "must" for us.

---

1. Sri Aurobindo Birth Centenary Library (SABCL), vol. 17 : *The Hour of God*, p. 7.

I

It has been said that the ultimate Reality is the Reality having two aspects — the aspect of the eternal or non-temporal (the silent *Brahman*) and the aspect of the dynamic universal (the active *Brahman*), or, in other words, the aspect of Being and the aspect of Becoming. These two aspects of the Absolute seem to be irreconcilable to each other from the dividing mental viewpoint. Actually speaking, the terms of one and many, formless and form, the indeterminable and the determinable are not really opposites; rather, they are complements of each other. Again, these are not "alternating values" of the Absolute. It is not to be said that the Absolute loses oneness in its creation of multiplicity, or rather it loses manyness by recovering oneness. Rather, one and many, formless and form are "concurrent values" explaining each other. They are, so to speak, "two faces of the one Reality," and the consciousness of both means the integral knowledge of *Brahman*. This knowledge is integral because here by possessing the Being we possess the Becoming.

Sri Aurobindo's yogic realization of the Reality unmistakably points to what is called "a Beyond of the beyond." This "Beyond of the beyond" is called "Non-Being," as we find it in the *Taittirīya Upaniṣad*. There it has been said, "In the beginning all this was the Non-Being. It was thence that Being was born" (II.7). Here Non-Being is not to be conceived as an inexistent Nihil; it is to be taken in the sense "of an X which exceeds our idea or experience of existence."[2] Actually speaking, Being and Non-Being are not mutually exclusive. The Reality as the affirmation of itself "as the free base of all cosmic existence" is called pure Being; and the same Reality is named Non-Being as "a contrary affirmation of Its freedom from all cosmic existence — freedom, that is to say,

2. SABCL, vol. 18 : *The Life Divine*, p. 28, footnote.

from all positive terms of actual existence, . . . "[3] Here by "freedom" is not meant the denial of all cosmic existence but the denial of limitation by all expression.

Becoming or the dynamic universal is another poise of the omnipresent Reality. The mere knowledge of the Becoming, without having knowledge of the oneness of the Being which is its base, is a partial knowledge. The consciousness of both Being and Becoming means the integral knowledge of the Truth. The way to having that knowledge is the way of possessing the Becoming by possessing the Being.

The idea of the one Reality as *saccidānanda* or Existence-Consciousness-Bliss is the idea found in the Upaniṣads, and Sri Aurobindo's yogic realization bears a further proof of what is eternally true. The pure reason tells us that as we are an aspect of the world-movement, this world-movement too is an aspect of something other than itself, of what transcends space and time, and this something is not dynamic but stable. The very idea of energy in action, as we find it in the dynamic universal, suggests invariably the idea of energy not involved in action. And the latter is said to be simply and purely absolute existence. This "absolute existence" is indefinable, infinite and not bound by space and time. It is without quality, quantity and form. When it is said that it is without them, it means that it surpasses them. The pure Existence is that into which form, quality and quantity pass and get so transmuted that they lose their identity and out of which they reappear as form, quality and quantity in the cosmic movement.

The Force or Energy causing the world-movement is inherent in Existence. This Force of Existence may remain concentrated or it may diffuse itself in varied forms. Again, this Force is not a mere Force, but a conscious Force. If the Force that is responsible for the emergence of the world is a

3. SABCL, vol. 18 : *The Life Divine,* p. 28, footnote, p. 28.

Conscious-Force, the world created by such a Force does not move aimlessly, but moves with a view to fulfilling some purpose, some end in view.

The supreme Reality is not only Existence and Consciousness-Force but also Bliss; it is the triune principle of Existence-Consciousness-Bliss, *saccidānanda.* As we cannot think of any deficiency or of any failure of Force in respect of absolute existence, so also we cannot think that there is dearth of delight in it. "All illimitableness, all infinity, all absoluteness is pure delight."[4] The pure Existence is boundless; it is "in full possession of its infinite and illimitable self-consciousness and self-power;" and self-delight is the other name of self-possession; thus bliss "consists objectively in the absence of limitation."[5]

The self-delight of the Supreme does not remain confined to its immobile and silent self-being. Out of its self-delight it luxuriates itself in the infinite flux or dynamism of Nature. Thus the key to the riddle of cosmic existence Sri Aurobindo finds in the principle of joy or delight. It is for the sheer joy of the thing that the infinite Spirit creates and sustains the world. "World-existence," says Sri Aurobindo, "is the ecstatic dance of Śiva which multiplies the body of the God numberlessly to the view: it leaves that white existence precisely where and what it was, ever is and ever will be; its sole absolute object is the joy of the dancing."[6] The incomprehensible Reality at once transcends and embraces and sustains the cosmic drama.

The process by which *saccidānanda* manifests itself is called "the process of differentiation." This process starts from the level of the Supermind. "Supermind is the vast self-extension

---

4. SABCL, vol. 18 : *The Life Divine,* p. 28, footnote, pp. 91-92.
5 Ibid., p. 92; & SABCL, vol. 12 : *The Upaniṣads,* p. 22.
6. SABCL, vol. 18, p. 78.

of the *Brahman* that contains and develops."[7] It is the real creatrix of the world, and hence "it must be not only state of knowledge, but power of knowledge, and not only a Will to light and vision, but a Will to power and works."[8] It is the creative medium through which the Reality involves itself in cosmic existence. The knowledge corresponding to the Truth is called a vast Truth-Consciousness; and that is the Supermind.

The Supermind as Truth-Consciousness is "an ordering self-knowledge" without which the manifestation of the One "would be merely a shifting chaos, precisely because the potentiality is infinite which by itself might lead only to a play of uncontrolled unbounded Chance."[9] What are created by this ordering self-knowledge out of the infinite potential multiplicity inherent in the divine are all pre-determined in its self-knowledge.

Out of the indivisible One the Supermind develops, by the Idea, the triune principle of existence, consciousness and bliss. The three, thus developed out of the One, are maintained in unity. The Supermind, by its differentiating power, is able to bring forward one or other of the three principles drawn out of the womb of the One, and that which is thus brought forward does not exclude the other two but contains them within itself by way of implying them. It is to be noted that the process of differentiation that takes place at the supramental level is made "the foundation of all other differentiations"[10] in the process of creation.

Now, as the Self-Delight of the One is infinite, it continues to manifest itself in order to see itself in a multitude of forms and also through each form separately. What is nearest to the

---

7. SABCL, vol. 18, p. 128.
8. Ibid., p 123.
9. Ibid., p. 132.
10. Ibid., pp. 128-29.

supramental Truth-Consciousness is an Overmind power which is "the first fountain of the creation of the Ignorance."[11] A line is drawn between the higher half and the lower half of the universe of consciousness. This line is the intermediary Overmind. The higher half consists of *sat, cit, ānanda* and *mahas* (the supramental), while the lower half includes Mind, Life and Matter. The intermediary Overmind itself is luminous, for it has the knowledge of the One as the essence of all things. Though itself "golden" by the luminosity of its knowledge of the One, it serves as a "Lid" covering the "face of the Truth" and thus keeping from us the full indivisible supramental Light. This action of the Overmind has been expressed in the *Ṛgveda* as *ṛtena ṛtam apihitam* (truth hidden by truth).

Division and multiplicity go on increasing as the supramental Consciousness descends from the overmental plane to the lesser planes of Mind, Life and Matter. The descending Consciousness takes a great plunge, through the lesser planes, into a dense material Inconscience. And the plunge, the involution of the Spirit, is followed by its emergence from the shackles of the inconscient Matter. Here the concept of the terrestrial evolution finds its place in the philosophy of Sri Aurobindo.

II

The foregoing discussion gives stress on the involution of the Spirit. Evolution, in the real sense of the term, is always preceded by involution. "The word evolution carries with it in its intrinsic sense, in the idea at its root the necessity of a previous involution."[12] The fact that all evolves from the inconscient Matter indicates its prior involvement in Matter. If we discern in Matter the promise and potency of all terrestrial Life, certainly, then, we shall not understand by

11. SABCL, vol. 18, p. 236, footnote.
12. SABCL, vol. 16 : *The Supramental Manifestation*, p. 235.

Matter the Matter of the physicist as a prior self-existing fact. If we accept what the physicist means by Matter, what will emerge out of Matter as real differences at every successive stage in the evolutionary process will remain unexplained. By at once endowing Matter with "the promise and potency" of all that eventually crowns the evolutionary process and taking Matter in the physicist's sense of the term, we are divesting the word "evolution" of its real meaning.

The involution of the Spirit in Matter not only makes the evolution necessary but also gives it a special meaning which is "an outrolling of a manifold Power gathered and coiled up in the crude intricacy of Matter."[13] This meaning of evolution specifies a direction of Nature's march through the evolutionary process towards the upward progression — a rise or an ascent — of the involved Spirit into larger and larger light of consciousness. The movement of evolution towards a progressive self-manifestation of the Spirit in a material universe has to square at every step with the fact of the involution of the Spirit in Matter.

Sri Aurobindo speaks of a "principle" or a method of the evolutionary process. His contribution in this respect is original and of much significance. The principle of the evolutionary process as stated by him is as follows:

> The principle of the process of evolution is a foundation, from that foundation an ascent, in that ascent a reversal of consciousness and, from the greater height and wideness gained, an action of change and new integration of the whole nature.[14]

The "principle" as stated above shows that the evolutionary process is a triple process, a threefold movement — "foundation," "ascent" and "integration."

---

13. SABCL, vol. 16 : *The Supramental Manifestation*, p. 238.
14. SABCL, vol. 19 : *The Life Divine*, p. 724.

By "foundation" Sri Aurobindo means an "involutionary foundation,"[15] a foundation in which the Spirit with all its powers gets involved. And that foundation which serves as the medium of the evolution of the Spirit is Matter. When Matter is an intermediary, it cannot be the ultimate foundation. If there be any ultimate foundation, that is the infinte Spirit, "the original force-substance"; and all other force-substances like Matter, Life and Mind are "degrees and modifications of the substance of Spirit."[16]

The question that arises here is: why is it so that Matter, and not Life or Mind, has been chosen as the foundation of the ascent of the Spirit? By positing eight principles Sri Aurobindo has shown that our existence is a sort of refraction of the divine existence, and that refraction takes place in an inverted order of ascent and descent. Thus we see:

Existence	Matter
Consciousness Force	Life
Bliss	Psyche
Supermind	Mind

Matter is the lowest form of being of the element of *sat* (Existence) in *saccidānanda.* When the Divine descends from the pure Existence through the creative medium of Supermind, it, by dint of its exclusive concentration, involves itself with all its powers in the inconscient Matter. And Matter which comes as a result of the exclusive concentration of Consciousness-Force serves as a foundation of the ascent of the Spirit "through a developing life, soul and mind and the illuminating medium of Supermind towards the divine being."[17]

15. SABCL, vol. 19 : *The Life Divine,* p. 703.
16. SABCL, vol. 17 : *The Hour of God,* p. 15.
17. SABCL, vol. 18 : *The Life Divine,* p. 264.

The difficulty of Matter consists in an obscured, a veiled consciousness which, though limited by its own movement, contains all the latent powers of the Spirit. This veiled, involved or somnambulist consciousness is called the "nescience of Matter."[18] "The awakening of a greater and yet greater consciousness in this Nescience is the miracle of the universe of Matter."[19]

The Matter which we experience by our senses is only an outermost sheath and crating, which, being more dense with "the atomic nescience," cannot be the ground of Life, Mind and other powers. Behind the outermost material sheath there are "other subtler degrees of physical substance which are less dense with the atomic nescience, and it is easier for life, mind and other powers to enter into them and operate."[20] If these finer invisible physical layers did not exist supporting this gross visible physical world, that world could not abide; "for then the fine operations of transmission between Spirit and Matter could not be executed at all and it is these that render the grosser visible operations possible."[21]

We have so far seen that there must be a physical foundation which makes evolution or an ascent possible. By an "ascent" is meant an upward progress or development from grade to higher grade. An evolutionary process must be a development of something that is involved in the basic principle of being or substance. Now, when that something involved in the first foundation appears as a new power of existence, its emergence or ascent cannot be totally free of the grip of the basic physical in which it was involved.

---

18. SABCL, vol. 17 : *The Hour of God,* p. 15.
19. Ibid.
20. Ibid., pp. 15-16.
21. Ibid., p. 16.

The ascent is followed by "integration" which constitutes the last phase of the triple process of evolution. When something emerges as a new principle of existence from its involved state in the basic substance, it gains a greater height and wideness, undergoes an action of change, takes a reversible turn and applies its force "to modify or change or to revolutionize the law and working of the original substance chosen as the evolutionary matrix. . . "[22] Its force to integrate or transform the original substance will depend upon its essential potency. As it is not the original Principle of Existence, it will not be able to bring about an entire transformation.

III

The terrestrial evolution of Nature, says Sri Aurobindo, has a double process — an outward visible process of physical evolution and an invisible process of soul-evolution. The first one is called cosmic evolution, the discussion of which will be followed by that of soul-evolution.

In cosmic evolution we find Mind and Life as evolved in Matter, but as they are subject to modification by the law and nature of the first substance which is Matter, they are limited. In their ascent, however, Mind and Life, by a reversible process, modify the law and working of the original substance according to their potentiality. Thus transformation of the original substance takes place first as living substance and then as conscious substance. As a result of this transformation we come to see that the inertia, immobility and inconscience of matter are changed into a movement of consciousness, feeling and life. But Mind and Life, though they use their force to modify the original substance, do not succeed in transforming it totally, because they are also subject to modification by the

---

22 SABCL, vol. 19 : *The Life Divine*, p. 704.

nature and law of the material substance; and so they become limited in their potentiality, in their power to modify the nature of material substance out and out. These limitations of Mind and Life go to prove that neither of them is an original creative Power. Mind and Life, like Matter, are also intermediaries, appearing successively in the cosmic scene through the evolutionary process.

There must be, says Sri Aurobindo, an original creative or evolutionary Power. The evolutionary process, as we have seen, starts from the first substance which is Matter. The material energy, as it is inconscient, cannot be the original and ultimate Power. If it were so, then the appearance of life and consciousness would not have been possible, because what is inconscient cannot give rise to consciousness, and what is inanimate Force cannot evolve life. Then there must be "a secret Consciousness greater than Life-Consciousness or Mind-Consciousness, an Energy more essential than the material Energy."[23] Since such Consciousness is greater than Mind-Consciousness, it must be a supramental Consciousness-Force. Again, as this Force is more essential than the material Energy, it must be the Power of that which is the inalienable unity of all things, i.e. it must be the Power of the Spirit.

Thus the original creative or evolutionary Power is the Spirit which, by the full emergence of its supramental law, can bring about the entire transformation of the material universe. As a result of this transformation the mental being will be changed into the supramental, the inconscient in us will become conscious, our material substance will be spiritualized. In short, in our whole evolutionary being and nature the supremacy of the law of supramental consciousness will be established. "This must be the culminating emergence or, at least, that stage in the emergence which first decisively

---

23. SABCL, vol. 19 : *The Life Divine*, p. 705.

changes the nature of the evolution by transforming its action of Ignorance and its basis of Inconscience."[24]

Thus we come to see that all things in this world are expression, form, energy, action of the Spirit, the ultimate Reality. Matter itself is the form of the Spirit, life the power of being of the Spirit and mind the working out of consciousness of the Spirit. All Nature is the self-creation of the spiritual Being.

IV

In enunciating the theory of the evolution of the individual soul Sri Aurobindo contributes something original to the general history of evolution. The evolution of Nature and the evolution of the individual soul are the two expressions of the same Reality. The human urge and the cosmic urge — both, through the integral process of evolution, seek to realize the same highest ideal, the ideal of the supramental Divine. Cosmic evolution provides the conditions in which the individual being, the soul, can progressively manifest itself till it reaches its goal.

The divine *saccidānanda,* in the supramental Consciousness, is so modified as to support the evolution of a diversified individuality. The supporting concentration of *saccidānanda* or the individual Self (*jīvātman*) gets involved in the evolutionary movement by projecting itself. Though the individual self as a supporting Self maintains its relation with its created forms called "souls," it maintains its relation with the universal Divine as well and knows itself as the One *saccidānanda.*

The involvement of the individual Self into the evolutionary movement is not direct but indirect, since in its essence it stands above the personal evolution. It is unborn and eternal, although it upholds the manifested personality from above. It

---

24. SABCL, vol. 19 : *The Life Divine,*

emanates from itself a "spark" called the soul which remains in the evolution and supports our whole evolution from within.

The soul, as a spark of the Divine Fire, contains all the divine possibilities within itself; and it undergoes the process of evolution so that those divine possibilities are brought out. Through the fulfilment of those possibilities the soul's terriestrial journey would be Godward. For the progress of the soul, for its evolution in the earth-existence, rebirth is "an indispensable condition." Each grade of cosmic manifestation which serves as a place for the indwelling Spirit is turned by rebirth as a means of progress for the individual Spirit is turned soul. Sri Aurobindo shows the necessity of rebirth by the simple reason which follows:

> If evolution is a truth and is not only a physical avolution of species, but an evolution of consciousness, it must be a spiritual and not only a physical fact. In that case, it is the individual who evolves and grows into a more and more developed and perfect consciousness and obviously that cannot be done in the course of a brief single human life. If there is the evolution of a conscious individual, then there must be rebirth.[25]

The soul, then, passes through the archway of birth and death from one state to another, thus progresssing "from life to life through an evolution" till it reaches "the human state and evolves through it all a being of itself which we call the psysical, a vital, a mental human consciousness as its instruments of world experience and of a disguised, imperfect, but growing self-expression."[26]

It has been said that the psychic being which is a conscious form of the evolving soul supports the evolution from behind

---

25. SABCL, vol. 22 : *Letters on Yoga*, p. 47.
26. Ibid., p. 438.

the veil and uses mind, life and body as its instruments. A time comes when the psychic being does not more remain covered by the veil; it comes out of the veil "to take command and turn all the instrumental nature towards a divine fulfilment."[27] This is what is called "the psychic change, the conversion of our whole present nature into a soul-instrumentation,"[28] this change or evolution of the psyche marks the beginning of the true spiritual life. For the complete emergence of the soul what is necessary as a first condition is a direct contact in the surface being with the spiritual Reality. The soul may attempt to get this contact through the thinking mind as an intermediary or through the heart.

As to the first approach it can be said that the soul creates a constant psychic impression on the thinking mind with a view to drawing it towards the impersonal. The thinking mind, being thus impelled by the soul, deepens its urge and becomes conscious of a spiritual essence or an impersonal Reality. This consciousness of the spiritual essence is an intimate and invisible awareness. The whole thinking mind gets moulded in the form of what it realizes; it attains purity, largeness, tranquillity and impersonality. This mental change does not remain confined to the mind only; its tranquillizing influence falls on the vital parts also.

The soul can also establish its direct contact with the spiritual Reality through the heart. This approach through the heart gives a more quick result since the spiritual Reality has its occult seat "just behind in the heart-centre, in close contact with the emotional being in us."[29] The soul's approach through the thinking mind or through the heart only for making a direct contact with the supreme Reality does not bring about

---

27. SABCL, vol. 22 : *Letters on Yoga.*
28. SABCL, vol. 19 : *The Life Divine*, p. 891.
29. Ibid., p. 902.

an integral transformation which is the object of spiritual evolution.

For a complete change in our thought, life and action the centre of consciousness is to be shifted from the surface to the inner being. There must be approach not only of the thinking mind and the heart but also of the will. The consecration of the will in works is possible if there be no ego-will and its motive-power of desire. Again, for the highest spiritual transformation the shifting of the centre of consciousness from the surface to the inner being or the openness to the psychic being within us is not enough. With this openness there must be "an opening upward to a supreme spiritual status or a higher existence."[30] The latter opening can be done by an ascent of consciousness into the supramental where the truth shines without being veiled. This ascent of consciousness is made possible by the psychic or psycho-spiritual change. It opens us not only to the cosmic consciousness but also to the superconscient which is hidden from us by the strong and hard lid of the dividing and separating mind. This "lid thins, is slit, breaks asunder or opens and disappears under the pressure of the psycho-spiritual change and the natural urge of the new spiritualized consciousness"[31] towards the superconscient.

The ascent of consciousness becomes possible through a series of intermediate gradations, through the Higher Mind, the Illumined Mind, Intuition and the Overmind. This series of intermediate gradations constitutes what is called the "spiritual-mind range."[32] The spiritual-mental range serves as an intermediary in the transition from the mental to the supramental. To pass from the mental to the mental-spiritual

30. SABCL, vol. 19 : *The Life Divine*, p. 910.
31. Ibid.
32. SABCL, vol. 18 : *The Life Divine*, p. 277.

means to pass from a consciousness based on an original Inconscience to a consciousness based on a secret self-existent Knowledge. The different grades of the mental-spiritual do not constitute a method or way of knowing; nor are they a faculty or power of cognition. These grades are "domains of being"; each of them signifies "the substance and energy of the spiritual being"; and each represents a field of existence by which is meant "a level of the universal Consciousness-Force" which constitutes and organizes itself "into a higher status."[33] Thus "the Higher Mind brings a greater consciousness into the being through the spiritual idea and its power of truth"; "the Illumined Mind brings in a still greater consciousness through a Truth-sight and Truth-light and its seeing and seizing power"; "Intuition is a power of consciousness nearer and more intimate to the original knowledge by identity."[34] And the Overmind carries in it "a delegated light from the supramental Gnosis"; it is "a power of cosmic consciousness, a principle of global knowledge."[35] In the spiritual-mind plane it is the Overmind which is regarded as "the highest possible status-dynamics of the Spirit."[36]

When the ascending consciousness reaches the plane of the Overmind, from that summit it can have a direct vision of Truth, of the Divine *saccidānanda*. When the individual soul enters into the Overmind, it becomes a part of the overmental action. Through the Overmind it can be united with the cosmic Self and can attain an action of universality in its nature. But the Overmind cannot lead the individual ascending consciousness beyond itself, "it cannot dynamise the Transcendence: for it is the Supermind alone that is the

33. SABCL, vol. 19, p. 938.
34. Ibid., p. 946.
35. Ibid., p. 950.
36. Ibid., p. 952.

supreme self-determining truth-action and the direct power of manifestation of that Transcendence."[37]

For a complete change in our thought, life and action, for our total transformation, "there must take place as the crowning movement the ascent into the Supermind and the transforming descent of the supramental Consciousness into our entire being and nature."[38] Without the descent of the supramental there can be a vision of infinite consciousness, force and bliss, but ultimately such a vision will not be lasting, there can be a faint memory of it in the mind. But once the ascent into the supramental is made possible, the "descent of the supramental is an inevitable necessity in the logic of things and is therefore sure."[39]

Sri Aurobindo gives reason as to why the descent of the supramental is "inevitable." As Mind, Life and Matter as grades of existence have manifested in the material world, so Supermind too as a grade of existence must manifest in that world.

The fact is that "a supermind is already here but it is involved, concealed behind this manifest mind, life and Matter and not yet acting overtly or in its own power. . . . "[40] It can be liberated from its involved state on "the approach and arrival of the descending Supermind,"[41] and after being liberated it can "reveal itself in the action of our material, vital and mental parts so that these lower powers can become portions of a total divinised activity of our whole being: it is that that will bring to us a completely realized divinity or the divine life."[42]

---

37. SABCL, vol. 19, p. 953.
38. Ibid., p. 891.
39. SABCL, vol. 22 : *Letters on Yoga*, p. 8.
40. SABCL, vol. 16 : *The Supramental Manifestation*, p. 43.
41. Ibid.
42. Ibid.

The divine life upon earth is the ideal that is placed before us. With the descent of the supramental the whole of humanity cannot be changed in a moment. "The descent of the supramental means only that the Power will be there in the earth-consciousness as a living force just as the thinking mental and higher mental are already there."[43] The supramental Power will be at first for the few, and afterwards it will spread from the first centres and take up more and more of the earth-consciousness. Those few will be called Supermen. The ideal of supermanhood and the ideal of divine life upon earth are really the same, since "Supermind is superman."[44]

Sri Aurobindo says that the ideal of supermanhood can be realized by Man. The greatness of Man does not lie in what he is but in what he makes possible. His aspiration, his consecrated will, his total surrender to the Divine, his purity devoid of any taint due to ego-will, in short, his psycho-spiritual change will prepare to rise into the supramental; he will be passing from evolution in the ignorance to an evolution in the Knowledge.

---

43. SABCL, vol. 22 : *Letters on Yoga,* p. 15.
44. SABCL, vol. 17 : *The Hour of God,* p. 76.

Part III
On Education

7

What it is to be Educated?
In the light of Sri Aurobindo's Philosophy

Indrani Sanyal

I BEGIN with a very basic but oft-asked question, viz. "What it is to be educated?" The most simple, obvious reply seems to be that to be educated is to acquire knowledge. Still it may be asked, "What does motivate us to acquire knowledge?" Indeed, in this twenty-first century, looking at the world scenario we find that education is considered to be a great weapon in the hands of the educated. Students all over the world are taught many subjects — some traditional, some very new branches of study and patterns and models adopted for imparting education are also varied and many. Most of the students are required to spend seventeen to eighteen years of their life in schools only to acquire knowledge. We learn history, geography, literature, mathematics, life science, physical science and so on. In this system of education the passing the examination and also passing the examination with good marks, getting a degree, and getting a job are all very intimately intertwined. But are we satisfied with this education? Does this education help us to cope with real situations of life? Does this education make us "more" humanly than our less fortunate uneducated counterparts? Very often the present patterns of education are looked upon with suspicion. Questions are raised about the true nature of education and their aim in human life. A highly qualified technologist proving his skill in building spaceships, moon bridges may miserably fail in tackling old age problems. An efficient author weaves stories of happiness and sorrows of hundreds of men and women but is not capable to meet his own life crisis. Rampant increases in the incidence of terrorism and violence show that increase in material prosperity has not educated men to love one another or to prevent unnecessary violence. It has become one of the regular features in newspapers to bring out reports of suicide by unsuccessful candidates in examinations. Psychologists report that the cases of students seeking professional help because of depression, anxiety and other mental illness are on the rise. So, the question recurs, why are we being educated? What place should we accord to education in the human life? The present paper is an attempt to answer this question after Sri Aurobindo, one of the rarest geniuses who wrote extensively on philosophy, politics, poetry, art, literature, *yoga* and education. Sri Aurobindo who was a teacher, first at the Baroda College during years 1899 to 1906, then in the Bengal National College, Calcutta in the years 1906 and 1907 was the acting principal of the college. He wrote many important articles on education in the *Karmayogin* during the year 1909-10 under the title "A System of National Education."[1] "A Preface to National Education,"[2] another article of Sri Aurobindo appeared in the *Arya* in 1920 in two parts. His book, *The Synthesis of Yoga*[3] contains many basic insights regarding education. Compared to the vast literature that Sri Aurobindo had produced, his

1. "A System of National Education," in *The Complete Works of Sri Aurobindo,* vol. 1, Sri Aurobindo Ashram Publication Department, Pondicherry, 2003, pp. 383-410.
2. "A Preface to National Education," in *The Complete Works of Sri Aurobindo,* vol. 1, Sri Aurobindo Ashram Publication Department, Pondicherry, 2003, pp. 415-27.
3. *The Synthesis of Yoga,* Sri Aurobindo Ashram, Pondicherry, 2002.

contributions directly bearing the title on education[4] may seem to be quite meagre. However, it would not be correct to assess Sri Aurobindo's contribution to philosophy of education in terms of papers on education. It is to be borne in mind and seen subsequently that the concept of education for Sri Aurobindo, connotation-wise is a very wide notion and it is very much linked with some of his basic insights relating to evolution, transformation and the *yoga*. Within the span of this paper no attempt will be made to cover the many facets of a prolific writer like Sri Aurobindo. He was a great philosopher no doubt, but he is one of the rarest among philosophers who is not confined within the constructed theoretical edifice. He was equally, if not more, interested in focusing upon the application of his theory. In fact, in his philosophy of education, if properly understood, we shall see an admixture of both theory and practice. He applies his philosophy to work out the themes of self-development and transformation of man on earth. In this paper an attempt will be made to provide an exigesis of Sri Aurobindo's views and their analysis.

From the age of seven Sri Aurobindo was nurtured and brought up in the British system of education and he was in and out familiar with the European model of education especially the British model. His views on education bear the stamp of being predominantly Indian in its perspective but for that matter it did not lose its uniqueness. In developing his philosophy of education, I would like to elucidate Sri Aurobindo's views in its generalities in the Indian context by reference to classical Indian philosophy and contemporary Indian views as well. Secondly, to understand the educational philosophy of Sri Aurobindo, in all its bearings, to comprehend the logical justification and interrelation of all its principles

4. "Address at the Baroda College Social Gathering"
"Education"
"The Brain of India" →

and practices, we must try to understand the basic vision of Sri Aurobindo as regards man, nature and the world process. "Man is there to affirm himself in the universe, that is his first business, but also to evolve and finally to exceed himself: he has to change his partial being into a complete being, his partial consciousness into an integral consciousness. . . ."[5] This statement of Sri Aurobindo brings out very clearly his regard for man and his belief regarding the objective of human existence. In developing his philosophy of education which is often known as Integral education[6] and putting it to practice he found in the Mother the most meticulous interpreter of his ideas and the ablest collaborator to implement these to practice. We would see that often Sri Aurobindo's ideas were more clearly explained through the Mother's interpretation.

Spiritualistic Turn in Education

In India education was never equated with the learning of

→ "A System of National Education"

"Message for National Education Week"

"National Education"

"A Preface on National Education," in *The Complete Works of Sri Aurobindo*, vol. 1, Sri Aurobindo Ashram Publication Department, Pondicherry, 2003.

5. *Sri Aurobindo Birth Centenary Library*, vol. 19, p. 684.
6. The term, "Integral Education" has been used by the Mother of Sri Aurobindo Ashram, Pondicherry in her message to Dr. K.G. Sayiddin, a member of the Education Commission (Kothari Commission, 1964-66) for National Development. She says: "India has or rather had the knowledge of the Spirit but neglected matter and suffered for it. The west has the knowledge of matter but rejected the Spirit and suffers badly for it. An integral education which could, with some variations, be adopted by all the nations of the world must bring back the legitimate authority of the spirit over a matter fully developed and utilized."

   Collected Works of the Mother, Sri Aurobindo Ashram, Pondicherry, vol. 12, p. 25.

books by heart.[7] Hence an educated man in that Indian model would differ from an uneducated man not on the summation of information that he has but rather in the manner of

---

7. Now, the question is, when we ask what it is to be educated, do we mean by it what it is to be *jñānavān*? Or do we mean by it to be *vidvān* or *śikṣita*? If we turn to Indian tradition and philosophy we find that knowledge and its allied concepts like *jñāna, śikṣā, vidyā,* etc., occupied a very important place. *Vidyā* is significantly contrasted with *avidyā* or ignorance. *Avidyā* creates in man a distorted vision, a wrong and perverted knowledge of things. According to lexicography *vidyā* is science, learning, scholarship; according to some there are four *vidyā*s or science:

   Trayī, the triple Vedas, such as *Ṛg, Yajur* and *Sāma,*

   Āṇvikṣikī, logic,

   Daṇḍanīti, science of government,

   Vārtā, practical arts such as agriculture, commerce.

   Manu adds a fifth *vidyā* which is *ātma vidyā,* Knowledge of soul or spiritual truth.

   The Buddhists talk of three types of training or *śikṣā*:

   Adhicittaśikṣā, i.e. training in higher thoughts,

   Adhiśīlaśikṣā, i.e. training in higher morality,

   Adhiprajña, i.e. training in higher learning.

   An important distinction has been drawn in Indian philosophy between two kinds of knowledge — lower knowledge or *apara vidyā* and higher Knowledge or *para vidyā.* The *para vidyā* is the knowledge of *ātman* or *Brahman* and *apara vidyā*, according to Śaṅkara, is the knowledge of *dharma, adharma,* their means, and fruits. The concept of *vidyā* as we find has both narrow and wide sense. In its narrow sense *vidyā* is more or less similar with the present-day notion of subjects taught in schools and colleges, whereas, in another sense *vidyā* comes closer to knowledge or *jñāna*.

   The word *veda* is derived from the root *vid*, which means "to know." The main objective of the Upaniṣads is to make human beings aware about the real life situation and to motivate him to seek knowledge about himself and the world. The Upaniṣads lay great emphasis on knowledge (*jñāna*), i.e., *jñāna-mārga* which is

→

development of his faculties. Rabindranath Tagore (1861-1941) is considered to be the most educated Indian in spite of his not possessing any formal degrees and diplomas from colleges or universities. For Tagore, the goal of education is to promote the fullest growth and development of the soul. Swami Vivekānanda (1863-1902) says quite clearly that education is not the amount of information that is put into your brain and runs riot there undigested all your life. The objective of education is to make a true man, to build life. If education were identical with just collection of information, then libraries would have to be ragarded as the greatest sages in the world, and encyclopaedia as the *r̥ṣi.* Gandhiji also believes that true education draws out and stimulates the spiritual, intellectual and physical faculties of the children. Gandhiji maintains that education is an all-round drawing out of the best in a child and man — his body, mind and spirit. Sri Aurobindo also looks upon education as a means for the awakening and developing of man's spiritual being. Sri Aurobindo's concern for true knowledge and his endeavour to bring out the exact connotation of education is very much Indian. His considerate outlook and respect for his own culture made him conscious about the worthiness of it. However, it would be wrong to consider him as conservative and as blind to his own culture. He never disregarded advancement of science and newer technologies nor did he advise us to go back to the periods of chariot and bullock carts. When Sri Aurobindo was struggling to spell out the theme of national education, the country was under the British rule. In fact, it was one of the most debated issues of the time whether Western education was a boon or a bane? Groups who were very much against Western education, considered any influence of the West upon Indian mind to be vicious and degrading.

→ one of the paths apart from *karma-mārga,* the path of work, and *bhakti-mārga,* the path of devotion. This shows clearly that Indian philosophy in general puts much emphasis on knowledge.

On the other hand, the other extreme group was blind in their admiration for whatever Western and applauded Western education and culture. Sri Aurobindo was the person who had direct knowledge of the model of Western education. He had appreciation, for the Western model but it was not blind unmixed appreciation for he was at places critical of it. He was not against accepting new ideas and knowledge from the West but he had at the same time deep regard for Indian values. He was very much against disregarding India's own culture and knowledge, its own requirement and temperament. His objective was to initiate a system of national education which would be as comprehensive as the European model and more thorough minus the associated evils of that system. In fact, it is very difficult to answer unambiguously without taking into consideration certain assumptions of what is the objective of education. What is to be considered as the goal or objective of education depends on one's conception of education. In the Indian conception of education as we see from classical philosophical texts, education is never for acquiring success in career or acquiring huge amounts of money. Sri Aurobindo agrees with the Indian conception of education and for that matter does not like to consider education as a tool only for success in career or for earning a huge sum of money. He thought that the intellectual side of education had received more importance because obtaining a job was considered to be the primary goal of education. However, Sri Aurobindo was very pragmatic in his approach to education and he did not deny or underscore the intellectual side of education; he objected against over-emphasising the intellectual aspect of education at the cost of other aspects of it. In India in classical text and literature, as we have already seen the desire for knowledge as a goal of education does exist. But this feature, i.e. desire for knowledge as the goal of education, we hardly come across in any other culture and country. In many civilized countries of the world the goal of education is conceived to be a desire to be wealthy or desire to be successful in career. But Sri Aurobindo would call that narrowly-held concept of education, where desire for knowledge is not a motivating factor, is a bad education. Sri Aurobindo further observes that this bad education creates a peculiar vicious circle, for under the influence of bad education the desire for knowledge never does arise; and the education remains bad as it does not emanate from desire for knowledge. Contrasted with bad education, a good education is to be viewed as that which along with providing knowledge to the students also generates in the student a power to use that knowledge. He was very much critical of the type of university education that was being provided to the students. He characterizes Indian University education under the colonial rule as "smattering of facts in each department of knowledge and this has led to degradation."

Regarding the type of education received from Baroda college, Sri Aurobindo remarked it was a "great and complex educational force, which is not solely meant to impart information." As we see that mere acquisition of information or knowledge is not to be equated with education, "the amount of knowledge is in itself not of the first importance; but to make best use of what we know." Very closely tied up with this notion of using knowledge is the idea of developing instruments for receiving knowledge.

Integrating Man, Nation and Spirit

Coming to the second point, as a prerequisite for grasping his notion of education, as I have already hinted, we need to have some idea about his views about the relation between man, nation and world process. Man, according to Sri Aurobindo, is a developing being and education accordingly is a process of development. Sri Aurobindo says that a true education integrates three basic things:

1. Man, the individual in his commonness and uniqueness,
2. Nation or People, and
3. Universal Spirit.

Sri Aurobindo sees in man the individual, a soul, a portion of the divinity enwrapped in mind and body, a conscious manifestation in Nature of the universal self/spirit; at the summit of his ascent man is bound to rise to something greater than his physical, vital and mental personalities, to his spiritual being. And herein lies the supreme manifestation of the soul of man, his ultimate divine manhood, his real *paramārtha* and the highest *puruṣārtha*. According to Sri Aurobindo, man is a transitional being. Sri Aurobindo had repeatedly said that man is a mind encased in a living body. He is only in the third stage in the upward movement above matter and life and there are four more stages to be ascended to reach the ultimate Reality. Though man is the highest of the created beings, he is not the last word in the evolutionary process. A great possibility awaits man. There is something beyond, something that mankind shall be. In his epic *Sāvitrī*,[8] we find a brilliant exposition of this thought:

> Thus shall be earth open to divinity
> And common natures feel the wide uplift,
> Illumine common acts with the Spirits ray
> And meet the deity in common things,
> Nature shall live to manifest secret God,
> The Spirit shall take up the human play,
> The earthly life become the life divine.

In this connection, true education has a significant role to play. Jugal Kishore Mukherjee while writing *Principles and Goals of Integral Education*,[9] very aptly remarks, " . . . We cannot but

8. *Sāvitrī*, Sri Aurobindo Ashram, Pondicherry, 2002.
9. *Principles and Goals of Integral Education*, Jugal Kishore Mukherjee, Sri Aurobindo Ashram, Pondicherry, 2005, p. 5.

feel eager to know how education can possibly play such a momentous role in the achievement of a total spiritual transformation of man and his life — his life outer as well as inner." Towards Sri Aurobindo's philosophy of education, two sorts of responses are possible. Some may feel that his notion of total spiritual transformation is a piece of abstruse metaphysical parable and any notion of education linked up with such absurdity may lead to mere disillusionments. The second response would come from those who are curious to know how genuine education may prepare "the future of humanity to receive the supramental light that will transform the elite of today into a new race."[10] In fact, many of us are educated in the sense that we have many tags of degrees and diplomas with our names. But have we ever been able to attain spiritual transformation through that education? Hence the question remains how is that spiritual transformation through education is possible at all?

Sri Aurobindo points out that in the Indian conception, a soul in an individual has been looked up from various angles: soul is regarded as mental, as intellectual, as ethical being; as dynamic and practical, as aesthetic and hedonistic, as vital and physical being. The interesting fact is that neither singularly nor jointly all these aspects extend over whole of the soul. Sri Aurobindo considers all these aspects of soul as power of the soul, and power of the soul manifests with the soul. Secondly, this power of the soul is dynamic, it has growth and development and in his opinion the power of the soul grows with the growth of the soul. But it is not the whole of the soul for soul is essentially a spiritual being. The aim of true education is to be understood in the light of this remark: "There is a supreme Divine Consciousness and we want to manifest this Consciousness in physical life."[11]

10. *Collected Works of the Mother*, vol. 12, p. 112.
11. Ibid.

Sri Aurobindo sees in the nation or the people not merely an organized state or an armed and efficient community well-prepared for the struggle of life. Nation for him is a great collective soul, and life that has appeared in the whole and has manifested a nature of its own and a law of that nature, a *svabhāva* and *svadharma*. A nation is to be viewed as a great communal soul. It is the idea of the universal manifesting in the human race. Sri Aurobindo's concept of soul and his concept of nation do not find universal acceptance. However, given the framework of Sri Aurobindo, for him true education is the instrument for real working of spirit in the mind and the body of the individual and the nation. It may be said that with respect to an individual, the goal of true education is the development of the soul and its powers and potentialities. The aim of true education with respect to a nation is preservation, strengthening, and enrichment of the nation's soul and its *svadharma.*

Sri Aurobindo sees in humanity the Universal spirit manifesting in the human race, evolving through mind and life with a high spiritual aim.

True education will be an instrument for real working of the spirit in the mind and body of the individual and the nation. Thus understood, education would be an instrument for social change. What are men trying to achieve in the world since antiquity? What is the purpose of human existence? Is he not trying to establish a perfect harmony within his own subjective being? Is he not trying to establish a perfect harmony between an individual and another individual? Is he not trying to establish a harmony between an individual and a group or groups to which he belongs? Is he not trying to establish a harmony between groups? Sri Aurobindo's answer to all these questions will be in all probability affirmative and he would emphasise the role of education in achieving this goal. To quote

Sri Aurobindo:

> . . . that alone will be a true and living education which helps to bring out to full advantage, makes ready for the full purpose and scope of human life all that is in the individual man, and which at the same time helps him to enter into his right relation with the life, mind and soul of the people to which he belongs, and with that great total life, mind and soul of humantiy of which he himself is a unit and his people or nation a living, a separate and yet inseparable member.[12]

Thus, it is quite evident that in Sri Aurobindo's philosophy of education much emphasis has been laid on the psychic aspect of man with his own being, with his fellowmen and with ordering of his individual and social life. Sri Aurobindo draws distinction between intellectual aspect of education, physical training and edification of character. In his opinion these three aspects together constitute education. Intellectual aspect of education is larger and more difficult but it is a mistake to consider this to be the whole aspect of education. He was critical of the present Indian University system for in it only the intellectual aspect has been given more priority to the utter neglect of other aspects. It was one of the limitations of the system that need to be rectified.

Some Fundamental Mistakes in Educating

The first fundamental mistake is to confine to the training of memory or the storing faculty and provide students with a store of facts and second-hand ideas.

Secondly, it is a mistake to neglect other manipulating faculties, viz. the power of reasoning, the power of comparison and differentiation, and the power of expression.

These powers demand cultivation for these would assist an individual to be properly educated. He also talks about

12. *SABCL,* vol. 17, p. 198.

training in the formation of habit of correct analogy: "The learner will inevitably draw analogies and argue from like to like." He gives importance to imagination as one of the indispensable instruments for education. The faculty of imagination has a triple-functioning mode, by formation of mental images, by creating images or new combinations of existing images or thoughts, and by appreciation of the "soul in things" like beauty, greatness, emotion and spirituality. According to Sri Aurobindo, we find that he has maintained that the true basis of education is the study of the human mind, and he does not specify whose mind it would be. The Lockean *tabula rasa* model of mind where impressions are impinged only from the outside is not acceptable to Sri Aurobindo. In his model of education it is required that teachers and parents help the child to educate himself, to develop his inner capacities and grow as an organic being. The individuality of each child and his potentialities for acquiring knowledge have to be given priority. No child should be regarded as a copy of another child. In his *A System of National Education* Sri Aurobindo focuses upon certain principles by following which the goal of true education may be reached.

"Nothing can be taught"[13] is one of the principles Sri Aurobindo advocated. This negative statement does not indicate any frustration on the part of Sri Aurobindo about the capability of human beings to learn. Sri Aurobindo's conception of subject that is being educated is not comparable with a piece of dead material over which a sculptor works with his chisel to give a shape and appearance of his choice. The educationist is working with a completely different entity with an "infinitely subtle and sensitive organism." Hence from the beginning, for Sri Aurobindo, in the process of being educated the subject is very active and not supposed to be

---

13. *A System of National Education*, p. 384.

inert and passive. For him all knowledge is within and has to be evoked by education rather than instilled from outside. This statement may sound really awkward and unrealistic to many. Sri Aurobindo was critical of our university education for its attempt to load the minds laboriously with information without any regard for the psychology of the man. In this system of education the faculties by which human beings can properly assimilate, create and grow in intellect, manhood and energy are destroyed. Hence collection of information will never suffice for that education. It would definitely require something more, and that has to be evoked from within, and in this regard how knowledge is to be evoked from within Sri Aurobindo has also given suggestions. For Sri Aurobindo a man is a homogeneous part of Infinite energy, *prakṛti, māyā* or *śakti,* by whatever name it is called and along with other forms like plant, insect, or animal a man is also merely a more efficient or less efficient *ādhāra,* i.e. substratum of this energy. The true education as conceived by Sri Aurobindo is one of the processes by which man can increase his capacity as substratum of this all-pervading energy. The teacher is not an instructor or task master. He does not impart knowldege to him, he shows him how to acquire knowledge for himself. "He does not call forth the knowledge that is within; he only shows him where it lies and how it can be habituated to rise to the surface."[14] One of the main reasons for his being critical of the European model of education is its non-recognition or lack of proper understanding of the psychology of human mind.[15]

The second thing that Sri Aurobindo would insist is that the process of providing education cannot remain insensitive or ignorant about the type of the mind that is receiving education. It should never be forgotten that everyone has his own *svabhāva* and *svadharma,* his intrinsic nature and the

---

14. *A Preface to National Education,* p. 422.
15. *The Brain of India,* p. 370.

characteristic turn of his being. Each individual mind has its very unique propensity and essence, and attempts to ignore that would not be regarded as proper education. The idea of hammering the child into the shape desired by the parent or teacher is barbarous. The warning of Sri Aurobindo is very much relevant in recent times: "There can be no greater error than for the parent to arrange beforehand that his son shall develop particular qualities, capacities, ideas, virtues or be prepared for a prearranged career. To force the nature to abandon its own *dharma* is to do it permanent harm, mutilate its growth and deface its perfection. It is a selfish tyranny over a human soul and a wound to the nation, which loses the benefit of the best that a man could have given it and is forced to accept instead something imperfect and artificial, second-rate, perfunctory and common."[16] The truth of Sri Aurobindo's insistence that the chief aim of education should be to help the growing soul to draw out that from within itself which is best and make it perfect for a noble use, can hardly be denied.

A child's heredity, his surroundings, his nationality, his country, his soul from which he draws sustenance, the air which he breathes, the sights, the sounds, habits to which he is accustomed should not be hastily separated. In Sri Aurobindo's words,[17] "We must not take up the nature by the roots from the earth in which it must grow or surround the mind with images and ideas of a life which is alien to that in which it must physically move. . . . A free and natural growth is the genuine development." But from this it should not be supposed that Sri Aurobindo was against taking any thing from sources other than one's native soil. He says very carefully that if anything is worthy of adoption may be adopted from other soils.

---

16. *SABCL*, vol. 17, p. 204.
17. *A System of National Education*, p. 385.

The Development of the Physical

According to Sri Aurobindo any education to be regarded as complete must aim at developing five main types of human activities like the physical, the vital, the mental, the psychic and the spiritual. These may be regarded as the five aspects of education and these physical, vital, mental, psychic and spiritual aspects may succeed each other in the growth of the individual. But it should not be supposed that once one aspect has been developed it will continue in that phase, but rather the process of developing each aspect must continue till the end of life. He has a detailed programme for imparting physical education for perfection of the body. Sri Aurobindo states that a development of the physical consciousness must be the aim of human life. The Mother in her article "Physical Education" reiterates the standpoint of Sri Aurobindo: "Health and strength are the first conditions for the natural perfection of the body."[18] Among the different domains of human consciousness, the physical domain is "most completely governed by method, order, discipline, and procedure." The total perfection of the body and nothing short of it would meet the requirement of Sri Aurobindo for whom education is the other name for evocation of potentialities, and when talking about physical body, it is to be understood that specifically the entire and full development of potentialities of the physical body is implied here. So he felt that any education relating to body must take into account these aspects of physicality and should accordingly be precise and methodical in procedure. There is no special time in life when physical education has to begin for it may begin at birth and continue throughout life. The education of the body to be methodical and orderly may proceed, as elaborated by the Mother, along three main ways.

---

18. "Education II — Physical Education" The Mother, in *A Scheme of Education*, Pranab Kumar Bhattacharya, Sri Aurobindo Ashram, Pondicherry, 1952, p. 79.

In the first place, it is to be directed towards control and discipline of bodily functions. In this connection a minimum knowledge about body and its organs and their normal functioning is required. For the balanced growth of muscles in the scheme of education there has to be provision for physical exercises and outdoor games. Secondly, it is necessary that all parts and their movements are methodically pursued. Thirdly, in a scheme of education there should be provision for rectifications of defects and bodily deformities, if any. "In any case, children should be taught to have respect for health, admiration for a healthy man whose body knows how to repel attacks of illness."[19] Among the stated requirements to be developed in a child from a very tender age are taste for cleanliness and respect for the rules of hygiene.

The Development of the Vital

The education of the vital is considered to be the most important and the most indispensable. Two aspects of vital education have received much consideration, one relating to the development and utilization of sense-organs and the other relating to acquiring mastery over one's character and transformation.

"The perfection of the senses as ministers to thoughts must be one of the first cares of the teacher."[20] Hence the training of the senses is very important. The development of a methodical and enlightened culture of senses among children would have a great impact on the character of the children. This will bring about psychological health, and he is a strong protagonist of the beauty and harmony of the sensations as much as a beauty of the body and its movement. He believes that with a proper discipline it is possible to widen the field

19. "Education II — Physical Education" The Mother, in *A Scheme of Education*, Pranab Kumar Bhattacharya, 1952,, p. 81.
20. *A System of National Education*, Sec V, "Training of the Senses," p. 397-401.

of physical consciousness and that may enable one to project himself out at a distance. The adoption of any coercive measures for suppression of senses is never encouraged; nor the course of stringent asceticism is ever advocated. An effective education was Sri Aurobindo's vision as a substitute for all those less-enduring processes. The most important thing for a child is to learn to observe himself, to note his internal reactions and impulses. In this connection the child must be provided guidance for the regulation of the breathing, *nāḍī-śuddhi* (nerve purification), development of the sensitiveness of *manas*, yogic discipline of *sūkṣma-dṛṣṭi* or subtle reception of the images; and purification of mental and moral habits (*citta-śuddhi*). Thus, Sri Aurobindo says "Sense improvement by practice." This process would be effective if with the growth and power of observation there is also a growth of will in the child towards progress and perfection. He acknowledges that there are different methods for different instances for awakening this will to progress and to develop. This brings us to the other aspect of the education of the vital: this concerns character and its transformation. The Mother has given an elaborate explanation of this vital education and sums up very succinctly the crux of his teaching as follows: "A methodical and enlightened culture of the senses can little by little remove from the child whatever has been vulgar, common place, and crude in him through contagion: this culture will have happy reactions even on his character."[21]

The Development of the Mental

The powers of the mind have to be developed. Educational operations are to put the growing soul into the way of its own perfection. Sri Aurobindo states that mind or *antaḥkaraṇa* consists of four layers:

---

21. "Education II — Physical Education," p. 81.

1. ***Citta***: The reservoir of past mental impressions or the storehouse of memory is the foundation on which all the other layers stand.
2. ***Manas***: The second layer is the mind proper or *manas*, the sixth sense of our Indian psychology. The function of the mind is to receive the images of things translated into sight, sound, smell, taste, and touch by the five senses and translate these again into thought sensations.
3. ***Buddhi or intellect***: The third layer is the real instrument of thought and that which orders and disposes of knowledge acquired by the other parts of mind. The intellect is an organ composed of several groups of functions: function and faculties of right hand and function and faculties of left hand.

   These important functions have all to be raised to their highest and finest working power, if the education of the child is not to be imperfect and one-sided.
4. ***Bodhi***: The fourth layer of the mind is not as yet fully developed in man, is attaining gradually to a wider development and more perfect evolution.[22]

In this connection, we find that he is drawing a distinction between active memory and passive memory. Within the fold of passive memory all experiences are preserved; on the other hand, active memory selects and takes whatever it requires from this storehouse. Active memory is functionally higher than the passive memory, and for its functioning to be perfectly developed it needs proper training. But the passive memory functions in its own way and does not require any training for its growth. The passive memory is supposed to be automatic and it preserves flawlessly whatever comes to it.

---

22. "The Powers of the Mind" in *A System of National Education.*

The active memory may fall victim to many errors and flaws, for in its search for the object it seeks it may pick up something which is not the required item. It may select some unimportant item as important and may fail to pick up the desired one. Hence with regard to active memory the question of being more developed or less developed arises. For that reason the training of memory is very important, for as one of the instruments of knowledge it needs to be sharpened and strengthened so that education processed through it is perfect.

We should not try, as we generally do now, to erect a huge superstructure of knowledge in the mind of the student without preparing a solid foundation to sustain that knowledge. "Information cannot be the foundation of intelligence."

Child's ethical-aesthetic nature too has to be developed. "The attempt to make a boy moral and religious by the teaching of moral and religious textbooks is a vanity and a delusion, precisely because the heart is not the mind, and instructing the mind does not necessarily improve the heart."[23] The subject of education is a student, a living and growing being, who is already carrying within him *saṁskāra*s or impressions which are both in-born and acquired. Hence when we are talking about the development of moral nature or aesthetic nature all these aspects have to be taken into consideration. Sri Aurobindo, a psychologist *par excellence,* made it clear quite categorically in his writings that the development of the moral nature and the development of heart are concerned with emotions, the *saṁskāra*s or formed habits and associations and the *svabhāva* or nature. In this connection the very pertinent question is, how to morally train an individual? Among human emotions some are regarded as good or some as bad. It is human *svabhāva* or nature that expresses itself through various courses of emotional

---

23. Sri Aurobindo's "The Moral Nature" in *The Complete Works of Sri Aurobindo,* vol. I, p. 389.

expressions. In the literature of classical Indian philosophy we often come across elaborate discussions and analyses of roots or springs of human action. The subject has been discussed in detail in the Yoga philosophy of Patañjali wherein he traces passions to three roots, viz. *lobha* (greed), *krodha* (anger) and *moha* (delusion). These passions play definite roles in directing human beings in their various activities. Some may fulfil their passion directly by performing certain acts or some may make others to perform those acts. According to Sri Aurobindo to train oneself morally should be similar to training oneself to be habituated to right emotions, to best physical/moral habits and to perform right actions according to essential nature.

The Development of the Psychical

Now in the scheme of education as suggested by Sri Aurobindo, the other two important aspects are psychical and spiritual. Sri Aurobindo had made it clear that in every man over and above his physical, vital and mental aspects there are aspects of psyche and soul. For Sri Aurobindo these earlier mentioned three aspects of education relating to physical, mental and vital, help in developing human personality as a "well-defined self-conscious entity." Psychic education helps one in being equipped in answering to questions about the motive of life or purpose of human existence. Education concerning physical, vital and mental is necessary, but one need not remain satisfied with that sort of education alone. In his view, from the ontological viewpoint, a psychic being is concretization in space and time of one supreme and universal consciousness. Psychic education is very much differernt from other sorts of education spoken earlier. He feels that mental education does not have any role in preparing one for the psychic life. Psychic education is required for making an individual conscious of his psychic presence "in the depths of your being that which carries in it the sense of universality, limitless expansion, termless continuity."[24] "It is through the psychic process that truth of an individual being comes into contact with him and the circumstances of his life."[25] Psychic education will facilitate the discovery of the psychic being, which requires "as much fortitude and endurance as the discovery of new continents."[26] Once truly psychically educated then the false barriers distinguishing one individual from the other collapses and egoism centring round centralized individual fades out and external personality dwindles. But he was aware that this path of psychic education was not an easy path. Psychic education begins the process of decentralization and the individual learns to extend himself by beginning to live in everything and in all beings. In the domain of psychic education, as suggested by Sri Aurobindo "Each one must, so to say, chalk out his own path through his own difficulties."[27] In this connection, it is worth pointing that for Sri Aurobindo in the province of this education the personal will of the individual has a decisive role to play. However, he does not rule out the possibility of success in being psychically educated by following the path of the successful person. Finally, however, as the Mother interprets, "the attempt is to one's own personal initiative: the discovery is a personal matter and a great resolution, a strong will and an untiring perseverance are indispensable to reach the goal."[28] This education releases the individual from all chains consisting of slavery to the flesh and all sorts of personal attachments. But Sri Aurobindo does not consider this to be the final state of education. Jugol Kishore Mukerjee very aptly describes "an attainment of divine perfection of human being and living

---

24. The Mother, "Education-V "The Psychic and The Spiritual Education," in *A Scheme of Education,* p. 102.
25. Ibid., p. 101.
26. Ibid., p. 103.
27. Ibid., p. 102.
28. Ibid.

here upon earth is the central aim of our existence."[29] To quote from Sri Aurobindo, "All life is a secret *yoga,* an obscure growth of Nature towards the discovery and fulfilment of the divine principle hidden in her which becomes progressively less obscure, more self-conscient and luminous, more self-possessed in the human being by the opening of all his instruments of knowledge, will, action, life to the Spirit within him in the world."[30] All this development is applicable to that which is within the human being and not to something alien or external to our being.

The Development of the Spiritual

The step that an individual has to take to reach the summit is through spiritual education, which has been regarded as another aspect of education. Sri Aurobindo insists on drawing a sharp line of demarcation between psychic education and spiritual education, though broadly speaking, both of these aspects of education are brought under "yogic discipline."[31] The objective of psychic education is not the same as the objective of spiritual education, for psychic education aims at higher realization in the earth, but the aims of spiritual education is to escape from all earthly manifestations. He talks of supreme liberation which is the result of merging into the formless. But we must carefully note that for Sri Aurobindo there was another implication for liberation. He was not supporting the type of liberation which is for the betterment of only one individual. It is not desirable that liberation would be for one individual whereas others suffer. "They dream that others should profit by the wonders they have discovered in their inner explorations."[32] It should not be supposed that

29. Jugal Kishore Mukherjee, p. 23.
30. *SABCL,* vol. 21, p. 590.
31. The Mother, p. 105.
32. Ibid., p. 108.

self-annihilation is the way for escaping from suffering, sorrow and death of this world.

The Development of the Supramental

This is followed by another state, i.e. the supramental education. The supramental education will progress from above downwards. Supramental education consists not merely in progressively developing human nature. It is transformation of the nature itself, an increasing growth of its latent faculties, heightening the consciousness and bringing down the higher consciousness into the lower.

The more and more we enter into the philosophy of Sri Aurobindo it becomes clear that his notion of integral education is the applied aspect of his philosophy of evolution. The Cartesian dualism of mind and matter may face a staunch critic in the philosophy of integral education as advocated by him. The age-old controversy between matter and problems relating to their association may be solved if integral education as advocated by Sri Aurobindo is accepted. For, if integral education is properly achieved, it is clearly a passage of man's consciousness encased in matter from inconscience, subconscience to super-conscience. Sri Aurobindo expresses it poetically as follows: "Man by himself is a little more than an ambitious nothing. He is a littleness that reaches to a wideness and a grandeur that are beyond him . . ."[33] *Yoga* and education come closer in Sri Aurobindo's philosophy. Sri Aurobindo does not identify *yoga* only with *haṭha yoga* for he considers that that sort of conception of *yoga* leads to the neglect of the psychological aspect of *yoga*. Nor does he accept the identification of education with professional training or vocational courses. Properly understood, in the light of Sri Aurobindo's philosophy *yoga* and education are one and the same thing. Sri Aurobindo explains the meaning of *yoga* as

33. *SABCL*, vol. 15, p. 94.

follows: "*yoga* is a methodized effort towards self-perfection by the expression of the potentialities latent in the being and a union of the human individual with the universal and the transcendent Existence we see partially expressed in man and in the Cosmos."[34] It is obvious from Sri Aurobindo's writings that the notion of transformation is one of the key concepts in Integral Yoga. He himself has clarified the meaning of transformation as follows: "I use transformation in a special sense, a change of consciousness radical and complete and of a certain specific kind which is so conceived as to bring about a strong and assured step forward in the spiritual evolution of the being of a greater and a higher kind and of a larger sweep and completeness than what took place when a mentalized being first appeared in a vital and material animal world."[35] The complete process of transformation as described by Sri Aurobindo is triple: psychic transformation, spiritual transformation, and supramental transformation. There is a distinction among transformation as there is a distinction between psychic consciousness and spiritual consciousness, there is distinction between spiritual consciousness and supramental consciousness.

According to Sri Aurobindo, the transformation when it is supramental, as a result of the descent of the supermind, the body, life and mind of man are also greatly transformed. With the descent of the supermind a radical transformation of all existence — material, vital, and mental takes palce and as a result of this man is transformed into superman or gnostic being. However, in this connection, it should be observed that "Our mental, physical, vital existence need not be destroyed by our self-exceeding, nor are they lessened and impaired by being spiritualized, they can and do become much richer, greater, more powerful: in their divine change they

34. *The Synthesis of Yoga,* p. 2.

35. *SABCL,* vol. 22, p. 98.

break into possibilities which in their unspiritualized condition could not be practicable or imaginable."[36] The process of supramental consists of following three steps:

1. Ascent to the supermind through the intermediary planes of consciousness — the higher mind, the illumined mind, the intuitive mind, and the overmind.
2. Bringing down the supramental through these planes of consciousness into the mental, vital and down to the physical.
3. Resulting in the reversal and the new integration of consciousness.

In this scheme supramental transformation and supramental education are the same thing. Supramental education is not confined to the mind for bringing about the potentialities of the mind. Supramental education is for the transformation of human nature itself, transformation of the being in its entirety. This supramental education, he believes, will bring about ascent of the species, superman, leading in the end to the appearance of a divine race upon earth. Thus, we find, for Sri Aurobindo, true education is a process of self-development, and this process of self-development through physical education, vital education and mental education may be the goal of all ordinary men. This process of self-development if carried further through the stages of psychical education, spiritual education and supramental education lead to a total transformation. The true education thus will establish life divine upon earth. Sri Aurobindo's philosophy of education is a reinterpretation, and rediscovery of the truth that is not sectarian but for humanity as a whole.

---

36. *SABCL*, vol. 18, p. 728.

References

Sri Aurobindo, *The Complete Works of Sri Aurobindo,* Sri Aurobindo Ashram Trust, 2003.

Bhattacharya, Pranab Kumar, *A Scheme of Education,* Sri Aurobindo Asharm, Pondicherry, 1952.

Joshi, Kireet, *Philosophy of Yoga of Sri Aurobindo and Other Essays,* The Mother's Institute of Research in Association with Mira Aditi, Mysore, 2003.

(The) Mother, *The Complete Works,* Sri Aurobindo Ashram, Pondicherry.

Mukherjee, Jugal Kishore, *Principles and Goals of Integral Education,* Sri Aurobindo Ashram, Pondicherry, 2005.

Saraswati, Acharya Vidyananda (Dr. Raghunath Pani), *Integral Education: Thought and Practice,* A.P.H. Publishing Corporation, New Delhi, 1997.

8

Relevance of Sri Aurobindo's Thoughts on Education to Teachers

Priya M. Vaidya

I

Indian Philosophy

SCIENTIFIC progress and technological advancement has made human life more comfortable. Material prosperity has amplified the possibility of progress. Yet, man's quest to know himself persists. Questions such as Who am I? What is my purpose in life? Seem to distract the common man and the academician, the rich and the poor, the old and the young some time somewhere. The need to explore the spiritual realm within encourages man to contemplate.

Indian philosophy as *darśana* occupies a special place in the scheme of progressive thoughts. It reveals to man the secrets of the spiritual world, which is indeed the basis of a meaningful life.

> The discipline that studies, or rather ventures to approach this experience, not only through understanding but also in faith and subservience, making the best of logic and epistemology, is what we know as *Darśana Śāstra* meant to

> train the mental faculty for *sādhanā* not for merely scholastic debates.[1]

Indian philosophers have studied and analysed human life from the spiritual perspective. This analysis has guided man to know the transcendental aspect of human life. Experiences of revelation, inner vision, spiritual awakening by seers and sages in India have unfolded the aspect of Divinity within. For instance, experiences shared by Swami Vivekānanda and Sri Aurobindo with people reveal this dialogue with the Divine.

According to Dr. Radhakrishnan, "It is not because India guards under her soil the bones of our fathers, but because she stands for eternal principles — that life is spiritual aspiration, matter the handiwork of spirit, and all Universe one in spirit."[2]

II

Sri Aurobindo's Philosophy of Education

Sri Aurobindo's philosophy is unique as it tries to comprehend the world by considering the Matter, the Spirit, Life, Mind, the Super Mind and their working in harmony with each other.

> In Sri Aurobindo's philosophy for the first time man and his terrestrial life have received their full recognition. He is the first to declare that it is possible for man in this terrestrial life, in this physical body, to attain complete Divinity.[3]

---

1. Maheshwari, H., "The meeting of the ancient and the modern in Indian philosophy today," *Indian Philosophical Annual*, vol. 18, [1985-86], University of Madras, p. 150.
2. Radhakrishnan, Sarvapalli, *The Philosophy of Rabindranath Tagore*, Baroda: Good Companions and Publishers, 1961, p. 179.
3. Maitra, S.K., *An Introduction to the Philosophy of Sri Aurobindo*, Pondicherry: Sri Aurobindo Ashram, 1986, p. 69.

The concept of Divinity according to Sri Aurobindo is unique as he emphasizes on seeking it by actually living in the physical universe. Sri Aurobindo is certain that man will become sooner or later, sooner rather than later, a Divine Man.

The philosophy of Sri Aurobindo with its entire centre being "man" and his potentialities to be Divine inculcates a feeling of optimism in man's present life. The same approach is perceived in his ideas on education.

The entire set-up of Sri Aurobindo's philosophy of education thus is based on a spiritual base, which is unique and is a rich blend of systematic and human approach to the field of education. The philosophy of education of Sri Aurobindo looks beyond the superficial aspect of education today and reflects on the intricacies of education and its close and complementary relation to life.

III

The Need for a Different Pattern of Education

A pattern of education closely depicts the society in the making. For the aims of education surely indicate the aim of the society. Sri Aurobindo's spiritual approach to life is lucidly focused in his philosophy and is carried forward in his philosophy of education. This may be the reason why he was against the European pattern of education, which was a contrast to it. The European pattern of education hardly has any Indian touch — the spiritual base. Sri Aurobindo emphasized on the Indian pattern of education unlike the foreign. This was so because, this kind of education was Indian in origin and philosophically profound.

The uniqueness of his philosophy of education was, he perceived education for the Indians with reference to the developing soul. By this, education would also take care of the future needs of the country.

Sri Aurobindo's stress on National education did not mean moving back to the mathematics of Bhaskar. The main focus was on the Spirit — the living and vital issue, which was important. He considered the mind/spirit to be the base of the foundation of education.

The educational system in the modern age has made us aware of the empirical world and its comforts so much that we have forgotten to look within. Although man has gained so much mastery over Nature, yet he has not been able to understand and control his Self. This may be the defeat of our educational system and humanity in total. The pupils are not made aware of the intricacies of life such as its subtle beauty, charm and inner worth. The pupils are not trained to recognize the true capacities of the body, the mind and the secret of the soul.

Advanced teaching technologies and still advanced information have only equipped pupils intellectually and helped them to develop the world scientifically. Hardly any effort is taken to help the pupil to become a loving child, an honest worker and a committed countryman.

Development and progress of the mind largely determines the progress of the country. Sad confused minds cannot construct a better world. Thus, the need is to revive the thoughts on education of great Indian thinkers in the modern age. Indian philosophers of the modern age can play a vital role in this process. They can train the educators and the pupils to grasp the true purpose of education as viewed by Sri Aurobindo. This will not only establish the lost links between philosophy and education but it will also give the educators a chance to analyse life gradually. These thoughts can progressively nurture a better system of education in India.

The paper attempts to suggest [HELP] a Holistic Educational Learning Programme for educators based on the thoughts of Sri Aurobindo.

IV

Holistic Educational Learning Programme [HELP]

A. THE AIM OF THE PROGRAMME

(a) To bring forward spiritual development in educators.

(b) To help educators to become effective facilitators of knowledge.

B. APPROACH

The approach adopted is holistic. It aspires to nurture in the educators a spiritual perspective about life so as to become effective facilitators by incorporating the views of Sri Aurobindo on education.

C. THE PROCESS DESIGN

(a) To acquaint the educators about the essence of Sri Aurobindo's thoughts on education.

(b) To arrange activities for the educators so as to grasp the theoretical and practical significance of Sri Aurobindo's thoughts on education.

The brief review of the process design:

(a) To acquaint the educators about the essence of Sri Aurobindo's thoughts on education

Sri Aurobindo's philosophy of education is different from others for its systematic approach, which gives equal importance to the material and spiritual aspect of life. Sri Aurobindo considers the true basis of education to be the study of the human mind. He states that nothing can be actually taught. Thus, the task of the teacher is not to impose but instead to suggest.

(i) *The role of the teacher:* The mind according to Sri Aurobindo has to be consulted in its growth. He considers that each person has something Divine, something which is his own, and he thus has also a chance of perfection. The task of the teacher is to help the growing soul to draw out that, in itself, which is best, and make it perfect for a noble use. He also suggests that a pupil should pursue a journey from within for transforming oneself. The educationist must consider the *citta* as an important layer to understand what lay within the human being actually.

(ii) *The mind proper or the manas:* The first business of the educationist according to Sri Aurobindo is to develop the five senses in the child. The training should be so perfect that the hand for instance should be trained to reproduce what the eye sees and the mind senses.

(iii) *The intellect or buddhi:* Sri Aurobindo calls the intellect or *buddhi* as the real instrument of thought. The intellect is an organ composed of several groups of functions divisible in two important classes — the functions and faculties of the right hand and the functions and faculties of the left hand.

(iv) *The highest stratum of knowledge:* The highest stratum of knowledge focuses on the peculiar powers present in man. Experiences of revelation, direct vision of knowledge, plenary inspiration of speech, etc. Sri Aurobindo stresses on the importance of this kind of knowledge unlike the modern educationist who dismisses it as meaningless.

(v) *The moral nature in man:* The modern pattern of education has ignored the importance of moral nature in man. Sri Aurobindo gives importance to the moral nature of man. He highlights the factors which play an important role in determining the moral nature such as (a) the emotions, (b) the *saṁskāra*s or formed habits, and (c) the *svabhāva* or nature.

The best emotional, mental and physical habit with its continuity in right action can help the individual to grow actually. Reading of biographies, setting forward personal examples, etc., can help the pupil to make changes in his moral nature. Self-training, *sādhanā* and exercise can prepare the individual for the religious living. Moral training is essential to help the pupil to realize the relation of his life to God, towards humanity, for the country, for others and also for oneself.

(vi) *Education-intellectual:* Sri Aurobindo feels that in India we have confused education with the acquisition of knowledge only. He accepts that giving knowledge to the pupil is necessary but the more necessary aspect than this is to build in the pupil the power of knowledge.

The presence of knowledge is not only an important aspect of education but with it the best use of knowledge possessed is equally necessary. The need of the hour according to Sri Aurobindo is to grasp the worth of intellectual alertness, quickness and originality.

(vii) *The perfection of the body from a spiritual angle:* Sri Aurobindo's philosophy of education does not limit itself to encouraging the growth of moral, intellectual capacities in the individual with special reference to the full use of sense-organs only. In fact, he tries to give importance to achieve perfection of the body through education itself.

Sri Aurobindo feels that if a divine life is possible on earth then broadening the powers of the body is possible. Perfection can be accomplished through Yoga. Yoga is a means — a path that is spiritual and psychic. The mind and the body are prepared to make them fit for the reception of the spiritual energy.

(viii) *Suggestions by Sri Aurobindo to improve the modern- day educational system*

[a] *Teachers io devote nine-tenths of their energy to education*: Teachers should focus more on the active mental faculties in the pupils. The three sisters in the family of knowledge, viz. humanities, mathematics and science should be the concern of the educational system. The powers in the pupil can be developed if the teacher educators encourage the mastery in these subjects.

[b] *Teaching needs reform*: Sri Aurobindo stresses not on imposing of knowledge but tries to encourage the process of self-education initiated by the child himself. He emphasizes that the true art of teaching is to awaken the interest in the pupil to master the subject.

[c] *Learning language*: Learning of language is not a casual process of learning. Sri Aurobindo suggests mastery over one's own language to master other languages later on. He considers the mother tongue to be the proper medium of education.

[d] *Appeal qualities in the pupil*: Sri Aurobindo reminds the educationist to give away the teaching by snippets. This does not help the development of the individual. He intends to focus on the process of education, which begins from within interacting with the material world outside.

[e] *Training of the logical faculty*: The logical faculty can be trained to work in a proper way. Sri

Aurobindo considers the training of logical faculty as one of the important aspects of education. The training of the logical faculty can guide the pupils to think correctly. Teacher educators should take effort to develop this faculty in the pupil.

(b) To arrange activities for the teacher educators so as to extend the theoretical and practical significance of Sri Aurobindo's thoughts on education

The activities are as follows:

(i) *Yoga training for teacher educators*: Yoga training sessions can guide the teacher-educators to be physically fit, mentally alert, and emotionally stable and spiritually awake. This session should be conducted everyday for one hour.

(ii) *Music appreciation session*: This session should be conducted for the teachers at least once in a week for a duration of one hour.

(iii) *Poetry reading session*: Self-composed poems or poems of great poets should be read and discussed amongst the teacher educators once in a month.

(iv) *Games*: Teachers should be encouraged to design educational games to enhance creativity within and extend concern towards the students apparently. Such games can also help the body and the mind to relax.

(v) *Meditation*: Teachers should be trained to meditate at least for one hour everyday. This will help the teacher educators to develop the art of introspection.

D. BENEFITS

- Teachers can become effective facilitators.
- This can help the teacher educators to be positive.

- This is indeed a cost effective and relevant programme in the modern age.

E. LIMITATIONS

Lack of commitment on the part of the teacher educators can hamper the scope of the programme.

F. UNIQUE

The programme is spiritual and relevant in the modern age. It can elevate human life in many ways.

G. GLOBAL SIGNIFICANCE

This programme can guide the teacher-educators from different countries to be effective facilitators and promoters of peace within and without.

V

Conclusion

The importance of spiritualism in education is more relevant today for it gives importance to the human heart and not to the human intellect only. The heart and the head together surely help the development of oneself and the society. The gains out of this pattern of education are, it inculcates a feeling of belongingness towards the society with a concern towards one and all. If the divine in man is realized with the help of education then our educational institutes can one day become the temples of knowledge actually. This would mean transformation in man and development of the society at large. Sri Aurobindo's thoughts on education can help and guide us to accomplish this goal in the modern age.

9

Education
A Faithful Transcription

Rashmi Sethi

"THE meaning we attribute to human life depends in the final analysis on the place we assign to man in the universe as a whole." This in turn will depend on our total attitude towards reality *without* and reality *within*.

When we look at the separative existence, found in strife-ridden relationship, excessive materialistic moorings, exclusive identities where personalities have become anonymous, shorn of authentic experience, one can gauge the quality of human existence generally operative as of now.

Further, trends in educational research focussing on themes like "teacher burn out," emolument related dissatisfaction in teachers, stagnation in teaching (otherwise a dynamic noble profession), increasing call to accommodate human rights education, value education, gender studies, etc. necessarily concern us about the state of affairs. Surely, something other than elected authority and provisions made for the welfare of mankind at the societal level is needed. There is a need to work upon the "state of consciousness in man's dealings with himself and his relationship with others."

This presentation is an attempt at the exposition of the concept of education enunciated by Sri Aurobindo and The

Mother. It also intends to look at how education can become a faithful transcription of the experience of reality in totality. Before proceeding further, a brief look at the concept of Integralism would help to situate the observations that follow.

1. Integralism or the inclusive totality is a world-view that visualizes reality in totality of existence, consciousness-force and bliss. This reality is seen as grades, viz. the physical, vital, mental, psychic, spiritual and supramental.
2. It is world-affirming as it affirms the individual, the universal and the transcendent, the aspects of Reality.
3. It admits the principle of involution-evolution as a delight of the Divine to relate matter and spirit in a spiral unfolding.
4. It is all encompassing as it does not leave out any aspect of reality (entity or event) as insignificant in its scheme.
5. It is all-accommodating as it does not reject any aspect of reality as inconsequential or unwanted.
6. It is comprehensive in its treatment as it harmoniously entertains the range of experiences while retaining the uniqueness, and commonality of each, simultaneously.
7. It addresses the cascade of conflicts in experience at the physical, vital and mental levels of mundane existence (mixed consciousness) and seeks to resolve them through the transformation of consciousness.
8. It takes note of the dissatisfaction owing to the gap in relating matter and spirit as the two extremes of the same spectrum.
9. It focusses on the dialectics of progress wherein stepwise relating of the matter to the spirit is brought

about at the individual, the universal and the transcendental levels intrapolating it at the level of the basic structuro-functional unit — the cell.

10. It resolves the numerous paradoxes that afflict the individual and the society on their way to progress and development. Caught in the paradoxes, the dynamic force gets paralysed resulting in the "tragedy of ineffective action."

11. Integralism contends that *Separation* is false in practice, unreal in essence and its basis can be transformed into unitive experience marked by the principle of harmony and rhythm.

12. Thus, it provides a strong *terra firma* for educational endeavour to promote the evolution of consciousness through the "action-ability paradigm" at the individual and universal levels.

Integralism sees man as an individual with a soul, a *refracted portion* of the Divine (consciousness). He is a physical, vital and mental being and operates at different levels of consciousness. Wrapped in matter as body, he is a conscious manifestation in nature of "the union of the self and spirit." Human personality is visualized as consisting of evolving components, namely, physical, vital, mental and psychic. Man's personality has a scope to evolve from three-dimensional to four-dimensional entity in which each component has the possibility of its realization necessarily through the other, under the stewardship of the soul (psychic).

Integral education works to restore the lost delight of Man (at present in fragmented existence). It can become a faithful transcription when it enables the Individual to identify with his self and translate this identity each moment in his actions such that each cell of his body identifies itself with the self (psychic). "Education that deals with man in whom the constituents of personality are governed by the psychic entity" enlarges the scopes for his union with the Divine. This premise unfolds the spiritual dialectics, here on earth as a field for Divine deliberation.

Education impacts the quality of existence at various levels through the principle of transformation, i.e. upward opening and expansion of consciousness. It prepares the individual for progressive change in the consciousness, "a turning towards" and contacting the all-pervasive reality. This makes integral education dynamic and evolutionary in nature. It is democratic as it holds that true teaching consists in consulting the instrument of knowledge in the progress of the individual. It allows an experience guided by integral principles. It has a progressive pedagogy well-cushioned by Integral Yoga which dissolves the limits of consciousness of the individual and the society in a methodical way. It has the promise to enable the individual to be free from misconceptions owing to the snippets of information, the world liberated from global chaos and mankind from evolutionary crises.

In fact, the *integral principles of teaching* express the self-willed principle of involution of *The Divine;* it is individual-centred and proceeds from existential to transcendental level of existence.

It guides the inward growth through the free progress system which regards the individual uniqueness with respect to the ascent from below and descent from above of the consciousness.

It aligns the physical, the vital and the mental faculties in such a way that the heart is trained to reproduce what the eyes see and mind senses, thus removing the discrepancy to decode the experience in its totality. All this through the education in physical culture, aesthetic culture and mental culture, leading to such a quietude in the mind that concepts get translated into an experience which is identical with the being. Aspiration and love contribute immensely to transact complete identity.

Religion can become an uplifting experience sans *communal* connotations associated with it when viewed integrally. It implies living for God, humanity, country and oneself, none being at cross purpose to the interest of the other.

Such an education provides for man's participation in higher and vaster life through greater consciousness.

At the social level too, it would help to manage the tension of the multi-marginal commitments of an individual as a member of diverse groups, each with its own objective, usually loosening the integrity of the individual.

Value component in this education would be taken care of when any action is prompted by concern; it becomes rational and just; this lends value and credibility to the lived experience.

Education which works for the realization of the self at various levels adopts the yogic pedagogy.

Yoga becomes a logical necessity when we accept the ontic principle of the Supermind which can be realized by transformation in the existing consciousness, the nature of which is piecemeal. As a practice in the development of inner consciousness of man it rationally arrives at the unitive perception of matter in relation to the spirit. "Integral Yoga is an experience that helps to regain the lost unity by opening up the consciousness" (SA20 39).

Identity and relation with higher consciousness systematically enables the consciousness of the individual to become aware of things, forces and the cosmos simultaneously to experience the unitive co-existence of diversity. Integral Yoga operationalizes the linkage conceived among the three facets of reality. Rhythm and harmony the quaint quotients of bliss (*ānanda*) become operative through *yoga* wherein form becomes complementary to the force in one's experience.

Integral Yoga psychologizes the metaphysical reality by *transcribing* the latter into the mental experience. Thus it lends **reality** to the transcendent aspect.

Education benefits through *yoga* as human relationship, when identified and enriched, would lift the quality of life meaningfully.

Education as *yoga* puts the principle of harmony in perspective to relook at actions prompted at the level of ordinary consciousness. Integralism which sees paradoxes as reflective of imperfection in relationship benefits from education which works to regain the lost delight in knowledge, will and action.

Nothing less than Divine union being the *motif* of Integral Yoga, gives impetus to self-perfection through *yoga* of the Divine work, *yoga* of the Divine knowledge, and *yoga* of the Divine love. It involves a series of transformations. *Yoga* of the Divine work seeks the union through action mediated by the *Principle of Sacrifice.* Sacrifice, as a common Divine action, helps to recover the oneness of the individual. It has the strength to sublimate the whole nature by perfecting action. Identification with sacrifice affirms the Divine presence here on earth.

Sri Aurobindo states that any consciously-guided sacrifice can become Divine on the condition that the heart, the will and the mind of the individual are associated with the law and gladly follow it. Gradually sacrifice leads to consecration, and conversion in consciousness. The contact with the universal energy enlarges and its presence becomes a reality for the individual. This constant work leads to psychic transformation. Thus selfless action becomes universal and later spiritual.

The *yoga* of the Divine work needs the *yoga* of the Divine knowledge as action is motivated by right identification of one's existence whose knowledge is important.

The *yoga* of the Divine knowledge enlightens the ignorance in experience as it understands paradoxes as boundless realization of the same Divine. By knowledge through the self, nature and works, it fulfils Man-Divine relationship, and furnishes the proper notion of the self and the world, which is essential to identify the self.

However, the integral vision to experience the universal and the transcendent Divine as a grasped Reality in the individual needs the *yoga* of the Divine love. In it, Love is treated as an elemental emotion shared by all. As relation with the Divine develops, all sensitivities integrate and get transformed leading to the effective experience of the Divine love — hitherto adventitious, survival becomes authentic existence.

Yoga prepares for the emergence of the soul centre of the individual and then a stage reaches when glimpse of the Divine descent becomes real to one's perception.

As *yoga* of the Divine work purifies, the Divine knowledge identifies, *yoga* of the Divine love inspires the working out in our living form and action of the inner consciousness, thus removing "the tragedy of ineffectiveness in action." Yogic experiences purport to empower the individual for transformation.

It is also called the *yoga* of self-perfection as it deals with the perfection in interrelatedness and inalienable harmony.

Education through yogic method (contact) transforms the *derivative experience* of reality into a *direct experience* as it deepens man's direct contact with the reality.

Integral education thus provides a comprehensive and convincing broad way for the *seekers* of spiritual transformation in life.

Part IV
On Poetry and Art

10

"The Word that Knows"
Sri Aurobindo's Metaphysics of Poetry

Pabitrakumar Roy

I

SRI Aurobindo has himself been a poet exercising his own theory of poetry. It was as a poet that he consistently saw himself, and it was to the writing of poetry that he always reverted whenever his other activities allowed. His poetic output is immense, he wrote poetry for over fifty years, and shortly before his death, in his 78th year he was concentrating on the revision of his epic, *Sāvitrī*. It has become the record of his own spiritual experience, and the vehicle for his teaching. Its epic theme is the adventure of consciousness. *Sāvitrī* is a sort of poetic philosophy of the Spirit and of Life. It is the visionary, revelatory element in *Sāvitrī* that gives it its unique quality. It is a new kind of poetry, and demands a new mentality. *Sāvitrī* is a record of a seeing. Whether one likes this *genre* of poetry is another matter.

Sri Aurobindo's theory of poetry is an argument for the new kind of poetry, its language and office. Parallel to the evolution of consciousness, language of poetry too evolves towards a discourse of an experience of the sun of Truth unmasked of the golden disc. The poet throws into significant form the truth he has seen. It is the vision of the creator that matters in poetry. Sri Aurobindo calls it "the *mantra* in poetry"(*FP*, p.9). Poetry *par excellence* is the rhythmic speech which arises at once from the heart of the seer, it is a discovery of the word, the form of thought proper to the reality. In this pursuit poetry goes beyond the visible, and as all art do, it reveals and shows us that which is hidden. It is in this light that Sri Aurobindo's theory of poetry is to judged and appreciated. Poetry in the past has done the miracle of revelation at moments of elevation. Rimbaud ordained that one must be a *seer*, make oneself a *seer* by a long, prodigious dedication. The poet's job is a self-search. *Je dis qu'il faut etre voyant, se faire voyant* are Rimbaud's own words.

In his letter to Paul Demeny, Rimbaud continues that a language has to be found. This new language would be of the soul, every word being an idea, the time of the universal language will come. Revelations from the unknown demand new language (*formes nouvelles*). Rimbaud mentioned Baudelaire as the first seer, king of poets (see *Rimbaud*, tr. Oliver Bernard, Penguin, 1962, pp. 7-16). In his theory of poetry, Sri Aurobindo explores the possibility of the seeing diction of poetry, a more conscious aim and steadfast endeavour. Hence, the future poetry.

II

Sri Aurobindo seeks to establish poetry as the *mantra* of the real. Ordinarily poetry is conceived as an aesthetic pleasure of the imagination, the intellect and the ear. Thus looked upon one is to miss poetry's inner aim and deeper law. It is not denied that imaginative pleasure is the first element of any art, the point is that pleasure is not enough for supporting poetry as the support for something greater beyond. Sri Aurobindo considers the intelligence, the imagination and the ear are not the true recipients of the poetic delight, nor are they true creators or hearers. They are only its channels and instruments. The more directly the word reaches and sinks deep into the soul, the greater the poetry. This is Sri Aurobindo's basic thesis. The pleasure of the instrument is to be raised and transmuted into the deeper delight of the soul. Or the ontological category of *ānanda* is that from which poetry arises, and it is to that soul it reposes. Sri Aurobindo views *ānanda* as a great formative and illuminative power of any creativity.

What role does the critics or the artist then play? Technique does make poetry. A deficient execution may not prevent the poet's soul from creating great poetry. Compared to its importance in other arts, technique occupies a smaller field in poetry. The rhythmic word as an element of poetry is subtle, complex and variously suggestive. It bears almost infinite possibilities in many directions. Sri Aurobindo distinguishes different values of the rhythmic word, its sound value, thought value and soul value. It may be recalled Rabindranath too had suggested a distinction between the truth-value and "the taste-value" of a work of art (see *Personality*, "What is Art?," 1965, p. 20). The taste-value is unanalysable, it lies in the unity that transcends the facts *about* a work of art. Moore perhaps had some such idea in mind when he spoke of beauty as an organic whole. Poetic discourse, in a similar mode, goes beyond the laws of technique and on its summits exhibits an element of the ineffable. The form of the poetic speech is determined from within, it is not imposed by any mechanical law external to it. The poet, in the heat of creation, comes to possess the form. The intellectual sense of "form" is a subordinate action or an undertone in the mind of the creator. It is in this sense that Plato, in his *Ion* said that the poets are possessed and inspired, poetry is a spontaneous projection. It is not by art that the poet sings, but by power divine. As Plato put the matter, God takes away the minds of poets, and uses them as his ministers. The priceless words of high poetry are uttered in a state of unconsciousness. God himself is the speaker, and through them he is talking with us (see *Ion*, 533f).

The word "inspiration" relates to breathing. The metaphor of breathing recurs in the Upaniṣads. The Vedas are projected as though they were breathed out by the real self (*Bṛhadāraṇyaka*, 2.4.10.). When Sri Aurobindo speaks of poetry as "the spontaneous form" of the poet's soul, he is in point of fact looking back to the creative act of the Spirit, which he takes and uses as the model of poetic creation.

Poetry then is "self-vision," and the discourse seeks to extend the visionary quality to all experience. An urge for transcendence marks poetry. It may start from the sensuous and sensible, and using it as a symbol and a source of images, it soars beyond the visible, and reveals that which is hidden. Sri Aurobindo is led to buttress this theory of poetry by considering the historical development of meaning of words. In ordinary language, which is utilitarian in its motive and intention, words are treated as conventional signs. Though useful for life, words are, as Sri Aurobindo points out, without life. The conventional word-signs are infused with life by the speaker's intonations of voice. But in the primitive usage, words had a real and vivid life, and speakers were conscious of the matter. Words were magically potent. In his study of the Vedic language, Sri Aurobindo has dwelt at length on this issue. Studied intellectually, we may not find any natural or inherent equivalent between any sound and its sense. There must have been an indefinable quality in the sound "to raise certain vibrations in the life-soul of the human creature" (op. cit., p. 13). When the word *vṛka* was used in the Vedic expression, it did not *denote* a wolf merely, it *meant* the "tearer." Such had been "the sensational relation" between the wolf and man. A certain quality in the soul associated it with the sensation of tearing. There have been great debates between Nyāya and Mīmāṁsā thinkers regarding the meaning of words. The Mīmāṁsakas hold that the word means primarily the universal (*jāti*), the Naiyāyikas maintained that it means the universal, the structure (*samasthāna*) that goes with the universal, and also the individual. The debate had given rise to two distinct views of sentence interpretation. The Nyāya view is called the doctrine of relation of the meanings of uttered words, *abhihitānvayavāda*, as against the Mīmāṁsā (Prabhākara's) view, called the doctrine of the uttering words, the meanings of which have already been related, *anvitābhidhānavāda*. Sri Aurobindo's point is something else. For him it is the primacy of the noun-words. The Nyāya and the Mīmāṁsā accounts are sophisticated intellectual treatment of the problem of the meaning of sentences and of words occurring therein, there is nothing primitive about their accounts. Sri Aurobindo goes further back in time in order to unravel the mystery of words in relation to meaning. A recovery of the original function of words is needed.

There have been kindred views that tell us that reason is not man's primitive endowment. Language, they go on to say, reflects man's myth-making tendency. Philosophy of mind involves much more than a theory of knowledge, it involves a theory of prelogical conception and expression. It may be worth our while to take note of some of the relevant views. Mythology, said Max Müller, is inevitable, it is the power of language on thought in every possible sphere of mental activity. But Sri Aurobindo will never endorse Max Müller's view that the mythical world is essentially a world of illusion, however original and necessary be the self-deception of the mind. One might feel quite amused to find a linkage between Max Müller's view and that of Wittgenstein's idea of bewitchment by language. Is myth really a darkening shadow which language throws upon thought? There is Hamann's dictum that poetry is the mother tongue of humanity, and it has also come to be held that speech is rooted not in the prosaic but in the poetic aspect of life, and hence its ultimate basis must be sought not in preoccupation with the objective view of things. Sri Aurobindo has brought out the difference between prose and poetry. Prose, he says, takes its stand on the intellectual value of the word. Adequacy of speech is its first object. As a style, prose carries speech to a higher power than its ordinary usage, in attaining a general fluid harmony of movement. Prose associates words agreeably and clarifies the intelligence, and strives after accurate, subtle, flexible and satisfying expression. It may even acquire an outward approximation to poetry, use figures of speech as figures of thought, i.e. for giving a stronger intellectual vision of the thing or the thought it defines. Prose always "has its eye on its chief hearer and judge, the intelligence. . . . Reason and taste, two powers of the intelligence, are rightly the supreme gods of the prose stylist" (ibid., p. 15). On the contrary, the privilege of the poet is to go beyond such powers of high prose as adequacy and effectivity and discover, in tenser illumination, the inspired word of inevitable utterance with a depth of sense and a power of infinite suggestion welling up directly from the spirit within. The highest trend of the poet's utterance is to seek for the inevitable word, and he finds it, he casts "into it some deeply revealed truth of the spirit itself," and what he thus utters is the *mantra*. We may note, in passing, what Longinus had spoken of such achievements of language: it "carries one up to where one is close to the majestic mind of God." (*On The Sublime*, Chapter 36, tr. T.S. Dorsch, Penguin, 1965, p. 147).

Sri Aurobindo puts a special value on the lyric as it comes closer to the *mantra* mode of utterance. For him, the lyric is the primary poetical motive and spirit. Ernst Cassirer has argued that lyric poetry is rooted in mythic motives, and keeps its connection with myth even in its highest and purest products. What he means by the lyrical is not just a general category of poetic literature. In this context what is of moment is the fact that the lyric is expressive of the mystical experience the poet or speaker undergoes at blessed moments. The hymn was among the first developed of the definably lyric genre. Apart from the *Ṛgveda*, the ancient bodies of the lyric poetry is the Hebrew, owing something to Egyptian and Babylonian sources. The Egyptian origin of the Hebrew lyric is evident from the fact that Moses was taught the whole theory of rhythm, harmony and meter by the Egyptians. The famous hymn of Moses in *Exodus* (15.1-2) is a case in point. The lyrical genius of Sappho was so great that Plato counted her to be the tenth muse beside the nine. She asked her daughter not to mourn her death, because in dying she was "to enter a home of poetry" (*Greek Lyric Poetry*, tr. Willis Barrstone, Bantam Books, New York, 1962, p. 94). The modern masters of the lyric, Yeats, Rilke and Rabindranath, have all used language to enshrine their visions of life and existence, suffused by the illumination of the spiritual.

III

What distinguishes Sri Aurobindo is his accent on the visionary quality of poetry, or the seerhood of the poet. *Satyadharmāya dr̥ṣṭaye* (*Īsa Upaniṣad*, 15) is the prayer proper on the part of the poet. It is not the psycho-physical person who could be said to be the seer. It is the soul which sees, says Sri Aurobindo. Everything else is to become the instruments of the soul. For high poetry to be there, there has to obtain a spiritual transmutation of the organs, and the expression comes out purified and uplifted. In the terminology of Nyāya, the organs are defined as the instruments, *karaṇa* of the *ātman*. Whatever the *ātman* uses for its own purpose is material in nature, unconscious, *jaḍa*. Sri Aurobindo employs the ideas of *bahiḥkaraṇa* and *antaḥkaraṇa*, or as he says, the eye, sense, heart and thought — mind, and renders them as instruments of the soul. Thus there are two elements, one the outward or instruments, and the other, the real or spiritual. In matters empirical we employ categories of the intelligence, which makes the data of cognition precise and definite. Thus we come to have the intellectual idea. But the soul idea is another story. It exceeds the intellectual, and brings into identity with the whole reality of the thing expressed. Keats wrote in a letter that when a sparrow came to his window, he shared its existence, and picked about the gravel. Sri Aurobindo has put the matter as follows:

> A knowledge which became what it perceived,
> Replaced the separated sense and heart
> And drew all nature into its embrace.
>
> — *Selections from Sāvitrī,* ed. Mary Aldridge,
> Sri Aurobindo Ashram, Pondicherry, 1975, p. 20.

It is a remaking of consciousness. *The Life Divine* contains the celebrated distinction of separative knowledge from knowledge by identity. Our knowledge of external things is separative, we do not identify ourselves with external objects, we do not enter into their existence as if it were our own. Whatever contact we have of them is through the senses. But this is no real directness or real intimacy with objects known. There is much that remains to be made up by a sense-mind intuition. Reason-organized knowledge is chiefly a knowledge of the surface of things.

What then is called for is a deeper and larger cognition, a knowledge by the direct contact of consciousness with its object. Apropos the Vedāntic theory, "consciousness is one in the subject and the object, and in the contact of existence with existence this identity brings to light or awakens in the self the dormant knowledge of this other self outside it" (*The Life Divine*, 1949, p. 483). This is knowledge as seeing. The poet makes us live in the soul as he himself sees by the soul beyond the sight of the surface mind, and thereby finding the revealing word.

Here we have Sri Aurobindo's radical thesis, namely that the poetic word makes us see, and it is only secondarily that it may make us think or feel. Sight, he says, is the primary consequence and power of poetic speech. The kindred arts of painting, sculpture and architecture appeal through significant images. For poetry, the image is verbal, or verbal icons, when we come across the inevitable word, it compels us to see, *mantra* starts from the revelatory poetic word.

The word has a graduation of its expressing powers of vision. Sri Aurobindo invokes the grade of speech (*vāk*) called *paśyanti vāk* which may have evolved out of the Vedic images in the hymn to us as, wherein the goddess is spoken of as uncovering her breast (*Ṛgveda*, 1.92); Agni is said as giving the poet clarifying vision (*Ṛgveda*, 4.5, 7 and 8); in another context (6.9), Agni inspires the poet to speak the right words. Even the epithet *kavi*, the poet, has a special use for Agni. Sri Aurobindo takes the term to denote "as the mystic fire." In the Upaniṣad it is declared, times without number, that *vāk* verily is the Reality, *vāk vai brahmā* (*Bṛhadāraṇyaka*, 4.1.2), that *vāk* is the fourth poise of the Reality, *vāgeva brahmanścaturthaḥ pādaḥ* (*Chāndogya*, 3.20.3) and *yā vāk sāma*, speech itself the revealed word (*Chāndogya*, 1.3.4.) for example. The argument runs as follows: If Reality is self-manifesting, and if speech is one with it, then speech reveals itself as the word. It remains for the poet to discover that.

The dicovery has to be gradual with the evolution of consciousness in the poet. Adopting the *Īśa Upaniṣad* image of the golden disk covering the face of the Sun we could say with Sri Aurobindo that such surface beauties as those of image, through an emotion, though not unspiritual in themselves, might stand in the way of a full and open disclosure. The task is to look beyond the image, and not to be seized by it. The pleasure we have from the outward beauty crafted in the body of poetry is not enough. It has to pass into or drowned in the *ānanda*, the ecstasy of poetic revelation. A transfiguration of the poetic devices has to take place, and language attaining to the height of bare and direct expression leaps into the infinite. Style, as a consciously intellectual mode of expression, is of no consequence in meeting the severe demand of *mantra*. It creates its own style. The Word is the essence of the poetic style.

What about the hearing? The thesis that poetic utterance is a discovery, and that poetic inspiration passes into an ecstasy of sight has to account for the alleged pleasure of the ear we derive from poetry. Let us consider the term *indriya*. It does not stand for the physical organs. It is the inner locus of the contact between *manas* and the sensation. Accordingly Sri Aurobindo speaks of an inner hearing. Poetry addresses itself to the inner senses. Even though he maintains that sight is the essential poetic gift, he appears to suggest that poetic truth is seen, while its word is heard. The evolution in poetry is from the objective to the inward, and from the inward to the spiritual. But the question arises: are seeing and hearing two different species of perception depending on the difference of the sense-organs involved? Is there a primacy of seeing over hearing? Or are seeing and hearing but the same modes of perceiving, only externally differentiated? Perceptuality of both seeing and hearing, according to the view of *pratyakṣatva* argued in the *Vedānta Paribhāṣā,* is not constituted by the sense-organs. The fact of being due to the organs is not the criterion of perception, *na hi indriya janyatvam pratyakṣatve*. Perceptuality entails that what is perceived does not have any existence apart from the *pramātṛ caitanya*, i.e. the consciousness associated with the subject. On grounds such as these, Sri Aurobindo may be taken as equating seeing and hearing, they are integrated, it is the soul, after all, which sees and hears.

Sri Aurobindo takes up the matter for a deeper understanding. Are not the poets of *mantra* seers of truth and hearers of its word? If that be so, then how can we sustain the claim that sight is essentially the poetic gift?

Rhythm is the founding element of poetic expression. The revealing word has its own unity of measure and speech.

Thought echoes with the native sound of its Ideas, as Sri Aurobindo puts it.

The tone builds the verse. There is a rhythm of thought and spirit that sounds within the poet, and in bringing it out, he suggests more than what is heard. The inaudible music floats above the vocal music. The unheard song (so favourite with Kabīr) is heard behind and in the inner silence. To catch some of its echo is the privilege and intention of poetical rhythm. It may be recalled that silence too is a status in the self. The word vibrates out of the nameless silence. One complements the other, "It is out of the Silence that the Word creates the worlds forever proceeds; for the word expresses that which is self-hidden in the Silence" (op. cit., p. 27). Poetry is the rhythmic voice, but it is the inner voice that enlivens the pulsations of the surface voices.

It is possible to say that Sri Aurobindo proposes what may be called the revelation theory (*a la* I.A. Richards, in *Principles of Literary Criticism*) as regards both seeing and hearing. He does not say much about music, but what has been offered in the above for the value of sound in poetry could be extended to music as well. Beethoven's great compositions were done when he had lost the power of hearing, and he considered his music as revelatory of the states of the soul as an incorporeal entrance into the higher world through tones that sound and roar and storm. There is some truth in Walter Pater's remark that all art constantly aspires towards the condition of music. Every art endeavours to obliterate the distinction of the matter from the form. There may be different degrees of achievement. Even Sri Aurobindo suggests that the poetic ideal is that in which the distinction is reduced to its minimum. In lyric we are least able to detach the matter from the form, and the lyric is, for him, the primary poetic motive. He quotes, approvingly of course, Keats' idea that the poet has to be a miser of sound and syllable, economical of his means in making the most of all its possibilities of sound.

A certain shedding of the verbal luggage is required on the poet's part in his journey towards discovering the *puissant* word. J.W.N. Sullivan in his study of Beethoven writes that in the Ninth Symphony there is a reaching out after something that should transcend what is called the human, an exploration into a new region of consciousness. It is a revelation of existence as seen from the vintage point a higher consciousness. The greatness of Beethoven's late music is unique, not only in music, but in the whole of art (see *Beethoven*, Pelican, 1927).

May be that Sri Aurobindo purposes a sort of synthesis of hearing and seeing. Both are as much revelatory of Truth, as when they are fused into and rooted in the Spirit. A work of art, be it poetry or music is, as Keats has put it, a "fosterchild of silence and slow time." What the piper painted on the Greek urn plays is to be heard by the inner ear:

> . . . Therefore, ye soft pipes, play on;
> Not to the sensual ear, but more endar'd,
> Pipe to the spirit ditties of no tone

When Rabindranath asks: "Have you not heard his silent steps?" the point at issue comes to life at once. Sri Aurobindo speaks of "soul sound" that all mystics hear, as did Mira, when she tells us of hearing the footfalls of Hari. Or, lately, as Jirbanananda Das, a Bengali poet of recent times says that he heard angels singing among the deodar trees. Such hearing is seeing as well.

Post Script

Indian philosophy has ever been concerned with language. Long before the philosophical schools were formed, the *Ṛgveda* and the Upaniṣads mused deeply on the mystery and manifestation of *vāk*, and its forms. Language is spoken of as rooted in Reality (*Brahman*). In turns of the metaphor of the inverted tree (*Gītā*), one could say that *vāk* has its roots above, while its branches spread below. The *Kena Upaniṣad* declares that Reality is the informing source of *vāk, yena vāgbhuyadate*. The *Atharvaveda* tells us that speech is inspired by the Transcendent, *apārveneśitā vācas*. This phrase was a great favourite of Rabindranath Tagore.

The *R̥gveda* mentions it numerous times that language is a mystery. A few of them may be cited.

The *R̥k* attributed to *Dīrghtamas* speaks of the fourfold poises of *vāk* (*R̥V*, I.164.45). Three of the poises are hidden in a cave, abide without manifestation, only the fourth one is spoken by humans. The idea that *vāk*, resplendent as lightning is hidden in a cave, but a part of it is uttered in assemblies: *sābhavati vidathyeva sam vāk* (*R̥V*, I.167.3) is obliquely referred to by Vālmīki, when in the Uttarakāṇḍa of the *Rāmāyaṇa* (97th Canto) he introduces Sītā in Rāma's court by saying that she looked like *vedaśruti* following Brahmā. The idea again recurs in Kālidāsa, when he speaks of Pārvatī (*Kumārasambhava*) as a grammatically faultless sentence, *saṁskāravatī vāk*. Centrality of language is a basic feature of Indian thought.

The *R̥gveda* (X.114.8) speaks of the infinite plenitude of *vāk: sahasradā mahimnaḥ*. It is co-extensive with Reality: *yāvad brahma visthitam tāvatī vāk*. Who can arrogate to himself the claim to have known *vāk* in its entirety? *Kaścasam yogamā veda dhīraḥ*. Who has ever grasped the core or essence of the sentences: *kodhiśnān pati vācam papāda*? In the *R̥k* the co-extensionality of *vāk* and *brahma* is really an important concept.

It may be noted that the terms *paśyantī, madhyamā* and *vaikharī* do not occur in the *R̥gveda*. We come across, instead Iḷā, Bhāratī, and Sarasvatī. These are R̥gvedic names of the three poises of *vāk*. As Sāyaṇa explains, Bhāratī is the *vāk* in heaven (*svarga*). Iḷā is the *vāk* at the empirical level, while Sarasvatī is the *vāk* in the mid-air (*antarikṣa*). These goddesses are manifestations of the mystic Fire, Agni (*R̥V*, I.142.9).

The Upaniṣads continue the talk about the ontology of *vāk,* though less about its manifestations. The argument involved in the Upaniṣadic thesis appears to be as follows : If *vāk* is *Brahman* (*yāvad brahma visthitam tāvati vāk, R̥V,* X.114.8), and *Brahman* is *caitanya* absolute then the involution of *Brahman* is the involution of *vāk.*

What Sri Aurobindo has achieved is this: Corresponding to the drop of consciousness (or *vāk*) there should also be a soar or an evolution (*Sāvitrī*). The twin processes validate each other. At this point he takes the tāntric view of *vāk* as descending from *paśyantī* through *madhyamā* to *vaikharī* and returning to the source in ascent. The *Māṇḍūkya* dwells on the involution of I-consciousness (*ātmā*) in terms of *suṣupti* through *svapna* to *jāgrata* states of the self. The presiding deities of the a states are named *Prajñā, Taijasa* and *Vaiśvānara* respectively.

In each case, the utterly transcendent, *parāvāk* as *oṁkāra* or the *devī* of Tantra or *ātmā* as *turīya* is not speakable. Language springs from silence and returns to silence.

It is possible to show four parallel descents cutting across the *R̥gveda,* the *Māṇḍūkya Upaniṣad,* the *Kāmakalāvilāsa Tantra* and Bhartr̥hari's *Vākyapadīya.*

R̥gveda		*Tantra*		*Māṇḍūkya-Yoga*		*Bhartr̥hari*
Vāk	↑	*Devī (Parā)*	↑	*Ātmā-Caitanya*	↑	*Śabda-Brahman*
Bhāratī		*Paśyantīdevī*		*Prajñā*		*Paśyantīvāk*
Sarasvatī		*Madhayamādevī*		*Taijasa*		*Madhyamā*
Il̥ā	↓	*Vaikharīdevī*	↓	*Vaiśvānara*	↓	*Vaikharī*

Sri Aurobindo's *yoga* is an adventure of consciousness. It is the evolutionary ascent from the *vaikharī* or *vaiśvānara* state to the *paśyantī* poise of the self. In his *yoga* of language, it is the ascent that renders mantric poetry possible. This is so because consciousness and language are co-implicates of each other.

The domain of poetry begins from *taijasa*. The *Māṇḍūkya* declares it as *avyavahāra*. This is quite significant. Language, in its ascent becomes divested of empirical import. It becomes *ātmapratyayasāra*, self-aware of itself. It is what *paśyantī vāk* stands for. When Sri Aurobindo speaks of the poetry of the future aspiring towards the "Seeing Word" or *paśyantī vāk*, he integrates the insights of Tantra, the *Māṇḍūkya* and *Vyākaraṇa darśana*. It calls for a deep and probing study. But a lot remains to be done.

Now as for the thesis that the Upaniṣads give us supreme poetry, two points can be made. First, it is a radical statement. The tradition does not look upon the *śruti* as poetry. Caitanyadeva regarded the poetry of Jaideva, Vidyāpati and Caṇḍīdāsa as spiritually authoritative. Our nineteenth-century thinkers spoke of the heightened passages of *Ṛgveda* and the Upaniṣads as great poetry. Vivekānanda admired the Nāsadīya-Sūkta as poetry of highest excellence. Rabindranath looked at the Upaniṣads as having passages of greatly moving poetical speech. Sri Aurobindo voices the renascent approach in a radical manner in looking upon *śruti* as poetry. Secondly, the language of the Upaniṣads takes off from *vaikharī* or *vaiśvānara* mode of speaking, and reaches out to such heights of expression as to embody ontology in all its descending and ascending movements. Expression and experience coalesce in breath-taking metaphors and turns of phrases. They record experiences of and encounters with reality in a direct manner. Since the mental categories of the subject and the object fall off and transcended, the seer-consciousness looks directly into the soul of things, and speaks in a language of discovery. One example of it would be the great assertion *so 'ham asmi*. At such height of experience pronoun (*sa*) and demonstrative (*tat*) become interchangeable. When one becomes what one sees, language or speech becomes *paśyantī*.

There is a prayer in *Ṛgveda* (X.9.83), *asme dehi dyumatim vācam*, give us brilliantly shining speech that is not polluted by obscurity, *anamīvā misirām*. Every poet prays for achieving *dyumatim vācam*. *Ṛgveda* X.79.1, 3 and 4 are especially relevant in respect of *paśyantī vāk,* as the language of integral consciousness (*kuṇḍalinī*) may have been an analogue of the ascent towards higher planes of being and awareness, breaking down rigidified, reactive modes of living, which are, more or less pathological.

As for examples of *paśyantī vāk* from Sanskrit and English poetry, I shall say that the journey from *vaikharī* towards *paśyantī vāk* has just begun. There can only be intimations of *paśyantī vāk,* and these will be few and far between. With the subjective turn in literature, possibilities of mantric poetry are on the horizon. These are sudden flashes breaking through the operation of the logical intellect and conventionalities of the art of poetry. When Bhavabhūti (*Uttamrāmacarīta,* 6.5) said that in the case of *ṛṣī*'s assertions *vācam artho anudhāvati,* meaning follows words, he struck the note of *paśyantī vāk*. For *laukika* sentences *arthavāgānuvartate,* word follows the meaning. This is the characteristic of *vaikharī vāk*. Bhavabhūti has a freer and higher function of poetic discourse. When Kālidāsa describes Śiva in meditation (in the third canto, verses 48 and 49) as having the *vaikharī* mode of speaking left behind. When Shelly's Apollo says "I am the eye through which the world beholds itself," we are struck by the lofty sense of identity pulsating in the sentence. When the Buddha said (in the *Dhammapada*) that he had found the house builder, who shall not build the house any more, the burden of his Enlightenment gets encapsulated in the metaphor, disclosing the secret of truth of our mortal experience.

The point is that my concern has been with showing the possibility of *paśyantī vāk*. It is shown to be a viable concept in terms of the metaphysics founded upon a critique of the operations of the mind in its empirical employment. If that be so, then instances of the manifestation or disclosure of the higher dimensions of the mind could be gleaned from the poetry of the East and the West. I would like to close with a fragment from the German poet, Rainer Maria Rilke's mantric conception of the "word":

> Where slowly from the long forgotten,
> Past experience rises up in us,
> Perfectly mastered, mild and beyond measure,
> And realized in the intangible:
> There begins the world, as we conceive it,
> And its meaning quietly surpasses us,
> For the mind that makes us lonely, wants
> To be sure that we shall be united.

The seer, the poet and singer, the spiritually creative, the physically receptive, the saint, they all know about the essentiality of form in word and sound, in the visible and the tangible. Through them the word becomes *mantra,* and the sounds and signs of which it is formed become the vehicles of mysterious forces. Through them the visible takes on the nature of symbols, the tangible becomes a creative tool of the spirit, and life becomes a deep stream, flowing from eternity to eternity. The tradition of the "inward" or spiritualized word and of the reality and actuality of the symbol has its prophets in our time. Sri Aurobindo has mentioned Tagore and Yeats, I like to add the names of Sri Aurobindo, Rimbaud, Baudelaire, Goethe and Rilke.

References

Adhvarindra, Dharmaraja, *Vedānta Paribhāṣā,* tr. Swami Madhavananda, Kolkata: Advaita Ashrama, 1989.

Bhavabhuti, *Uttamarāmacirita.*

Barnstone, W. tr. *Greek Lyric Poetry,* New York: Bantam Books, 1962.

Longinus, *On The Sublime,* tr. T.S. Dorsh, Penguin, 1965.

Richards, I.A., *Principles of Literary Criticism,* London: Routledge and Kegan Paul, 1960.

Rimbaud, J.A., *Rimbaud*, tr. Oliver Bernard, Penguin, 1962.

Selections from Plato, ed. R.W. Livingstone, London: Oxford University Press, 1945.

Selections from Sāvitrī, ed. Mary Aldridge, Pondicherry: Sri Aurobindo Ashram, 1975.

Sri Aurobindo, *The Future Poetry*, Pondicherry: Sri Aurobindo Ashram.

Sri Aurobindo, *The Life Divine*, New York: The Grey Stone Press, 1949.

Sullivan, J.W.N, *Beethoven*, Pelican, 1927.

Tagore, Rabindranath, *Personality*, Kolkata: Macmillan, 1961.

11

Sri Aurobindo's Understanding of Indian Art

Supriyo Bhattacharya

I

"So wonderfully has God made the world that a man using a simple combination of lines, an unpretentious harmony of colours, can raise this apparently insignificant medium to suggest absolute and profound truths with a perfection which language labours with difficulty to reach. What Nature is, what God is, what man is, can be triumphantly revealed in stone or on canvas," wrote Sri Aurobindo in the *Karmayogin* in 1909 in course of discussing the national value of art. Commenting on the enormous value of art to human evolution, he wrote in the same journal:

> The system of education which, instead of keeping artistic training apart as a privilege for a few specialists, frankly introduces it as a part of culture no less necessary than literature or science, will have taken a great step forward in the perfection of national education and the general diffusion of a broad-based human culture."[1]

---

1. Sri Aurobindo, *The National Value of Art*, 1st edn., 1922; 3rd impression 1999.

And if art is to reach towards the highest, Sri Aurobindo believed that "the Indian tendency must dominate.[2]

II

Now, what is the "Indian tendency?" What is the basic nature of artistic vision in India, as revealed in her classical or ancient art? Sri Aurobindo explained at length about this Indian artistic vision and motifs and subjects of Indian art of the past in his brilliant book *The Foundations of Indian Culture*, written in the *Āryā* (1918-21) mainly as a detailed rejoinder to and point-by-point refutation of William Archer's criticisms of Indian culture in his provoking book *India and the Future* (1917). Sri Aurobindo noted that a considerable amount of work had already been done in the clearing away of misconceptions about Indian art by Havell and Coomaraswamy and others, but he felt that a "more general and searching consideration of first principles" is necessary for any "complete view of the essential motives of Indian culture."[3] Recently much work has been done by modern scholars like Partha Mitter, Tapati Guha Thakurta and others on classical and nationalist phase of Indian art. In their work they have referred to the traditional and modern specialists in the field, but have not discussed anywhere the significant contributions of Sri Aurobindo to the understanding of certain basic aspects of ancient Indian art and artistic vision. This assumes special importance when we see that people from many parts of the world come to India and try to grasp the meaning and the roots of Indian culture by studying classical Indian art. One example may be the physicist Fritj — of Capra, author of the best-selling *The Tao of Physics* and *The Turning Point*, coming to India with the purpose:

---

2. Sri Aurobindo, *The National Value of Art*, 1st edn., 1922; 3rd impression 1999.
3. Sri Aurobindo, *The Foundations of Indian Culture* 6th edn., 1975, 2nd impression, 1980.

> From the beginning I had tried to approach the Eastern spiritual traditions not only cognitively but also experimentally, and in the case of Hinduism my experimental approach had been mainly through Indian art.[4]

III

What, then, is Indian art, according to Sri Aurobindo? "All Indian art," says Sri Aurobindo, "is a throwing out of a certain profound self-vision formed by a going within to find out the secret significance of form and appearance, a discovery of the subject in one's deeper self, the giving of soul-form to that vision, a remoulding of the material and natural shape to express the psychic truth of it with the greatest possible purity and power of outline and the greatest possible concentrated rhythmic unity of significance in all the parts of an indivisible artistic whole."[5] Sri Aurobindo compares this Indian method of giving "soul-form" to "self-vision" and the "remoulding of material and natural shape" to express the "psychic truth" with the method of the orthodox Western artist who works by a "severely conscientious reproduction" of the forms of outward nature.[6] Even when the Western artist brings in conceptions which are more properly of another kingdom, the "Stress of the physical world" is always with him and Sri Aurobindo notes that an "idealized imaginative realism" is as far as he can ordinarily go in the method of his work when he would "fill the outward with the subtler inner seeing."[7] "The farthest he has got," Sri Aurobindo grants, "in the direction of a more intimately subjective spirit is an impressionism which still waits upon her (i.e. nature's) models but seeks to get at

---

4. Fritjof Capra, *Uncommon Wisdom,* Flamingo, 1989.
5. Sri Aurobindo, *The Foundations of Indian Culture,* 1980.
6. Ibid.
7. Ibid.

some first inward or original effect of them on the inner sense, and through that he arrives at some more strongly psychical rendering, but he does not work altogether from within outward in the freer manner of the oriental artist."[8] The emotion and artistic feeling in this form are not a "pure spiritual or psychic emotion," but usually an "imaginative explanation derived from the suggestions of life and outward things with a psychic element" or an "evocation of spiritual feeling initiated and dominated by the touch of the outward."[9]

The Indian artist, argues Sri Aurobindo, starts off from the "other" end of the scale of values of experience which connect life and spirit. "The whole creative force comes here," says Sri Aurobindo, "from a spiritual and psychic vision" and the emphasis of the "physical" is secondary and "everything is suppressed which does not serve this purpose or would distract the mind from purity of this intention."[10] Sri Aurobindo admits that Indian painting expresses the soul through life, but he adds that life is only a "means" of the Spiritual Self-expression.[11] In this context, Sri Aurobindo brings up another important point. Many art-historians (in our country, the famous Niharranjan Ray) fix on the grand strongly outlined figures and the feeling for life and character (as evident in, say, the Ajantā frescoes) as the signs of the Indian character of some of the major Indian paintings (and also sculpture). But Sri Aurobindo points out the difference of the feeling for life and character in Indian art from the abundant vitality and the power and force of character such as we find in, say, an Italian painting, a fresco from Michel-Angelo's hand or a portrait by Titian or Tintoretto. In their

8. Sri Aurobindo, *The Foundations of Indian Culture*, 1980.
9. Ibid.
10. Ibid.
11. Ibid.

works we find a revelation of the glory and beauty of the "Sensuous appeal of life" or of the "dramatic power and moving interest of character and emotion and action."[12] This is the common form of aesthetic work in Europe. But in Indian art it is never the "governing" motive. The sensuous appeal is there, admits Sri Aurobindo, but he goes on to add that it is refined into "only one and not the chief element of the richness of a soul of psychic grace and beauty"[13] which is for the Indian artist the true beauty, *lāvaṇya*. The dramatic motive is "subordinated" and made only a purely "secondary" element, only so much is given of character and action as will help to "bring out the deeper spiritual or psychic feeling."[14]

Sri Aurobindo shows that this is also true in the Indian treatment of the human figure. All corporeal filling in of the outline by insistence on the flesh, the muscle, the anatomical detail is minimized or disregarded: "the strong subtle lines and pure shapes" which make the humanity of the human form are alone brought into relief.[15] Sri Aurobindo shows that the filling in of the line is done in another way: it is achieved by a "disposition of pure masses, a design and coloured wave-flow of the body, *bhaṅga*, a simplicity of content" by which the artist floods the whole with the significance of the "one spiritual suggestion, feeling, emotion" which he wishes to depict, his intuition of the "moment of the soul, its living self-experience."[16] To help us see this point, Sri Aurobindo draws our attention to the "almost miraculously subtle and meaningful use of the hands" and the subtle repetition of the suggestion of the

---

12. Sri Aurobindo, *The Foundations of Indian Culture*, 1980.
13. Ibid.
14. Ibid.
15. Ibid.
16. Ibid.

face and the eyes, which are a common feature of Indian paintings to express the psychic suggestion.[17] Every turn of the body, the pose of each limb, the relation and design of all the masses are filled with the same psychical feeling. Colour too is used, points out Sri Aurobindo, as a means for the spiritual and psychic intention and we can see this well enough if we study the suggestive significance of the hues in a Buddhist miniature. This power of line and subtlety of psychic suggestion in the filling in of the expressive outlines is the stamp of the whole work of Ajantā and continues in Rājpūt painting. As a particular example, Sri Aurobindo picks up the adoration group of the mother and child before the Buddha, one of the most profound, tender and noble of the Ajantā masterpieces.*[18] And to illustrate the difference between the

17. Sri Aurobindo, *The Foundations of Indian Culture*, 1980.

* "If we look long, for an example, at the adoration group of the mother and child before the Buddha, we shall find that the impression of intense religious feeling of adoration there is only the most outward general touch in the ensemble of the emotion. That which it deepens to is the turning of the soul of humanity in love to the benignant and calm Ineffable which has made itself sensible and human to us in the universal compassion of the Buddha, and the motive of the soul-moment the painting interprets is the dedication of the awakening mind of the child, the coming younger humanity, to that in which already the soul of the mother had learned to find and fix its spiritual joy. The eyes, brows, lips, face, poise of the head of the woman are filled with this spiritual emotion which is a continued memory and possession of the psychical release, the steady settled calm of the heart's experience filled with an ineffable tenderness, the familiar depths which are yet moved with the wonder and always farther appeal of something that is infinite, the body and other limbs are grave masses of this emotion and in their poise a basic embodiment of it, while the hands prolong it in the dedicative putting forward of her child to meet the Eternal. This contact of the human and eternal is repeated in the smaller figure with a subtly and strongly indicated variation, the glad and childlike smile of awakening which promises but not yet possesses the depths that are to come, the hands disposed to receive and keep,

→

usual European and Indian imagination, between the "mental, vital and physical stress" of the art of Europe and the subtle, less forcefully "tangible spiritual stress" of the art of India, Sri Aurobindo draws our attention to the picture of "Great Renunciation of the Buddha" in the Ajantā murals.**[19]

IV

The same method of execution and the stress of inner spiritual vision hold good in Indian sculpture too. Here, Sri Aurobindo brings in the best of Greek sculpture and shows how Indian art goes beyond Greek art in this sphere. The highest greatness of Greek aesthesis in sculpture subsisted so long (and it was not for very long) as a "certain satisfying balance was struck

---

→ the body in its looser curves and waves harmonizing with that significance. The two have forgotten themselves and seen almost to forget or confound each other in that which they adore and contemplate, and yet the dedicating hands unite mother and child in the common act and feeling by their simultaneous gesture of maternal possession and spiritual giving. The two figures have at each point the same rhythm, but with a significant difference. The simplicity in the greatness and power, the fullness of expression gained by reserve and suppression and concentration which we find here is the perfect method of the classical art of India." — *The Foundations of Indian Culture*, Sri Aurobindo.

18. Sri Aurobindo, *The Foundations of Indian Culture*, 1980.

** It is not at all his own personal sorrow but the sorrow of all others, not an emotional self-pity but a poignant pity for the world, not the regret for a life of domestic bliss but the afflicting sense of the unreality of human happiness that is concentrated in the eyes and lips of the Buddha, and the yearning there is not, certainly, for earthly happiness in the future but for the spiritual way out, the anguished seeking which found its release, already foreseen by the spirit behind and hence the immense calm and restraint that support the sorrow, in the true bliss of *nirvāṇa*."— *The Foundations of Culture*, Sri Aurobindo.

19. Ibid.

and constantly maintained between a fine, but not very subtle, opulent or profound spiritual suggestion and an outward physical harmony of nobility and grace."[20] But, concludes Sri Aurobindo, what Greek sculpture expressed was "fine, gracious and noble," but what it did not express was that "spiritual depth and extension which the human mind needs for its larger and deeper self-experience."[21] The Olympian gods of Phidias are "magnified and uplifted human beings" and they have a certain "divine calm of impersonality or universalized quality, divine type, *guṇa*"[22]; but the gods of Indian sculpture are "cosmic beings, embodiments of some great spiritual power, spiritual idea and action, inmost psychic significance"[23]; here, the human form is a vehicle of the "soul meaning, its outward means of self-expression."[24] Not the "ideal physical or emotional beauty," but the "utmost spiritual beauty or significance" of which the human form is capable, is the aim of this Indian creation.[25] In the statue of a king or a saint, we do not get merely the idea of a king or saint or meet some dramatic action or a character portrait in stone, but what is embodied is a "soul-state or experience or deeper soul-quality," as for example, not the outward emotion, but the "inner soul-side of rapt ecstasy of adoration and God-vision in the saint or the devotee."[26] Sri Aurobindo draws our attention to the great Buddhas (not the Gāndhāran) in cave-cathedral or the divine figures or groups in temple, the best of the later south Indian bronzes (as can be seen from the remarkable collection of plates in O.C. Ganguly's famous

---

20. Sri Aurobindo, *The Foundations of Indian Culture,* 1980.
21. Ibid.
22. Ibid.
23. Ibid.
24. Ibid.
25. Ibid.
26. Ibid.

book), the Kalasanhara image of Śiva, and of course, the Naṭarājas.

In this connection, Sri Aurobindo refers to one important point often raised by foreigners: he says that William Archer[27] doubts E.B. Havell's suggestion that these Indian artists knew the anatomy of the body well enough, but chose to depart from it for their own purpose. Sri Aurobindo replies that it does not matter much, since art is not "anatomy." The one point that counts, says Sri Aurobindo, is that the Indian artist had a "perfect idea of proportion and rhythm" and used them in certain styles with "nobility and power" and in others like the Javan, the Gauda or the southern bronzes with that or with a "perfect grace added and often an intense and a lyrical sweetness."[28] What was achieved was not an "outward naturalistic" beauty, but a "spiritual and a psychic beauty" and to achieve it the sculptor was right in suppressing the "obtrusive material detail" and aimed instead at "purity of outline and fineness of feature"[29] and in that purity and fineness he was able to work "a mass of force, or delicacy of grace, a static dignity or a mighty strength or a restrained violence of movement" or whatever he chose to convey.[30]

The application of this psychic vision to the human form sometimes offends the critics of Indian sculpture. There is the familiar objection to such features as the multiplication of the arms in the figures of gods and goddesses, the four, six or ten arms of Śiva, the eighteen arms of Durgā, because they are a "monstrosity," a thing not in nature. But Sri Aurobindo points out that he cannot see why this freedom should be denied in

27. Sri Aurobindo, *The Foundations of Indian Culture,* 1980.
28. Ibid.
29. Ibid.
30. Ibid.

the representation of Cosmic beings like the Indian godheads.[31] And he also raises the relevant question whether it is capable of "artistic representation, a rhythm of artistic truth and unity" which need not be that of "physical nature."[32] As for the "contorted postures" of some figures, the same law holds. There is often a departure from the anatomical norm of the physical body or sometimes an unusual pose of limbs or body; but the question is, Sri Aurobindo rightly argues, whether it is done without sense or purpose or whether it serves some significance and replaces the normal "physical metric" of Nature by another "purposeful and successful artistic rhythm."

To see this point, one can, for example, have a close look at the Ajantā mural of Avalokiteśvara Padmapāṇi. As the noted writer Narayan Sanyal has shown in his justly famous book *Ajantā Aparūpa*, an X-ray plate of the gesture of the palm and fingers of the Buddha's hand holding the lotus shows that the artist departed from anatomical accuracy. Why? Because, on close inspection it is found that the gesture of the palm and the fingers conforms to the form of a flower-bud and that was what was uppermost in the artist's mind while he was thinking of the hand of Avalokiteśvara Padmapāṇi.

V

Coming to architecture, Sri Aurobindo shows where the Western critic of Indian architecture goes wrong. Unable to see the true motive behind, he cannot discern wherein lies the unity that is essential in all works of art. He sees in it merely the work of a skillful craftsman who has executed a mass of incoherent details, with no apparent object whatsoever. Archer, whose ill-considered criticism of Indian culture generally elicited Sri Aurobindo's brilliant defence in *The Arya*, is blinder than

---

31. Sri Aurobindo, *The Foundations of Indian Culture*, 1980.

32. Ibid.

other European critics and most loud-spoken in his denunciation of Indian architecture. He dislikes massive structure as a rule. Naturally the huge temples of South of India have failed to evoke his admiration except as marvels of construction. He realizes that they are huge, but fails to see in that hugeness either unity or sublimity. But, Sri Aurobindo asks, how can there be a marvel of construction without any unity of design, or a mighty massive structure without greatness. Archer complains that ponderousness prevails everywhere, everything is over-wrought, all parts writhing with bizarre half-human figures which are senseless and seem to have no connection with the whole. The temples of northern India, which have not quite such a lavish display of ogres and demons and bizarre scroll-work on them, have not gained quite such a strong disapprobation as the temples of the south. The mixed Moslem architecture known as Indo-Saracenic has, alone, escaped the general condemnation of being barbaric. Sri Aurobindo shows, however, why the foreign critics fail to see our idea of oneness. They have been used to "the Greek unity gained by much suppression and a sparing use of detail and circumstance or the Gothic unity got by casting everything into the mould of a single spiritual aspiration,"[33] which are quite different from the Indian conception of it. The sacred architecture of India always aims at depicting the "eternal oneness of the Divine underlying and upholding the wonderful diversity of the created universe." This applies to architecture as much as to sculpture and painting, applies to those works that are epic in thier grandeur as well as to structures smaller in size which Sri Aurobindo calls a lyric of the Infinite. Sri Aurobindo suggests that one should go to a temple far from human habitation where the background and environment are quite natural. He suggests two names, Kalahasti and Siṁhacalam, both belonging to south India. The

---

33. Sri Aurobindo, *The Foundations of Indian Culture*, 1980.

two temples are alike in motive, but different in execution. They should be seen, Sri Aurobindo says, not detached from the environment, but in unity with the sky and the landscape; low-lying or hilly. Thus regarded, these man-made structures will appear as one in motive with their setting. Sri Aurobindo describes the two structures in these lucid words:

> One of these buildings climbs up — bold, massive in projection, up-piled in the greatness of a forceful but sure ascent, preserving its range and tune to the last; the other soars from the strength of its base, in the grace and emotion of a curving mass to a rounded summit and crowning symbol. There is in both a constant, subtle yet pronounced lessening from the base towards the top, but at each stage a repetition of the same form, the same multiplicity of insistence, the same crowded fullness and indented relief, but one maintains its multiple endeavour and inclination to the last, the other ends in a single sign.[34]

The massive base resting on the earth, the gradual taper as the edifice rises, the thronged figures indicative of infinite mutiplicity, the symbolic ending at the top, against the vast expanse of the sky, all express, not absence of unity, but a tremendous unity. When the whole is seen thus, every detail becomes easy of understanding.

The method of interpretation set forth above applies to all Dravidian temples from Madurai and Tanjore down to small but beautiful shrines by the way-side. The motive is the same for all. The architecture of the north is not quite of the same kind, the basic style is different; but in interpreting them we have to use the same method — intuitive and spiritual.

The European critic is constantly bringing up his objection to the thronging details and ornament so common in temple

34. Sri Aurobindo, *The Foundations of Indian Culture*, 1980.

architecture, urging that this emphasizing of detail mars the unity of design. But this argument only shows that the critic has allowed his mind to dwell on the details first without relating them to the original oneness in the spirit. It is the same with regard to the world. If we allow our mind to dwell on and stress the many in the universe, we find only "a crowded plurality."[35] To arrive at unity we have to reduce or suppress what we have seen and go back to realize the self, the infinite reality underneath. The rich ornament and detail in an Indian temple represent the infinite variety of creation on all planes and suggests infinite oneness of the endless multiplicity of things.

Archer in his attack on Indian architecture repeated again and again that the profusion of ornamental work in the Hindu temples, especially of south India, was barbarous and bizarre, and that it gave no relief to the eye and allowed no calm. Sri Aurobindo answers that the "unity on which all is upborne carries in itself the infinite space and calm of the spiritual realization"[36] and that consequently no unfilled spaces of a superficial kind were necessary, the eye being there only as an entry to the soul of the art. The massiveness of the southern temples has been discussed. They could not be otherwise than massive — representing, as they do, the cosmic scene as a whole. Some of the sacred edifices in the north, says Sri Aurobindo, have "a singular grace, a luminous lightness . . . a rich delicacy of beauty in their ornate fullness."[37] Not lightness and clarity of the Greek kind, "clarity of naked nobleness," but a remarkable blending of opposites such as characterizes the spirit of Indian religion as well as art. There is one comment however of Mr Archer that deserves mention here because it has been made also by more broad-minded critics like

35. Sri Aurobindo, *The Foundations of Indian Culture*, 1980.

36. Ibid.

37. Ibid.

Professor Geddes. It is this, that in these huge buildings there is always a "monstrous effect of terror and gloom." The comment is totally unwarranted. The Indian knows that terror and gloom are incompatible with his religion, art and literature. Even when they appear, says Sri Aurobindo, "they are always sustained by a supporting and helping presence, an eternal greatness and calm or love or Delight behind."[38] Take the Great God Mahādeva for instance. He is Rudra the fierce, Maheśvara the austere *mahāyogī*, but he is also Śiva the auspicious, Āśutoṣa the auspicious, the support and refuge of men. Again, take Naṭarāja, the dancing Śiva, wrongly described as Śiva destroying the universe. If the poise of the body, the mad fling of the limbs frightens anybody he has only to look at the serene beauty of the face in repose to be reassured immediately. In the image of Kālī, where even the face is afire with the zeal of destroying the powers of Evil, we have the two right hands in the poses of *abhaya* and *varada* — one saying "fear not" and the other promising a boon to the faithful. Only one word more on this subject. In the ornament of the sacred temples we find depicted various unhuman and half-human figures. The European critic probably does not know, or does not believe that these formidable-looking creatures actually exist on certain planes other than our own and it is perfectly consonant with the spirit of Indian art not to exclude them from any comprehensive design representing creation. They form part of the wonderful diversity of the universe.

Sri Aurobindo closes his chapter on Indian architecture with a couple of pages on Indo-Moslem architectural art. All over India we find mosques and other edifices of what is called Indo-Saracenic design, most of them, at least the best of them, belonging to the Mogul period. Sri Aurobindo finds in many of them "an impress of the robust and bold Afghan and Mogul temperament." Still, on the whole, he considers them a

38. Sri Aurobindo, *The Foundations of Indian Culture*, 1980.

typically Indian creation.[39] The decorative skill that one sees in these buildings are to be found in many Hindu temples of northern India. A lyric grace was developing in north India even before the Moslem advent (in the indigenous sculpture, as in the schools of the north-east and of Java), and this found its place in the Indo-Saracenic buildings blended with purely Islamic motives.[40]

In this connection it must be mentioned that Sri Aurobindo does not consider the "Mogul School" of paintings as an "exotic." His words on the Mogul paintings deserve our special attention:

> (In Mogul Paintings) there is rather a blending of two mentalities: on the one side there is a leaning to some kind of externalism which is not the same thing as Western naturalism, . . . but the central thing is still the domination of a transforming touch which shows that there, as in the architecture, the Indian mind has taken hold of another invading mentality and made it a help to a more outward-going self-expression that comes in as a new side-strain in the spiritual continuity of achievement . . . [41]

VI

Sri Aurobindo, we know, was one of the great founding fathers of National Education that was inaugurated in Bengal. But he was also its best critic. He pointed out that in the beginning that was made (in this education) by the importance attached to drawing and clay-modelling as elements of manual training, there was, the "absence of an artistic ideal,"[42] the misconception of the true aim of manual training. What he observed then

---

39. Sri Aurobindo, *The Foundations of Indian Culture,* 1980.
40. Ibid.
41. Ibid.
42. *The National Value of Art.*

bears repeating even today:

"The nation and the individual can gain nothing by turning out figures in clay which faithfully copy the vulgarity and ugliness of English commercial production, or by multiplying mere copies of men or things."[43] What Sri Aurobindo wanted was a "free and active imaging of form . . . and hue within oneself, . . . the inward vision of the relation and truth of things, an eye quick to note and distinguish, sensitive to design and to harmony in colour . . . "[44]

Sri Aurobindo's understanding of Classical or ancient Indian art helps us perceive these qualities in Indian art and develop them in our own consciousness for its fuller flowering, depth and richness.***

---

43. *The National Value of Art.*

44. Ibid.

*** In this paper, we have not launched upon any discussion of the nationalist phase of the art in Bengal and its great painters. Sri Aurobindo made some pertinent observations in this sphere in some places of his works. The modern discourse on this subject is also rich. To look into this area is a promising field of research.

12

The Myth of Sāvitrī and Satyavān
The Four Boons

Vladimir

THE story of Sāvitrī, as we first find it, is narrated in Vana Parva of *Mahābhārata* by Mārkaṇḍeya in answer to Yudhiṣṭhira's question about Draupadī: "was there any other woman in the history of men who being dedicated to her husband suffered so much as Draupadī?," and the *ṛṣi* says: "Yes, there was one. It was Sāvitrī."

It is interesting to note that Ṛṣi Mārkaṇḍeya, according to the Purāṇas, himself had gained the boon of immortality from Mahādeva in the first *manvantara* of this *kalpa*. Having become immortal, he went into a deep trance lasting for six *manvantaras*, awaking only now in the seventh one of our time, called *vaivasvata*. He is also known as the author of the *Mārkaṇḍeya Purāṇa*, which consists of the most magnificent and profound *mantras* dedicated to the Divine Mother, called *Devī Māhātmya*. Mārkaṇḍeya, the immortal worshipper of Śiva-Śakti, narrates here in *Mahābhārata* the story about Sāvitrī, the incarnation of the Divine Mother, who conquers Death.

The story is about a princess of Madra, Sāvitrī, who was born as an incarnation of the Goddess Sāvitrī, as a result of her father, king Aśvapati, performing a severe penance over 18 years, wanting to have progeny. Being pleased with his *tapasyā*, the Goddess bestowed upon him a boon of a birth of one daughter instead of his request for many (a hundred) sons.

Sāvitrī was so beautiful in her youth that none could approach her for marriage, being afraid of her splendour as of a supernatural power, *devakanyeti.* So the girl had to find a husband for herself. The *svayaṁvaram* was announced and she went around the world in a golden chariot in search of her mate. She travelled through all the kingdoms, lands and forests, but there was none to match her divine qualities, except Satyavān.

When Sāvitrī announces that she has chosen Satyavān, Nārad exclaims that she has made a wrong choice, a big mistake, *doṣa.* "Although he is the best among men," says Nārad, "he will die in one year from now, and nothing can be done about it." After hearing such shocking news, King Aśvapati asks Sāvitrī to find another person to marry. But Sāvitrī refuses, saying that she cannot choose twice, when her heart and mind have once decided.

Thus she marries Satyavān and moves into his house in the forest. She serves him and his parents in every way without complaint, remembering the words of Nārad and counting the days of his life. Neither Satyavān nor his parents know about it. The time goes by very quickly, and three days before the destined day, Sāvitrī performs a *mahāvrata tapasyā,* standing for three days and nights without sleep or food, like a pillar in deep meditation. On the morning of the fourth day, after completing the vow, she notices that Satyavān is going to the forest to cut wood. She also goes with him, after some debate with him and his parents who want her to take rest after performing such a difficult *vrata,* but she requests them to let her go with Satyavān and they cannot resist her will.

In the woods Satyavān suddenly feels dizzy and lies down with his head on her lap. He feels as if thousands of knives are piercing his body and falls unconscious. Then she feels the presence of someone else. She sees a dark figure with red eyes approaching them. It is Yama, the God of Death, who comes to fetch Satyavān. He takes his soul out of his body and goes away into his kingdom. But Sāvitrī follows him without delay. She speaks to him in a perfect poetic Sanskrit, surprising him with her high knowledge and deep understanding of *dharma.* So the Lord of Death, being at the same time the Lord of *dharma,* is immensely impressed with Sāvitrī and bestows upon her four boons:

1. return of sight for Satyavān's father, Dyumatsena and return of the kingdom which he once lost,
2. one hundred sons for her father Aśvapati, which he was aspiring for,
3. one hundred sons for Sāvitrī and Satyavān,
4. and finally the life of Satyavān.

In the morning Sāvitrī and Satyavān return home and see that the king Dyumatsena has got both his sight and his kingdom back. Neither Satyavān nor his parents knew what has actually happened. Only *ṛṣi*s were aware, praising Sāvitrī for her Divine Power of Love and Truth. This is briefly the story, where a destiny predicted as inevitable was changed by the determination of her will.

Sri Aurobindo's Interpretation of the Myth

Sri Aurobindo in the preface to his epic poem *Sāvitrī* gives us a brief introduction to the legend as it was narrated in *Mahābhārata.*

> The tale of Satyavān and Sāvitrī is recited in the *Mahābhārata* as a story of conjugal love conquering death. But this legend is, as shown by many features of the human tale, one of the many symbolic myths of the Vedic cycle. Satyavān is the soul carrying the divine truth of being within itself but descended into the grip of death and ignorance; Sāvitrī is

> the Divine word, daughter of the Sun, goddess of the supreme Truth who comes down and is born to save; Aśvapati; the Lord of the Horse, her human father, is the Lord of *tapasyā*, the concentrated energy of spiritual endeavour that helps us to rise from the mortal to the immortal planes; Dyumatsena; Lord of the Shining Hosts, father of Satyavān, is the Divine Mind here fallen blind, losing its celestial kingdom of vision, and through that loss its kingdom of glory. Still this is not a mere allegory, the characters are not personified qualities, but incarnations or emanations of living and conscious Forces with whom we can enter into concrete touch, and they take human bodies in order to help man and show him the way from his mortal state to a divine consciousness and immortal life.

To better understand the symbolism of the story, we should take a brief look into the Vedic metaphysics and especially cosmogony, and to explore the symbolism of this story in terms of Evolution as the "divine Event." According to Sri Aurobindo the Night of our consciousness, which is to be illumined, is "not our beginning nor our end." It was the outcome of the Supreme's Involution as a gradual withdrawal of His Aspect of Knowledge from His Aspect of Power. The Night which lay "across the path of the divine Event" is to be crossed by the evolution of consciousness, building up the consciousness of Another, as it were — the consciousness of Individual.

The Myth of Sāvitrī is about the Event in the Evolution of Consciousness which should end the time of Night and Death and Suffering, and bring mankind out of Darkness into Light, from Non-being into Being, from Death to Immortality. Sāvitrī is the Saviour, the Divine Mother, who by herself plunging into the Darkness brings the four Creator's emanations back to the Knowledge of the Supreme in themselves, and, what is even more important, a birth of a new being: the Divine Child, the Supreme Individual.

The Vedic Cosmology

(*Śatapatha Brāhmaṇa, Taittirīya Āraṇyaka, Bṛhadāraṇyaka Upaniṣad*)

BEGINNING

"At the beginning was the Self (*ātman*). He was Alone. He looked around and didn't find anybody else except himself. He said: "I Am . . . " But there was no other name to say, for he was alone. . . . So He felt lonely. He wanted Another." — *Bṛhadāraṇyaka Upaniṣad* 1.4.1-3.

THE FIRST INVOLUTION

"So out of Himself, as it were, he cast all these worlds, *sa imān lokān asṛjata.*" (*Aitareya Upaniṣad* 1.1, etc.) It is only by denying Himself and fully forgetting Himself, that He could start a new life of Another. The Supreme Knowledge-Power appears in this Creation as a gradual disappearance of knowledge whereas the aspect of power continues to be present and carries out the Creation. This was his first Involution. We call it involution because it was out of him, where he didn't know about himself anymore, outside his self-awareness, so to say.

According to the Mother's story, at the beginning of Creation there were four Beings emanated from the Supreme: Consciousness in Light, Bliss, Truth and Life. After refusing to be one with the Supreme and deciding to be independent, they fell into their opposites. So, there was a degradation from Light to complete Darkness, from Bliss to Suffering, from Truth to Falsehood, from Life to Death.

Death is therefore nothing but Life, Falsehood is Truth and suffering is Bliss carried.

THE SECOND INVOLUTION

When the first Creation was done, it became as if unsteady, *adhruvam iva*, says *Taittirīya Āraṇyaka* (1.23.8-9); so, in order to make it stable, the Supreme had to enter it. He has penetrated

Himself by Himself *ātmanātmānam abhisamviveśa*, and the Creation became steady. From this point the Evolution takes place.

What is evolving then?

1. It is He who has penetrated Himself by Himself and is growing through His own Denial of Himself in order to become Supreme Another. He is becoming an Individual Supreme, a Prince Satyavān. And this is the aim of all Creation. So if this prince Satyavān is to die, then the creation will lose its meaning and purpose.
2. It is also He, who has become his first Cosmic Creation, Nature (from his first Involution), which now is to become the Manifestation of his immortal mind, vital and body.

In the Mother's story, in order to repair the fall of these four beings, so to say, the Supreme Mother, Aditi, delegated out of herself the force of Love which has plunged into darkness and thus has entered the first Creation. In the Vedas it is Agni, the first *avatāra*, who lay down and hid himself within the darkness. It is because of his presence within the Creation that every creature is seeking after Knowledge and evolving towards the Supreme.

Vedic Symbolism of the Story

Here I would like to briefly elaborate on the main characters of the story, in the light of Vedic symbolism given by Sri Aurobindo.

There are two Kings, representing the two kingdoms of Knowledge and Power.

1. *Dyumatsena* — the Lord of the Shining Hosts, (lit. "with the army of rays or luminous beings"), the King of Knowledge (the rays of light, *gāvaḥ, usrāḥ,* in the Vedas are the symbols of Consciousness in its aspect of

Knowledge) here, in the lower hemisphere, falls blind, and thus loses his Kingdom. He has a son, Satyavān, a growing Soul of Man, a prince, a king to be, who cannot live without the support of light and truth in the Darkness of this Creation and therefore is to die within a year. Nor as a prince has he any future, for his father has already lost his kingdom.

2. *Aśvapati* is the Lord of Horse (*aśva,* horse, in the Vedas is a symbol of power, energy, force in opposition to *gauḥ,* cow or ray of light, as a symbol of knowledge: the cow is to be in front of the horse, the Knowledge is to rule the Power, according to the Vedic Vision). Here in the lower hemisphere Aśvapati is involved in *tapasyā,* concentrated spiritual efforts, dedicated to the Divine Mother, Sāvitrī, "goddess of the supreme Truth," calling for Her to support his spiritual work on earth with heirs. Otherwise his work has no future, since he has no son to continue it.

3. Satyavān is true but powerless in this darkness, for Truth has lost its power and he needs support from above.

4. The Goddess Sāvitrī, promising Aśvapati any boon he likes, does not give him the progeny he asks (100 sons), because she knows that without Dyumatsena first regaining his sight and kingdom there would be no future for Aśvapati, and all his endeavour would be fruitless. The goddess actually fulfils his wish by giving him a daughter Sāvitrī, who, by saving Dyumatsena and his Kingdom of Knowledge, opens the opportunity for Aśvapati, the King of Power, to have hundred sons. Once this is achieved, she asks Yama a boon of 100 children for herself and Satyavān (the symbol of the Divine Race on earth), which is granted by Yama without questioning, as inevitable after she has gained

the three previous boons. And only now does she ask for the Life of Satyavān, which basically implies a conversion of Death into its Origin: the Supreme Life. We can understand these boons in terms of symbolic action of the Divine Mother upon the four fallen Divine Beings (according to the Mother's story of Creation):

(a) Return of sight and kingdom for Dyumatsena, the Lord of Knowledge, could be seen as a symbol of return of "Consciousness in Light" from the state of Darkness;

(b) Hundred sons for Aśvapati, the Lord of Power, is probably a symbol of a return of Bliss to its Origin. In the story of Mārkaṇḍeya it is mentioned that Aśvapati, being a perfect king, loved by all his subjects, suffered a lot, *saṁtāpam upajagmivān,* from having no progeny, *anāpatyam.* In order to recover from that suffering he performed his *tapasyā* for 18 years. (It is interesting to note that the world of bliss, *ānandaloka,* being emanated from *sat* and *cit* is the world of the multitude of souls, the world of eternal and infinite becoming, we may say. In Purāṇas it is called *mahar-loka* or *janar-loka,* the world of Vast or the world of Genesis.)

(c) Hundred sons of Sāvitrī and Satyavān might be a symbol of a conversion of the Falsehood into the Truth. It is a symbol of the Supramental Manifestation upon Earth, with all its multitude of souls. Here Sāvitrī is becoming the Divine Mother and all men are her children: psychic beings.

(d) The Life of Satyavān, the Soul of Man, will not die; it is a symbol of conversion of Death into its counterpart — the Divine Life.

Sri Aurobindo and the Mother spoke about pre-Vedic and pre-Chaldean tradition. The story of creation, for example, told by the Mother is based on the knowledge of that pre-historic tradition. The myth of Sāvitrī has also some of those features, which cannot be fully understood within the Vedic tradition. It is only within the most archaic images and symbols of the oldest parts of the Veda that we can find a clue to these symbols in Sāvitrī. Sri Aurobindo writes in the *Secret of the Veda*: "In images of an energetic incongruity reminding us of the sublime grotesque and strange figures that have survived from the old mystic and symbolic art of the pre-historic world, Vāmadeva describes the *puruṣa* in the figure of a man-bull, whose four horns are the four divine principles, . . ." (SV, 308) "For all this creation has been, as it were, ejected into the subconscient by the four-horned Bull, the divine *Puruṣa* whose horns are infinite Existence, Consciousness, Bliss and Truth." (SV, p. 307). We can clearly see the correspondence of these four with *sat-cit-ānanda-vijñāna* of the later Vedic and Vedāntic tradition. These four horns of divine *puruṣa* are perhaps the pre-historic symbols of those four original divine beings, mentioned by the Mother in her story of Creation. Infinite Existence corresponds to Life in the Mother's story, and all others follow the same order.

There are some interesting implications which follow from this kind of identification. The order of these beings falling into their opposites and the order of their recovery is the same; it is: Consciousness, Bliss, Truth and Life. The Life or infinite Existence (*sat*) is falling last, and it is being recovered last. The Consciousness is falling first and is recovered first, which is fully understood within the Vedic tradition.

The conundrum of the story regarding the third boon of 100 sons for her and Satyavān is impossible to understand unless we see a bigger picture. How could she ask for the sons from Satyavān, if the very life of his was not granted?

And how could He, the Lord of Death, give her such a boon, if he refused to give her his life?

It is only when we know that the Existence, *sat*, is to be recovered last, that we understand what has actually happened. For, infinite Existence consists of all other aspects of Consciousness, Bliss and Truth (Supermind) and cannot come into existence without them being manifested first in the world.

The Truth or Supermind, as the Divine Manifestation in Matter (100 sons of Sāvitrī and Satyavān), should be granted before the infinite Existence can be effectuated. This was the secret knowledge, which made the narration of Mārkaṇḍeya seem irrational from the point of earthly wisdom. But from the point of the Infinite it is a perfect account. It also suggests that the whole Transformation will be fulfilled before it becomes finally effective and visible. It is probably this which makes Sri Aurobindo write about it in such a mysterious way:

> A Voice ill-heard shall speak, the soul obey,
> A Power into mind's inner character steal,
> A charm and sweetness open life's closed doors,
> And beauty conquer the resisting world,
> The Truth-Light capture Nature by surprise,
> A Stealth of God compel the heart to bliss,
> And earth grow unexpectedly divine.
> In Matter shall be lit the spirit's glow,
> In body and body kindled the sacred birth;
> Night shall awake to the anthem of the stars,
> The days become a happy pilgrim march,
> Our will a force of the Eternal's power,
> And thought the rays of a spiritual sun.
> A few shall see what none yet understands;
> God shall grow up while the wise men talk and sleep;
> For man shall not know the coming till its hour,
> And belief shall be not till the work is done. — Sāvitrī,
> p. 55

13

Some Reflections on Sri Aurobindo's "Essays on the Gītā"

Sarnath Basu

EVERY founder of the special schools of the Vedānta philosophy had to write his commentary on the *Gītā*. The *Gītā*, we know, was regarded as the *smṛti prasthāna* of these systems. Its authenticity was like that of the Upaniṣads. It is not a fact that only the Vedānta philosophers held it with high esteem. Other *āstika* philosophers also had the same attitude towards this great scripture. If the Upaniṣads are full of the luminous lights of the spiritual experiences, so is the *Gītā* for Sri Aurobindo. That is why he wrote extensively on its teaching.

Before we go into some aspects of its teaching, we should know the occasion in which he wrote the *Essays on the Gītā*. To know this background, we think, is necessary for the proper understanding of his mind. From the biography of Sri Aurobindo by A.B. Purani, we know that Sri Aurobindo had "the experience of the Silent *Brahman*" in January, 1908 while he was practising *yoga* under the instruction of the Maharashtrian *yogī* Viṣṇu Bhāskar Lele. In the month of May of the very same year he was arrested and put in Alipore Jail as an undertrial prisoner. For full one year in the jail he spent his time mainly practising *yoga* and reading the Upaniṣads and the *Gītā*. He had the realization of the *vāsudeva sarvam*, (the God in all becomings) in this jail. After one year of his acquittal and release he left British India and arrived at Pondicherry on 4 April 1910 mainly for finding out a new path for the humanity. A monthly philosophical review, *Arya* began to be published from 15 August 1914, under the joint editorship of Sri Aurobindo Ghosh, Paul Richard and his wife Mirra Richard later known as the Mother of the Pondicherry Ashram. Sri Aurobindo wrote almost all his major works (excluding *Sāvitrī*) in this journal till January, 1922. The world is indeed indebted to this couple without whose inspiration and endeavours the vast Aurobindo literature could not perhaps have seen the light of the day. The writings of Sri Aurobindo including his *Essays on the Gītā* were much later published in book form.

We have made a little digression from the original subject only to show the meditative and spiritual background of his writings. His *Essays on the Gītā* as the very name suggests is not a commentary (*bhāṣya*) in the traditional sense. The traditional commentaries sought to explain the teaching of the *Gītā* from a particular philosophical point of view. Śaṅkara, Rāmānuja and other Vedāntins wrote their excellent commentaries. But the excellence that was exhibited by them was more intellectual than spiritual. Sri Aurobindo's view on the *Gītā* is entirely a different one. He explicitly emphasizes that "The *Gītā* is not a weapon for dialectical warfare, it is a gate opening on the whole world of spiritual truth and experience and the view it gives us embraces all the provinces of that supreme region." "It maps out but does not cut up or build walls or hedges to confine our vision." He recognizes the *Gītā* as the product of a "vast synthetic mind," "a rich synthetic experience and therefore to approach it analytically from a particular system will be to miss the very essential teaching of it."

According to Sri Aurobindo, Indian mind and her culture are always synthetic in nature. In the past India has done three great syntheses — the Vedic, the tāntric and the synthesis of the *Gītā*. The *Gītā* starts from the synthesis of the Upaniṣads and makes a further synthesis of love, work and knowledge as means of liberation. Its teaching is universal because Truth itself is universal, not limited to any country, race, nation or religion. There are very little local or temporal elements in the *Gītā*, and the very little that it has can easily be universalized. For example, its reference to *cāturvarṇya, yajña,* and *śāstra* may seem at first sight to be narrow but in deeper analysis they too have a universal connotation. The *Gītā* itself has repeatedly said that the classification of people under the four heads of brāhmaṇa, kṣatriya, vaiśya and śūdra is based on the natural and inborn qualities of them. The fourth chapter of the *Gītā* elaborately deals with the several kinds of *yajña*, and it can easily be shown that no people can live without performing some or other kind of the sacrifices. And about the *śāstra pramāṇa* in respect of duties, Sri Aurobindo says that by it the *Gītā* does not limit itself to any particular system of code or rule of conduct. It is true that *śāstra* as a system of fixed rules of conduct may be necessary for the average man. But with the progress of our outlook, new *śāstra*s replace the old ones. The kinetic man is never satisfied in following the old codes as a routine, he may discover new values and want to live in accordance with them. So the *śāstra*s are liable to change but the central meaning of the term remains the same. It means the rule or code that one has to follow for his upliftment from the downward tendencies. Sri Aurobindo says, "the Vedic law becomes a convention and a Buddha appears with his new rule of eightfold path and the goal of *nirvāṇa*; and it may be remarked that he propounds it not as a personal invention, but as the true rule of Aryan living constantly rediscovered by the Buddha, the enlightened mind, the awakened spirit. But this practically means that there is an ideal, and eternal *dharma* which religion, philosophy, ethics and all other powers in man that strive after truth and perfection are constantly endeavouring to embody in new statements of the science and art of the inner and outer life, a new *śāstra*. The Mosaic law of religious, ethical and social righteousness is convicted of narrowness and imperfection and is now, besides, a convention; the law of Christ comes to replace it and claims at once to abrogate and to fulfil, to abrogate the imperfect form and fulfil in a deeper and broader light and power the spirit of the thing which it aimed at, the divine rule of living. And the human search does not stop there, but leaves these formulations too, goes back to some past truth it had rejected or breaks forward to some new truth and power, but is always in search of the same thing, the law of its perfection, its rule of right living, its complete, highest and essential self and nature."

Thus we see that Sri Aurobindo has often taken some important concepts of the *Gītā* and given to them wider connotation. Throughout the Essays we find ample examples of it. While explaining the meaning of *vedaiśca sarvairahameva vedya vedāntakṛt vedavideva cāham* by "Veda" he has meant the "inner Veda," the scripture is only a verbal form of it. The eternal Veda — the supramental light of knowledge is in the heart of every being and no *śāstra* be it the Veda, the Upaniṣads, the Koran, Bible or the books of the Chinese or the sayings, teachings of any prophet or *avatāra* can exhaust this infinite and eternal fountain of knowledge.

Similarly Sri Aurobindo while commenting upon the *śloka* — *bhaktya tvananyayā śakya ahamevamvidorjuna jñātuṁ draṣṭuṁ ca tattvena praveṣṭuṁ ca parantapa* says that as the *yoga* of the *Gītā* is comprehensive, the liberation it speaks of is also integral, it is *sāyujya, sāmīpya* and *sādṛśya* all at once. "The orthodox *yoga* of knowledge aims at a fathomless immergence in the one infinite existence, *sāyujya*; it looks upon that alone as the entire liberation. The *yoga* of adoration envisages an eternal habitation or nearness as a greater release, *sālokya, sāmīpya*. The *yoga* of works leads to oneness in power of being and nature *sādṛśya*: but the *Gītā* envelops them all in its catholic integrality and fuses them all into one greatest and richest divine freedom and perfection."

In the view of Sri Aurobindo, the "divine teacher" has taught this Integral Yoga of knowledge, devotion and action to "the human disciple" on the occasion of the Kurukṣetra war. Sri Aurobindo does not doubt the existence of the human-divine Kṛṣṇa or of Arjuna but rather argues at some length for their existence. He accepts the possibility of human avatārahood but is of the opinion that the *Gītā* has emphasized on the transcendent, the cosmic, the internal divine avatārahood. It is the internal divine who removes the ignorance from the heart of his devotees by kindling the lamp of knowledge. It is the same internal divine who gives the *buddhiyoga* to his devotees so that they may be on the right track in their worship. But it is also true that the Lord manifests Himself (*ātmānaṁ sṛjāmyaham*) in the human form and acts in an inscrutable way to establish the social and moral order. Only the fortunate few can properly understand (*vetti tattvataḥ*) this divine birth and action of the Lord and thereby live in Him. The *Gītā* is full of many philosophical terms. But Sri Aurobindo gives us the caution, which we have already noted, that they should not be interpreted from any angular standpoint. Both in the past and in the modern age the *Gītā* has been much misinterpreted because the synthetic character of its teaching was overlooked. Thus about the "modern misreading" of the *Gītā*, Sri Aurobindo says that the modern mind being divorced from the ancient Graeco-Roman culture and the medieval Christian devotionalism has sometimes treated the *Gītā* merely as a "Gospel of works." The *Gītā* teaches us action, no doubt, but this action must be based on a divine and spiritual life. So the disinterested performance of duties is not enough. The *Gītā*, says Sri Aurobindo, "does not ask the awakened moral consciousness to slay itself on the altar of duty as a sacrifice and victim to the law of social status. It calls us higher and not lower . . . it bids us ascend to a supreme poise above the mainly practical, above the purely ethical, to the Brahmic consciousness. It replaces the conception of social duty by a divine obligation."

Similarly Sri Aurobindo warns us against some traditional misinterpretations. The *Gītā* says much about the Sāṁkhya and Yoga, and uses many concepts allied to those systems. Unless we are careful enough, we may fall into the error of considering the *Gītā* as a work of the Yoga or of the Sāṁkhya philosophy. The *Gītā* is, according to Sri Aurobindo, in its foundation a Vedāntic work — its Vedāntic ideas are propounded by means of concepts prevalent in the Sāṁkhya and the Yoga systems. Sri Aurobindo's discussion on this point is highly illuminating and so we shall try to see how he establishes his thesis that the *Gītā* with its concepts of Puruṣottama makes the Vedāntic synthesis of the Sāṁkhya and Yoga ways of thinking.

At the outset Sri Aurobindo reminds us that the Sāṁkhya of the *Gīta* is not the system of the *kārikā*s because the traditional Sāṁkhya admits the plurality of *puruṣa*s, while the *Gītā* does not so admit. Secondly, the *Gītā* advocates that the One *puruṣa* or *Īśvara* is the cause of the universe but the Sāṁkhya deprives the Self of its power of creation and dissolution. Similarly, the Yoga that the *Gītā* speaks of is not, according to Sri Aurobindo, the Yoga system of Patañjali. Patañjali gives us mainly the practical method of *rājayoga* but the *yoga* of the *Gītā* is many-sided of which *rājayoga* is only an element. Moreover, the *Gītā* speaks of *samādhi* and *brāhmīsthiti* but its idea of *samādhi* is different from that of Patañjali. And lastly, the *Gītā* puts a permanent importance on action but Patañjali considers it as necessary only at preliminary stage.

The Sāṁkhya and Yoga of the *Gītā* are not in the view of Sri Aurobindo two incompatible systems. They differ only in their methods and starting points. The Sāṁkhya proceeds by knowledge. Yoga on the other hand proceeds by works. The *yoga* of the *Gītā* teaches us to offer our works as sacrifice (*yajña*) to the Eternal Master but this is possible only if there is a devotion to the ultimate in which knowledge also culminates.

Sri Aurobindo in his exquisite exposition of the dualistic system of the Sāṁkhya remarks that modern science also has arrived at the same conclusion regarding the presence of inconscient will and intelligence in the natural phenomena. "But Sāṁkhya explains what modern science leaves in obscurity, the process by which the mechanical and inconscient takes on the appearance of consciousness" in the human mind. Sri Aurobindo's comment on the traditional Sāṁkhya carries much philosophical significance. Thus he says that as a rational explanation of the cosmic universe and man's liberation from it, the Sāṁkhya is "as good and as effective" as the explanations offered by any other ancient system of philosophy. But there are certain points which the traditional Sāṁkhya could not satisfactorily explain. "The Sāṁkhya was bound to evolve pluralism by its rigidly analytical observation of the principle of thing." As the individual experiences vary, the Sāṁkhya had to postulate the multiplicity of the selves. Moreover, if we are to consider liberation as something real and also to admit that with the liberation of one all are not liberated then we cannot but admit the plurality of the selves.

After pointing out the mertis of the traditional Sāṁkhya, Sri Aurobindo passes on to his most important thesis that the theory of the plurality of selves can be avoided and has actually been avoided by the *Gītā* "by bringing into its Vedāntic Sāṁkhya the ideas and principles of Vedāntic Yoga." But he says that the solution of the problem about the multiplicity of the selves has actually been suggested by the Upaniṣads. The Gītā has only explicitly propounded that thesis by its theory of Puruṣottama. It is with the idea of the triple status of the One Conscious Self that the Sāṁkhya difficulty can be removed. Nature, the witnessing human soul and the Lord are not, in this version, three different entities. They are, on the other hand, triple status of the One Supreme Lord — the *uttama puruṣa* or *puruṣottama* who is the foundation of both the *kṣara* and *akṣara* status of His existence.

Sri Aurobindo emphasizes again and again that an actionless immutable existence is not the last word of the *Gītā*. One must pass beyond the state of actionless quietude of the *akṣara puruṣa* and realize the Puruṣottama as the governor of all existencies. When one realizes this, his human personality is transformed into a spiritual impersonality. So long as a man acts as a human person, who is nothing but a sum of natural qualities in the ultimate analysis, he is not liberated. But when he gives up his egoism and learns completely to surrender to Puruṣottama who is a Divine Person, his actions are taken up by Him. Such a man becomes the living mask of the Puruṣottama. The essence of *karma-saṁnyāsa,* thus, lies not in the external renunciation of works but in the offering of them as sacrifices to the Lord in the calm joy of the Impersonal. In the view of Sri Aurobindo, it is only when we see that the Puruṣottama is the foundation of the Divine life and works that we can understand the meaning of such *śloka* as *gatasaṅgasya muktasya jñānāvasthitacetasaḥ, yajñāyācarataḥ karma samagraṁ pravilīyate*. Here we have the suggestion that actions are possible even after liberation (*muktasya*). But then the ego or any kind of attachment is no more the cause of such actions (*gatasaṅgasya*). On the contrary, these actions are said to proceed from Divine knowledge (*jñānavasthitacetasaḥ*) and are preformed out of a spirit of sacrifice to the Lord (*yajñāyācarataḥ karma*). They arise from a free spirit and disappear without modifying it like waves that arise and disappear on the surface of conscious immutable depths.

In Sri Aurobindo's view, the teaching of the *Gītā* is not merely the stilling of the emotive and the thinking mind. It is true that the *Gītā* suggests in the first part of the sixth chapter the special *rājayoga* methods for controlling our emotions and thoughts. But it immediately suggests that they are meant for something higher, viz. the perception of One in the many and the consequent devotion (*bhajati*) for the Lord (*mām*). The state of the soul after its release from the bondage of Nature is described by the *Gītā* variously as *brāhmīsthiti, brahmanirvāṇa, brahmayoga, samādhi,* etc. Its ideas of *samādhi, brahmanirvāṇa,* etc. are of immense significance and they are in no way incompatible with actions in the world. Sri Aurobindo points out that it is significant that the *Gītā* often speaks of *brahmanirvāṇa* and not *nirvāṇa* merely which suggests that *nirvāṇa* which is peace supreme has its foundation in the Lord Himself (*śāntiṁ nirvāṇparamāṁ matsaṁsthām*). When the human soul attains the supreme status of its being, such status has been described by the *Gītā* as *matsaṁsthā, madbhāva, mama sādharmyamāgatāḥ,* etc. The soul in its dwelling in the Puruṣottama does not necessarily cease to work. Rather by attaining this transcendent and universal consciousness, he gets luminous knowledge other than mental thought, and power other and mightier than the personal will, and actions come spontaneously out of it.

Sri Aurobindo, thus, considers the idea of the Puruṣottama as the key concept of the *Gītā,* which in his opinion has exercised a definite influence on the Indian religious consciousnness for centuries. It is with the help of this idea that the "*Gītā* founds its synthesis of Vedānta, Sāṁkhya and Yoga, its synthesis of knowledge, works and devotion."

Part V
On Man and Relation

14

Sri Aurobindo's Concept of Man

Kh. Gokulchandra

MAN is not a mere animal though he is like an animal in many superficial respects. Ordinarily man is distinguished from animals not only by his superior capacities but also by his immense possibilities, by opening himself to the cosmic forces. Aurobindo's concept of man is somewhat different from what we know of man in a limited sense. Man is a "soul that has housed itself in a mind and body made of its own elements," as he puts it. He himself is an integral *yogī* and all his philosophization is brought from the realization of his yogic experience. Hence, common man will face difficulties in entering into his realm of thought in the first place. Sri Aurobindo thinks that the man whom we ordinarily know through our sense experiences is not the real man. Here we are not considering his view of Collective man or Society as we find in some of his writings. He also maintains that human beings are composed of many different parts, each part contributes something to the total being of our consciousness, such as, thinking, feeling, doing and so on. As in a machine, the parts perform their respective functions and at the same time, they contribute to the functioning of the whole. So, Sri Aurobindo considered the concept of man in terms of the concepts of the evolution, Gnostic consciousness which we call Supermind and Reality. He believed in the supreme union of spiritual experience and intellectual activity. This union is his vision of the future evolution of man.

The principle of evolution is the most important principle in Aurobindo's cosmology, his principle of evolution is not only the governing principle in his social philosophy but also his metaphysics. The process of man's social development in terms of goal, methods, nature, meaning and trend is the principle of evolution. Evolution presupposes involution.

According to Sri Aurobindo, matter is the starting point of the evolutionary process. As an integral *yogī* Aurobindo tried to synthesize matter with spirit. He pointed out that matter was not different from spirit. Unlike many rationalist philosophers, he treated matter as an important element of evolution of man. Matter and spirit are the different levels of evolution and different aspects of one omnipresent reality. Matter evolves in pure spirit. So, he considered man as the key to the evolutionary movement because only man could become conscious of the Reality. He thought that evolution helps a man to transform from a mere physical and a mental being into a spiritual being. According to him, "Evolution is nothing but progressive unfolding of spirit out of the density of material consciousness and the gradual self-revelation of God out of this apparent animal being."

In this philosophization on the concept of man, there are three aspects of man — the external or outer, the inner and the Divine. The external, according to Aurobindo, is that which is apparent to us. It is closely related to our physical nature. Physical nature is mainly concerned with the mentality of the physical man. "Objective," "customary," "practical," and "tradition" are his ideas. In this aspect, it also has our waking — conscious — existence. The second, the inner soul, which constitutes mainly the inner physical, the inner vital and the inner mental aspects, is the spiritual aspect of man in evolution and this soul is not always aware of the external becuase it is veiled from it. This inner being of man reveals the central being; it is used in the Vedāntic perspective as *ātman*. According to Aurobindo, there are two aspects of the so-called central being of man. One is upper and the other is the lower. He talks about the upper as nothing but the *jīvātmā,* transcending the self. "*Jīvātmā* is the individual self, the central being." It is that aspect of man which is prior to human evolution and which also transcends the process of ascent as well as the human expressions in terms of life and mind. *Jīvātmā* is also conceived as the spark of the Divine. It integrates the whole consciousness. It also presides over the evolution of the psychic being but itself does not evolve. Because *jīvātmā* is beyond spatio-temporal relation, it is formless and nameless, featureless, blissful, self-sufficient and internally satisfied with pure being. According to him, the lower aspect of central being of man is psychic being — subliminal self. This psychic being is the inner being of man. It is the evolutionary principle in man. It enters into the body at the time of birth and exists at the time of death also. This lower aspect is almost a deputy of the *jīvātmā,* expressing itself in individual life and existence and supporting it. This psychic being is always inside the evolutionary process. For him, "The psychic being realizes its oneness with the true being, the *jīvātmā,* but it does not change into it." The last aspect of man is the Divine soul which is the potentiality of Divinity. Aurobindo thinks that everything is the manifestation of the Divine, such as both the two aspects of the central being of man, i.e. *jīvātmā* and psychic are also the expression of the Divine. He also gives the identification of *jīvātmā* with that of the Divine that whereas there can be relation of identity-in-difference between the psychic being and the Divine, the *jīvātmā* can merge itself in identity with the Divine. As an integral *yogī* he clearly describes the concept of man as "The being of man is composed of these elements — psychic behind supporting all, the inner, mental, vital and physical, and the outer — quite external nature of mind, life and body which is their instrument of expression. But above all is the central being (*jīvātmā*), which uses them all for its manifestation, it is a portion of the Divine self."

Sri Aurobindo also talks about the concept of man in terms of the Gnostic Being or Supermind. According to Aurobindo, only a Gnostic Being is a perfect and complete man/individual. He must be the consciousness of the Reality, the Being, the Spirit that is secret in us. The Gnostic being is a completely divinized spirit and man of knowledge, who is not caught in the evolutionary process. Being a Gnosic, his whole way of being, thinking, living and acting would be governed by the power of a universal spirit. The nature of Supermind essentially becomes a unitary character of a Gnostic being. Supermind is one of the eight principles for Aurobindo which belong to the higher hemisphere. In this higher hemisphere, it represents the stage into which evolution is going to enter. It is the end and the ideal of mind. The consciousness of a Gnostic being is integral and therefore it will be able to create, harmonize and unify many diversities. All the activities of the Gnostic being are always based on knowledge. Body for the Gnostic being becomes an instrument of spiritiual activities. Therefore, he defines the Gnostic being as a man of knowledge, the man who has risen above the realm of ignorance. Thus, ordinary man "is a transitional being,"and he is not "final." He has to ascend to the level of what is called a supramental consciousness that is in eternal possession of Truth. But the present state of man is one of Ignorance. So, the question is asked, "is it possible for man to live a divine life?" Sri Aurobindo answered that though knowledge and ignorance appeared to be opposites, they are not really so. In the realm of spiritual wisdom there cannot be pairs of opposites. In this way, Sri Aurobindo gives us hope for Divinity.

So far, what is given is only a fragmentary idea of man. Sri Aurobindo was a scholar "philosopher," a *yogī* and a perfectionist. We cannot therefore enter into his intellectual and philosophical enterprise easily. That is why his philosophy is defined and redefined, interpreted and reinterpreted time and again and it still continues. Here one may ask a very basic question that how far the philosophy of Sri Aurobindo is related or relevant with our present-day crisis of existence. The present situation of the world in general and India in particular becomes more and more dangerous. The evil spirit of disintegration is knocking on the doors of every reason. There is starvation, unrest, regional conflict in many parts of the country. Man has created a system of civilization for meeting his mental, vital and physical claims and urges. But it now proves itself to him as "a too dangerous servant of his blundering ego and his appetites." It is said that all our intellectual enterprise can be fitted and interpreted through the given paradigm of Sri Aurobindo. But can this system be able to solve the acute problems faced by the farmers in the fields or the starving mothers with their children in their laps. In short, can the evolution of the spiritual man in the human mental being solve the present prevailing problems of the society? If the spiritual tendency in humanity cannot solve the problems confronted by man in his life then it is of no value. Because it is the individual man that suffers pain and sorrow, hatred and jealousy.

Answer to such kinds of attack is that spiritual evolution does not aim at solving human problems. It aims at forming a new foundation of our consciousness, a new basis of our being, our life and knowledge. A mystic is led by the law of harmony and concord and carries a sense of unity of all beings. Love and compassion is core to the life of the spiritual man. Being assisted by the spark of divinity, spiritual becomes real help to humanity since the solution of the problems offered by spirituality comes to us not by external means but "by an inner change, a transformation of consciousness and nature." The inner transformation and spiritual perfection is taken to be the most important thing to do. But, for that the importance of the society is not to be minimized. The society influence the individual and the individual pass through the social status of his being so that his pursuit of knowledge and right living are fulfilled. According to Sri Aurobindo, a perfect community can exist only by the perfection of its individuals. By leading a life in the social sense of the term an individual earns his fitness for leading a true spiritual life. The world around us is the manifestation of Reality and in all these manifestations of the world the individual alone is "the key to the evolutionary movement" for it is the individual who becomes conscious of the Reality in himself. Man's manhood lies in fulfilling God in life. So, let us try to develop our minds and awaken our spirituality. Now is the high time for it.

References

Banerji, Sanat K., *Sri Aurobindo and the Future of Man*, Sri Aurobindo Society, Pondicherry, 1974.

Chattopadhyaya, D.P., *Marx and Aurobindo.*

The Hour of God, Selections from His Writings, Compiled by Manoj Das, Sahitya Akademi, 2000.

Letters of Sri Aurbindo, 1st Series, Sri Aurobindo Circle, Bombay (1950).

SABCL, *The Life Divine.*

Philosophy of Supermind and Contemporary Crisis, Souvenir, ed. Kireet Joshi, ICPR, 2003.

Roy, D.K., *Sri Aurobindo on Man*, an Article on Man and Freedom, ed. S.K. Sen, 2001.

Sri Aurobindo, *A Practical Guide to the Integral Yoga*, Pondicherry, 1959.

Sri Aurobindo, *Lights on Yoga.*

Sri Aurobindo, *Sri Aurobindo Mandir*, Annual No. 6 (August 1947).

15

Towards a Theroy of True Human Relation

Jean Paul-Sartre vis-à-vis Sri Aurobindo

Susmita Bhattacharya

I

RABINDRANATH Tagore makes a significant comment in his *Religion of Man*: "The history of civilization is the history of human relationship." Relationship is the fundamental truth of this world of appearance. Creation has been made possible through the continual interrelationship of different beings. An individual starts on the long career of his evolution with his needs and desires. Then he gradually identifies partially his life with the life of a certain number of other individuals with whom he is associated by birth, choice or circumstances. So, an individual has in him two distinct master impulses, the individual and the communal. The possibility of their opposition and the attempt to find their reconciliation lie at the very roots of human evolution.

This paper is trying to probe the views of two great minds of the world who very distinctively visualized the human reality, the prospect or future of humanity as well as the inward journey of an individual being.

Jean Paul-Sartre, renowned French Existential philosopher in his famous writing *Being and Nothingness* (1943) has pictured the individual man as alone, insecure and somewhere alienated from everybody, everything as well as from his own self. At that time Sartre strongly believed that whenever two persons get related with each other, after some time they discover that their relation absolutely fails to be called a relation at all. According to Sartre, all these human relations ultimately turn into a subject-object relation, i.e. a man is at the same time a subject to oneself and becomes an object in the view of another man. And this subject-object dichotomy finally leads to an endless conflict. Everyone likes to enjoy his own freedom; thus he does not simply tolerate other's existence within his own orbit, since an individual is always suffering from a fear of losing one's own freedom. But at the same time, he also realizes that he has to be related with the other, since the other is an inevitable part of his world. So, here arises a tension between two individual beings which has made Sartre to say, "Man is a useless passion" (*Being the Nothingness*, p.149).

In 1945, Sartre gave a lecture titled "Existentialism and Humanism" at Paris. This lecture is fundamentally a defence of Existentialism as a doctrine true to Humanism. In this lecture Sartre very clearly defines the concept of individual subjectivism, the notion of inter-subjectivity as well as the aspect of humanity. He mentions in this lecture:

> Our aim is precisely to establish the human kingdom as a pattern of values in distinction from the material world. But the subjectivity which we thus postulate as the standard of truth is no narrowly individual subjectivism . . . it is not only one's own self that one discovers in the *cogito*, but those of others too . . . when we say "I think" we are attaining to ourselves in the presence of the other, and we are just as certain of the other as we are of ourselves. Thus the man who discovers himself directly in the *cogito* also discovers all the others, and discovers them as the condition of his own existence. He recognizes that he cannot be anything unless others recognize him as such. I cannot obtain any

> truth whatsoever about myself, except through the mediation of another. The other is indispensable to my existence, and equally so to my knowledge I can have of myself . . . the intimate discovery of myself is at the same time the revelation of the other as a freedom which confronts mine, and which cannot think or will without doing so either for or against me. Thus, at once, we find ourselves in a world which is, let us say, that of "inter-subjectivity." It is in this world that man has to decide what he is and what others are.
>
> — *Existentialism and Humanism*, p. 45.

But what is humanism? In reality, the word "humanism" has two very different meanings. One may understand by humanism an aspect which views man as the end-in-itself as the supreme value. But an existentialist will never take man as the end, since man is not any static concept, he is still to be determined. The existentialist admits another sense of the word "humanism." According to Sartre the fundamental meaning of this word is this,

> Man is all the time outside of himself: it is in projecting and losing himself beyond himself that he makes man to exist; and on the other hand, it is by pursuing transcendent aims that he himself is able to exist. Since man is thus self-surpassing, and can grasp objects only in relation to his self-surpassing, he is himself the heart and centre of his transcendence. There is no other universe except the human universe, the universe of human subjectivity. — Ibid., p. 55.

In 1980 Sartre in his *Last Dialogue* with Beni Levis, stressed the point that the ultimate truth of the human relation is not the conflict. Beyond this conflict there must be "something" which one has got to find out. So what is that "something" where a man can surpass his own religion, belief, all presupposed ideas and discover his true or real identity? To answer this question, Sartre referred to the concept of "myth" of the primitive men. Each primitive group had its own myth symbolized in the "totem." Through their very own totem, the members of the group could discover their unity and mutual relation with each other. According to Sartre, these myths and totems helped to establish a sense of solidarity within the members of the group. They felt that they were a total unit, different from another. This sense of unity helped them to survive unitedly. Sartre mentioned in his dialogue that they (primitive men) invented an animal as a totem (they adopted it as an emblem), they believed that this totem was the genetic source of a particular group. So, in that way they developed a belief of brotherhood. Thus, when they talked to each other they seemed to feel themselves to be the children of the same "Mother." So Sartre stressed the point that "brotherhood" is nothing but a sense of realization that all men are the offspring of the same earth-mother. Whatever Sartre wanted to say in his *Last Dialogue* is a sense of "Secret Solidarity." But what is the rudimentary source of this secret solidarity — this question was never satisfactorily answered by Sartre.

II

Sri Aurobindo discusses the different phases of human relation from a new dimension in *The Human Cycle* and in *The Essays on The Gītā*. Sri Aurobindo's vision as reflected in *The Essays on The Gītā* is as follows:

> But the individual being begins with ignorance and persists long in ignorance. Acutely conscious of himself he sees the ego as the cause and whole meaning of life. . . . He misses the true meaning of life and, since he does not use life and works for the enlargement and elevation of his being through sacrifice, he lives in vain.
>
> Only when the individual being begins to perceive and acknowledge in his acts the value of the self in others as well as the powers and needs of his own ego, begins to perceive universal nature behind his own workings . . . is he on his way to the transcendence of his limitation by the ego. He begins to give more value to the claims of the self in

> others and less to the claims of his ego; he admits the strife between egoism and altruism and by the increase of his altruistic tendencies he prepares the enlargement of his own consciousness and being.
>
> But this is only a long intermediate stage. It is still subject to the law of desire, to the centrality of all things in the conceptions and needs of his ego. . . . All this is still within the domain, though the very much enlarged domain, of the mutable, finite and personal. — *The Essays on The Gītā*

Sri Aurobindo admits that the will to be, the will to power and the will to know are perfectly legitimate. But he points out that their satisfaction cannot be achieved by any egoistic endeavour — not because of any moral or religious reasons but simply because they cannot be so satisfied for the attempt always gives rise to an eternal clash with other egoisms, a mutual wounding and hampering, even a mutual destruction. The reason is that we exhaust ourselves and corrupt ourselves in the very attempt to live by the destruction and exploitation of others. Therefore, Sri Aurobindo points out "only that which lives in its own self-existence can endure."

So, Sri Aurobindo concludes, the real self-knowledge and the right mode of living lies beyond. That can only come when an individual perceives that "that self in him and the self in others are one being and this self is something higher than this ego, an infinite, an impersonal, a universal existence in whom all move and have their being. . . ." (*The Essays on The Gītā*, p. 120).

Therefore, the brotherhood which Sartre was searching for and man dreams of attaining can be discovered from Sri Aurobindo's vision of true individual who is other than the ego. In *The Human Cycle* Sri Aurobindo mentions,

> The solution lies not in the reason but in the soul of man, in its spiritual tendencies. It is a spiritual, an inner freedom that can alone create a perfect human order. It is a spiritual,

> a greater than the rational enlightenment that can alone illumine the vital nature of man and impose harmony on its self-seekings, antagonisms and discords. A deeper brotherhood, a yet unfound law of love is the only sure foundation possible for a perfect social evolution; no other can replace it. But this brotherhood and love will not proceed by the vital instincts or the reason where they can be met, baffled of deflected by opposite reasonings and other discordant instincts. Nor will it found itself in the natural heart of man where there are plenty of other passions to combat it. It is in the soul that it must find its roots; the love which is founded upon a deeper truth of our being, the brotherhood or, let us say, — for this is another feeling than any vital or mental sense of brotherhood, a calmer more durable motive-force, — the spiritual comradeship which is the expression of an inner realization of oneness. For so only can egoism disappear and the true individualism of the unique godhead in each man found itself on the true communism of the equal godhead in the race; for the spirit, the inmost self, the universal godhead in every being is that whose very nature of diverse oneness it is to realize the perfection of its individual life and nature in the existence of all, in the universal life and nature. — *The Human Cycle*.

Question might be raised that what Sri Aurobindo says is the realization of one's own deeper self is a traditional realization, so what is new in Sri Aurobindo's view except a mere repetition? But Sri Aurobindo's contribution lies in pointing out that spiritual realization of inner oneness should not be a static realization, it must be a dynamic one. Such a dynamic truth-consciousness higher than the mind is called by him "Supermind" or "Supramental consciousness."

This will be clear from what he says regarding the nature of this dynamic consciousness:

> The Supermind is in its very essence a truth-consciousness, a consciousness always free from the ignorance which is the foundation of our present natural or evolutionary

> existence and from which nature in us is trying to arrive at self-knowledge and world-knowledge. . . . The Supermind, because it is a truth-consciousness, has this knowledge inherent in it and this power of true existence. . . . This is because its very nature is knowledge: it has not to acquire knowledge is always true, so too its will is always true; it does not fumble in its handling of things or stumble in its paces. In the Supermind feeling and emotion do not depart from their truth. . . .
>
> — *The Supramental Manifestation upon Earth.*

Sri Aurobindo shows that,

> Supermind is the grade of existence beyond mind, life and matter and, as mind, life and matter have manifested on the earth, so too must Supermind in the inevitable course of things manifest in this world of matter. In fact, a Supermind is already here but is involved, concealed behind this manifest mind, life and matter and not yet acting overtly or in its own power: if it acts, it is through these inferior powers and modified by their characters. . . . — Ibid.

In fact, from Sri Aurobindo's analysis we find that,

> mind is in its origin from Supermind is itself a power of Supermind . . . it is used by the Supermind principally for the work of differentiation which is necessary if there is to be a creation and a universe. In the Supermind itself, in all its creation there is this differentiating power, the manifestation of the One in the Many and the Many in the One; but the One is never forgotten or lost in its multiplicity which always consciously depends upon and never takes precedence over the eternal oneness. In the mind, on the contrary, the differentiation, the multiplicity, does take precedence and the conscious sense of the universal oneness is lost and the separated unit seems to exist for itself and by itself as a sufficient self-conscious integer or in inanimate objects as the inconscient integer. — Ibid.

Therefore, it follows that for human relation to be free from ignorance and all sorts of errors or conflicts that jeopardise it, it can be made secure and come to its full flowering only when, as Sri Aurobindo shows, "all the movements of thought, impulse and action are governed and directed by a self-existent and luminously automatic truth-consciousness and our whole nature comes to be constituted by it . . ." (Ibid.).

This is not a mere hope, for our evolution reveals that it is a secret self-existent knowledge and truth that is working to manifest itself in the creation here.

Part VI
On State and Politics

16

Sri Aurobindo and the Uplift of Humanity

Sushmita Bhowmik

INDIA, during the nineteenth and the twentieth century witnessed a renaissance not only in the form of the birth of nationalism and a high standard of rational thinking in every sphere of our social life, but also through the attempts towards the reawakening of humanity and the reconstruction of the life of the entire mankind. Such efforts towards the regeneration of the entire human race have been made by many of our eminent social thinkers. And Sri Aurobindo has been one of the major figures among them.

Besides being a patriot who has rightly been regarded as the prophet of Indian nationalism, and a poet, Sri Aurobindo has been, above all, a *mahāyogī* or a great spiritual seeker. He has devoted himself and put great endeavour towards the reconstruction of not only the Indian society, but of the entire human race and his attempts towards the same is dominantly spiritual. He has envisaged the dawn of a perfect life on earth which, according to him, would become possible through a gradual transformation and transmutation of our inner being and thereby also of the outer being, by the power of the Divine Light. Sri Aurobindo has thus propounded a new theory of human evolution and worked incessantly to realize that glorious future destiny of mankind, which has been revealed to his vision at a certain stage of his spiritual development and which thenceforth has become the all-engrossing mission of his life.

Now, the question is, what precisely is the nature and significance of this vision and work of Sri Aurobindo for the future evolution of man and society? Herein comes the metaphysical aspect of Sri Aurobindo's thought.

Reality for Sri Aurobindo is supremely spiritual. It is of the nature of *Brahman* or *Saccidānanda* and since everything is *Brahman,* matter also is *Brahman* and hence real. This Supreme Spirit or the Divine Reality is all-pervading. It is already present within us as well as in the external material world. The aim of human life, according to Sri Aurobindo, is to discover the Divine and then to work for its manifestation. Such realization and thereby the manifestation of the Divine will in the life of the individuals, as well as in the life of the nations and thereby in the entire material world, would lead to the divine transformation of our entire mode of existence and that would gradually lead towards a perfect life of peace, unity and harmony on earth. This would become possible through a gradual process of evolution of consciousness. The growth of consciousness, for Sri Aurobindo, is the supreme secret of life, the master key to earthly evolution. He upholds the theory of the spiritual evolution of Man into Superman and Nature into Supernature.

The evolution of the world has so far-reached the level of mind, crossing the stages of matter and life. But time has now come, says Sri Aurobindo, when evolution must take a leap into the next higher spiritual realm — into the Supermind. Mind is conscious and as mental beings we have no doubt attained certain perfections in different spheres of our life. But at the same time, we find that we are still suffering from various forms of ignorance, which is the cause of all our basic troubles. To overcome it, what is needed is a further expansion of our consciousness. The mental state cannot therefore be the end-state of our being. And according to Sri Aurobindo, mind has an inherent tendency to go beyond itself, an inherent urge to rise higher. Mind therefore is the stage wherefrom we need to ascend towards the higher level of consciousness beyond mind, which has knowledge inherent in it and that is the Supermind. Therefore, for Sri Aurobindo, if we want fulfilment of life, we need fulfilment of knowledge and for that ascent towards the Supermind is essential.

Now, the ascent towards the higher spiritual realm, towards the Supermind, would become possible with the descent of the higher principle — the Truth-consciousness or the Supermind into the lower realm. As a result of such descent of the Divine Light in our earthly life, there will be a radical transformation of our terrestrial existence, of our mind, life and even the physical body and the material world. It is an important aspect of Sri Aurobindo's theory of evolution that he maintains the transformation and evolution of not only the mind or the life but also of the matter or the physical body. As a result of such transformation, man would evolve into Superman and Nature into Supernature. Such transformation brought about by the power of the Truth-consciousness is known as the Supramental transformation. And Sri Aurobindo maintains that the Supramental transformation of the entire human race would lead to the emergence of the Divine Life on earth, which is the ultimate goal or the destiny of evolution.

But for the ascent towards the Supermind and divinization of our life, besides divine grace, supreme effort on the part of the human beings is also necessary. Mind, life and body are the instruments of the Divine manifestation on earth. The Supermind will descend into the lower nature — the mind, the life and the body, only if the latter is prepared to receive the Divine Light from the above. There must be an intense aspiration on our part and a readiness to surrender the whole of our being for the purpose of receiving the Divine Light to illumine our consciousness. And according to Sri Aurobindo the practise of integral yoga would help in such preparation of our entire being.

Yoga means union with the Divine. But for Sri Aurobindo that cannot be the ultimate aim of *yoga*. After realizing the Divine-unity, the Divine power must be brought down on earth for the divinization of the entire human life on earth. The aim of integral yoga is therefore to enter into the Divine-consciousness by merging into it the separative ego and to bring down the Supramental-consciousness on earth to transform mind, life and body. Thus the aim of Sri Aurobindo's *yoga* is not mere individual liberation but of the liberation of the entire mankind. And herein lies the distinct and the significant aspect of Sri Aurobindo's concept of *yoga*. With the liberation of the entire human race, the Divine Life would emerge on earth.

The Divine Life is the emergence of a perfect life on earth, a life not of separation or isolation but one of unity and harmony. It consists of a race of gnostic beings who are completely spiritualized and perfect beings. Being guided by the Supreme principle of unity — the Supermind — the life of the Supermen will be those of unity, harmony and mutuality. The realization of one's true self to be identical with the Self of the Universe or the Absolute Spirit and with the self of every other being, would form the basis of a feeling of unity within the gnostic beings in the Divine Life. From the perception of this basic unity will result mutual understanding and perfect reciprocity. Every being will realize himself in other beings and other beings within himself. He will always act in awareness of the harmony of his individual self with the total self, of his individual will with the total will and of his individual action with the total action. In other words, there will be a vivid and intimate consciousness of others — "a consciousness of their mind, life and physical being which are felt as if they were one's own."[1] This would inevitably result in love, brotherhood, unity, fraternity and harmony between each and every being in the earthly life. The establishment of the Supermind in the earth-nature will then mean not only the emergence of perfect individuals, but also of the creation of an ideal society from which all strife and struggle, all discord and disparity, will be eliminated.

Sri Aurobindo has thus visualized a society of the future — a society of the prefect people, living in peace, enjoying bliss and harmony with the environment.

A perfect world of unity and harmony is what, according to Sri Aurobindo, the future evolution of mankind would bring about and for its realization, according to him, what is important is not the working out of a perfect ethic, but the spiritual transformation of man and society. He holds that, "to be ourselves liberated from ego and realize our true selves is the first necessity, all else can be achieved as a luminous result, a necessary consequence. That is one reason why a spiritual call must be accepted as imperative and take precedence over all other claims, intellectual, ethical, social, that belong to the domain of the Ignorance. Nothing can be a sufficient substitute for the spiritual change that can realize the true and integral good, because through the spirit we come to the root of action and existence."[2] Performance of selfless work for the good of humanity is undoubtedly a lofty ideal. It is a highly valuable self-preparation and it carries a man a long distance towards spiritual fruition. But until one realizes the Divine who dwells in the heart of

1. Quoted from: B.K. Lal, *Contemporary Indian Philosophy*, Motilal Banarsidass Publishers Pvt. Ltd., Delhi, 1st edn. 1973, p. 216.
2. Quoted from: M.P. Pandit, *Sri Aurobindo: Studies in The Light of His Thought*, Sri Aurobindo Ashram, Pondicherry, p. 233.

humanity and also transcends it, one remains in the realm of ignorance. It has got to be clearly realized that there can be no career of genuinely selfless work without dynamic self-identification with the Divine Will. Until one realizes the unity of mankind within the identity of the transcendent Spirit, the humanitarian ideals would fail to become effectual protests against the separatist tendencies and mutual destructiveness of collective human existence. Nothing short of spiritual self-realization, which brings in its train universalization of being, can pull down the walls of division that separate man from man, country from country, nation from nation.

Thus, Sri Aurobindo has tried to provide the entire mankind, a solution towards the different crises of life and existence. He is convinced that it is the present egoistic consciousness that is responsible for most of our conflicts and difficulties. As long as man would be under the influence of egoism and as long as he would feel himself to be separate from others, oppression, exploitation and inequality that have been troubling mankind from the early period of human history, would persist in the society. And this is because of the fact that it is the rule of egoistic life to aggrandize itself at the expense of others. Only when man would find his true self to be the Spirit in which he is essentially one with all other men and with the Absolute Reality, there can be true fraternity. For then everyone will seek the happiness of others as much as of himself, and no one will feel himself to be perfect unless similar perfection is attained by his fellow beings. The political, the economic, the humanist, the international, the institutional, the ethical and the religious solutions are all inadequate for the purpose of global human fellowship for they are all partial. The real solution lies in the overcoming of animal propensities and physical-vital tendencies, in the spiritual efforts for collective liberation, in the total spiritual and Supramental transformation of the human nature with the power of Truth-consciousness. Humanity as a race will then present the figure of perfect unity in diversity with an overall harmony and integration as its foundation.

Spiritual reawakening of the mankind has therefore been the supreme guiding force in Sri Aurobindo's attempt towards the resurgence of the enitre humanity. And it has worked as a major guide even in his struggle for the freedom of his motherland. He, in fact, undertook yogic *sādhanā* during his involvement in the nationalist movement of India, in the early part of his life, to empower the masses with an inner power for political use. He was able to infuse a new spirit and awaken a new dynamism in the life of the Indian nation through his revolutionary messages based on "Spiritual Nationalism" and the concept of "Mother India." And later he left active politics and involved himself in intense yogic meditation, not because he lost interest in the work of liberating and rebuilding the Indian nation and of helping humanity, or because he was disheartened in the face of the formidable difficulties on the way, or for any other reason, but because his yogic activities gave him a surer light, a more effective power and new ways of working upon the outer events and circumstances by inner spiritual means and methods, by which he can work more effectively for the uplift of mankind.

In Sri Aurobindo's view, humanity is destined to evolve into Supermanhood wherein lies the highest good of the human race and in this great evolutionary leap forward, India who possesses a deep and abiding spiritual thought and practice, would take the lead. It has been quite evident to his profound vision of humanity's future evolution that after its prolonged engrossment in material existence in the present age under the influence of modern European civilization, it has become necessary for it to awaken to the spiritual call and rise to a higher level of spiritual existence. And it has also been clear to him that it is from Asia, and especially from India, that modern humanity is to receive that call for spiritual awakening and right direction in its upward spiritual ascension. This vision of Sri Aurobindo influenced his nationalist ideal. He maintained that since India would take the lead in the spiritual awakening of the humanity, the political liberation of India is of utmost necessity. And finally when India attained political independence on 15 August 1947, Sri Aurobindo said that it has a significance not only for us, but for Asia and the whole world, for, India has a great part to play in determining the political, social, cultural and spiritual future of humanity. According to him, India was rising not to serve her own material interests but to live also for God and the world as a helper and leader of the whole human race. Thus reconstructing the entire national life has not been the only aim of Sri Aurobindo, rather the resurgence of the whole of humanity has been his main concern that guided his life, thought and action.

Although the total aim of Sri Aurobindo has always been the perfection not only of the individual but also of the society and eventually of the whole of humanity, but it might be pointed out that in his thoughts and writings there is a greater primary emphasis on individual perfection than on social perfection. But here it has to be noted that, since according to Sri Aurobindo individual is the key of the evolutionary movement, he has had to focus his attention initially to a greater degree on the problem of individual perfection than on social perfection. This of course does not mean that the social side has been neglected altogether. On the contrary, the social life of man has been given an extensive and thorough consideration by Sri Aurobindo in his writings. The problem of social development and the issues connected with that problem has received special consideration and has been given a systematic and exhaustive treatment by Sri Aurobindo in his work, *The Human Cycle*. In *The Human Cycle* he has formulated three major stages of social evolution, which are the infrarational stage, the rational stage and the suprarational or spiritual stage.

Sri Aurobindo has thus tried to show the entire mankind a way towards the dawn of a new age — an age where peace, harmony and progress would reign supreme as the crowning fulfilment of human evolution. On the one hand he maintains that humanity is suffering from different limitations; this limitation is fundamentally a limitation of consciousness which is the cause of all our basic troubles. But at the same time he points out that mankind already possesses that *śakti* or power by which it can overcome all the limitations through a gradual expansion of consciousness. And this is one of the significant messages that Sri Aurobindo conveys to humanity. Further, discovering our inner spirituality and transforming the entire material existence by the spiritual light and power, through the practice of integral *yoga,* is what Sri Aurobindo wants mankind to try for. And it is important to note that he never aspires for the awakening of spirituality within humanity by completely denying the material life and existence, for, the latter too, in Sri Aurobindo's view, has its own importance and significance. Divinity, as he has shown, can be attained in the physical world itself, continuing to dwell in this physical body and having interaction with all our fellow beings. Materialism and Spiritualism have therefore been reconciled by Sri Aurobindo. And this makes his attempt towards the spiritualization of human life and existence distinct from the similar attempts made by the ancient mystics of India whose spiritual endeavour consists in the complete rejection of all phenomenal existence. Man and his terrestrial existence have therefore received their complete and significant recognition in the thoughts of Sri Aurobindo.

It is in response to the most fundamental problems relating to the very destiny of our earthly existence that the spiritual endeavour of Sri Aurobindo becomes relevant. He is convinced that with the establishment of the Truth-consciousness in our earthly existence, mankind will be liberated forever from the grip of all kinds of ignorance, evil and suffering. But, it may still be asked, however valuable Sri Aurobindo's work may be for the solution of the ultimate problems of life, how can his thoughts and work effectively help the world to overcome the immediately pressing problems and urgent difficulties? Today humanity is intensely suffering from the crisis of values — the values of love, peace, unity and brotherhood. And this is evident from the different forms of corruptions, exploitations, violence, oppression and injustice in every sphere of our life. The gradually increasing mechanistic and materialistic tendencies are turning man into machines, devoid of feelings and emotions and determining everything in terms of material benefits and comforts. The frequent march of destructive forces in the form of wars has brought human existence at stake. In short, certain evil forces are gradually engulfing human life trying to bring it to its end.

Now, we may try to determine what has brought humanity to such a critical situation. Unless we know the real causes that have led us into this critical situation, all our efforts to set it right will be in vain. And if we look deeper, we shall find that the basic factors behind all the external socio-political events affecting us are always inner, in the sense that they are the results of the different acts of our consciousness. The fact is that mankind in the contemporary society and culture has devoted much of its energy in improving the external aspects of life and has also achieved incredible progress in it. But it has failed to pay equal endeavour in developing the moral and the spiritual aspect of our inner being; consciousness therefore has not received its proper expansion. The result is that the egoistic tendencies of division and disharmony, in our individual and social life, are gradually becoming prominent and leading to strife and conflict, rivalry and violence. Since the basic cause responsible for the crises permeating our present life and existence is something internal, the solution to it must also lie within. This has rightly been realized by Sri Aurobindo. And thus he has shown a way towards the spiritual transformation and transmutation of our inner being and the gradual evolution of consciousness. With the evolution of consciousness of the entire human race, a perfect life of unity and harmony, that is, a Divine Life, would emerge on earth.

Therefore, according to Sri Aurobindo, the contemporary crisis of mankind is neither economic nor social nor political but evolutionary in character. The complexity and speed of the contemporary life demand of man the development of consciousness which is so integral and comprehensive that it surpasses the piecemeal and analytical and slow consciousness of the human reason. This demand, on the one hand, and the human refusal to transcend the limitations of the reason, on the other, create an impasse and the resultant crisis. This crisis, according to Sri Aurbindo, must be resolved, if mankind has to survive and fulfil its highest aspirations. And this can be done only by an upward evolution by a process of integral transformation. But the most fundamental task is to awaken the aspiration among increasing number of individuals, for the discovery of the inner spiritual reality and thereby transforming the life integrally by spiritual light and power. Those individuals will serve best the future who will hold out the possibility of spiritual transformation and work for it. In the words of Sri Aurobindo, "They will especially not make the mistake of thinking that this change can be effected by machinery and outward institutions, they will know and never forget that it has to be lived out by each man inwardly or it can never be made a reality for mankind."[3]

---

3. Quoted from: An article by Kireet Joshi, Sri Aurobindo, "India and the Future," *Sri Aurobindo and the New Age: Essays in Memory of Kishor Gandhi*, Sri Aurobindo International Centre of Education, Pondicherry, 1997, p. 22.

17

The Problem of State in Sri Aurobindo's Political Philosophy
A Brief Introduction

Dasharathi Sengupta

I

THE State, in common parlance, is regarded "as a people organized under a sovereign power within a definite territory." From this standpoint every state contains a democratic (demos being its core constituent element) as well as an authoritarian element (as the demos is divided into power-holder and power-subject). It is the largest multi-functional unit operating through an administrative apparatus that exercises legitimate coercive power. It can very well be equated with this apparatus — the state-apparatus — for all practical purposes. Its authority is all-pervasive and, perhaps, leaves no area of our material life untouched — from birth till death. We have to register our birth with it. Otherwise we do not legally exist. We cannot have a decent funeral if our death is not registered with the state.

One of the prime attributes of the State is its territoriality. Territory is the material base on which the functional edifice of the State is structured. Political power — power to extract obedience — is exercised within a defined territory and not outside it. The State regards its territory as sacrosanct, impenetrable and impermeable. Citizenship is defined in terms of permanent residence within its territorial limit and undivided loyalty to its authority. It unites the citizens under its overarching authority and divides them from the rest of human society — legally as well as politically. It assigns a definite collective identity to its citizenry, whose members are not — in the eyes of the State — individuals *per se*.

The State may be regarded as an association as well as an organization. These two, however, are not mutually exclusive denotations. For an association cannot do without an organization — loose or tight, formal or informal, democratic or oligarchic. The State as an association, however, cannot survive without a tight and formal organization, which tends to be oligarchic even under a configuration of democracy. Organization detests disorder and always seeks to impose, with varying degrees of success, ordered uniformity. Individuals are allowed rights and freedoms only as citizens and not as individuals. Their limits, however, are defined by the State itself. It is the latter which determines when the limit has been crossed and decides upon the penalty for deviance. One is welcome to be panegyric about the English Rule of Law. It is true that under its first proposition, as interpreted by Prof. A.V. Dicey, "No man is punishable or can be made to suffer in body or goods, except for a distinct breach of the law established in the ordinary courts of the land." But one should also keep in mind that this offers no protection against the rule-making and rule-adjudicating arms of the State. This state-apparatus, whatever be its form, claims legitimacy on two grounds — functional and representational. All those who have espoused its cause — right from Plato and Aristotle, Marsiglio and Hobbes, Hegel and Green down to modern publicists like Evans, Rueschmeyer and Skocpol — have assigned expansive functional role to the State, sometimes in highly abstract philosophical terms (Hegel) and sometimes in concrete utilitarian terms (Skocpol et al.). The other claim is that the State is the political embodiment of the Nation. It represents the will of the Nation and is the sole custodian of national interest. Nation, on the other hand, has grown into the capstan of the State ever since the end of Thirty Years' War in Europe. Statism and nationalism, as they stand now, are intertwining ideas; they complement each other and thrive on each other.[1] Thirty Years' War ended with the Treaty of Westphalia (1648). The idea of territorially sovereign national state, already in the air since the days of Machiavelli (CE 1469 –1527) finally received the stamp of legitimacy. Enlightenment endorsed it as a progressive rational principle, operating in the arena of politics. As the French Revolution unleashed the forces bent on replacing dynasty by nation as the substance of the State, the whole historical trend was hailed as the expansion of Reason's dominion.

The best exposition of State as the final triumph of Reason is to be found in Hegel. To him, meaningful human life can only be an ethical life. Ethical life, the true basis of freedom, is a dialectical unity represented by the State. The latter resolves the conflict between the unity of family and particularity of civil society into the harmony of universality. That is to say, the national community finds its final embodiment in the State.

Individual's existence, as mind, is determined by and becomes meaningful only as a part of the national community.

---

1. There is an exhaustive literature on the subject of State as a political institution. If one wants to avoid the run-of-the mill textbooks, value-oriented accounts, highly philosophical or ideologically biased treatises, he may start with the following:

   (a) *Introduction to Politics,* Pickles Dorothy, Methuen, 1976.

   (b) *Introduction to Modern Political Theory,* Barry Norman. P, Macmillan, 1982.

   (c) *The Idea of the Modern State,* McLellan et al. (ed.), Open University Press, 1990.

   (d) *Bringing the State Back* in, Evans, Roueschmeyer and Scokpol (ed.), Cambridge, 1989.

The age of anarchic individualism and endless interrogation, Hegel believes, has given way to an age of action in which the enlightened individual would realize himself in proportion to the extent of his surrender to the State. Nothing short of State, Hegel declared confidently, is the actualization of freedom.[2] It is these claims on behalf of the State, particularly the idea of State as the final end of human development, that Sri Aurobindo puts under scanner in two of his outstanding works — *The Human Cycle* and more articularly in *The Ideal of Human Unity*. His approach to the problem may easily be mistaken as Hegelian, as he also finds the State to be an outcome of human development. It transcends the earlier forms of group-life, — just as the State, in Hegel's political philosophy, unites and transcends both the family and the civil society. Aurobindo, in other words, accepts the State and assigns it a legitimate place in the scheme of spiritual evolution of mankind. State is a form of organized collective life which man needs at a certain stage of his development. But Sri Aurobindo refuses to accept the Hegelian proposition that the State marks the end of human development. He would, perhaps, agree with Hegel that the State is the march of God upon the earth. But he would also assert that the Divine marches beyond the confines of State. Thus, he writes, "Our progress may be a devious round leading from the easy and spontaneous uniformity and harmony which reflects Nature to the self-possessed unity which reflects the Divine."[3]

---

2. For Hegel's theory of State, the beginner may see the following:
    (a) *Political Thought* (Chapter III), C.L. Wayper, London: Hutchinson, 1965.
    (b) *Masters of Political Thought* (vol. 3), L.W. Lancaster, OUP Paperback (India).
    (c) *A History of Political Theory* (Chapter XXX), G.H. Sabine, Oxford and IBH Publishing Co., Indian Edition (1968).
3. *The Ideal of Human Unity*, (Chapter III), Sri Aurobindo Ashram, Pondicherry (1970), Paperback.

The State, in other words, cannot be the be-all and end-all. One may be tempted at this point to compare summarily the views of Rabindranath with Sri Aurobindo. Both reject the notion of an all-powerful, all-pervasive and all-comprehensive collectivist authority as the final arbiter of human destiny. Rabindranath juxtaposed State and Society in the context of India's history and cultural tradition. He saw no interacting relationship between them as in the West. He assigns greater value and role to the society, whose unity does not impose uniformity. Hence, to him, it is society and not State that has a liberating influence on the individual. Control by the State and dependence on State have, on the other hand, a debilitating impact.[4] Sri Aurobindo seems to agree, for he writes that in the old infra rational societies, what governed the human beings was not the State, but the group-soul, that is, the collective social mind, through customary institutions and self-regulations. Conformity to them was habitual. He further writes that subjection to society was not felt. This was partly because individualism was yet to emerge and social norms were effortlessly internalized. In the second place, diversities were tolerated and a remarkable latitude was shown to social variations. State, on the other hand, tends to suppress variations beyond a narrow limit. In support of this observation, it may be pointed out that pre-modern societies did not bother much about normal/abnormal dichotomy. Nor did they consign the abnormal persons to lunatic asylums.

Sri Aurobindo, however, appears to be more charitable than Rabindranath to the phenomenon of State. It is a human aggregate introduced by the gradualist process of Nature. At the same time, it represents efforts of man to realize his human

---

4. A fair idea of Rabindranath's approach to society and state can be had from such pieces as *Ātmaśakti*, *Swadeśī Samāj*, *Bhāratvarṣīya Samāj* and the series of writings known as *Śāntiniketan Prabandhamālā*, etc.

   See *Rabindra Racanābalī* (vol. 12), Centenary Edition.

self in ever larger social aggregate, the same vital drive — Aristotle would simply call it moral impulse — which impels man to proceed, step by step, towards "largest possible human aggregate, the whole of united humanity."[5] The State, then, is one such step — important and significant, though not final. It is one of the stages, like other lesser aggregates preceding it (family, commune, city-state or tribal formations).

Rabindranath, for all his poetic sensibilities and spiritual insights, did not have that historical vision which Sri Aurobindo applied to his analysis of State. Thus, to Rabindranath, not only all progress and development in Europe has been state-centric, it is also a typically European phenomenon. He appears to ignore the historical fact that the State, or more particularly, the Nation-State, is not even a five-hundred year old aggregate. It emerged as a negation both of Christian Universalism and feudal localism. Following Sri Aurobindo's line of argument we can say that nationalism and nation-state emerged in Europe because human consciousness — at that stage of European history — stood far below the level of aspirations represented by Christian Universalism, but had raised itself to a level that strained against the restraining framework of feudal localism.

Why does man form lesser and inadequate associations like State? It is not because his vision is clouded by prospects of some immediate gain, by greed and ignorance, but because the formation of lesser aggregates is commanded, rather impelled, by the very nature of man's spiritual evolution. The latter never follows a straight line. Its progress is through twists and turns. The lesser aggregates (like tribal states or nation-states) act partly as aids at a lesser stage of development; but they also become barriers and have to be overcome to reach the next higher stage. Sri Aurobindo is very clear on this point: it has been necessary to form the lesser aggregates

5. *The Ideal of Human Unity* (Chapter II).

in the progressive stages of human culture, for "the obstacles of space, the difficulties of organization and the limitations of human heart and brain have necessitated the formation first of small, then of larger and yet larger aggregates. . . ." But these are also training grounds. The progressive approach represented by them prepare human beings for the final universality. One reason behind the differences between Aurobindo's and Rabindranath's evaluation of State may be found in their distinctly different approaches towards the ideal of human unity. Both were firm believers in the spiritual unity of mankind — a unity that cuts across racial, religious, cultural and political divides. To both, the political division of the globe makes the realization difficult if not improbable. To Rabindranath this spiritual unity is something given. Man, born with a soul, has the whole physical world as his residence — his *svadeśa*, the whole spiritual universe as his *ātmik loka*. This unifying principle is independent of time and space. The State is a hindrance to its realization, which has to be endured, as it cannot be cured. Hence Rabindranath has no theory of political transformation. His condemnation of state is moral and does not issue from any historical judgement.

To Sri Aurobindo, on the other hand, this unity should be treated as the end-product of a long, twisting, spiral, and dialectical process of evolution which is initially blind and instinctive, but conscious and participatory in its final stages. It is a Divine cosmic plan whose execution is regulated by Nature. The latter operates through human beings. The thrust of Nature is not towards isolation, but towards aggregation. Sri Aurobindo refers to the intellectual and material circumstances that have brought the goal of human unity within human reach. . . . [6] But further progress demands a spiritual transformation. Man has to rise above his animal nature, above his vital and physical being and direct the central will of his

---

6. *The Ideal of Human Unity,* (Chapter I).

life towards a higher consciousness. Only then the turn towards unity would become a drive towards unity.

If this be the case, then human actions, human institutions and human aggregations have a relevance. Human unity is not something given. It is an ideal that has to be conceived in and perceived by human consciousness. It is a goal that has to be worked out by and achieved through human efforts. The relevance and role of the state have to be evaluated only in the light of how far it helps or hinders the achievement of that goal.

Sri Aurobindo, thus, did not reject the State like Bakunin[7] and Gandhi,[8] nor could he like Hegel and his followers advocate total surrender and submission to the State. The State is to him a product of historical development, of human efforts seeking material well-being and expansion of life into ever-greater aggregation. Yet as a firm believer in the spiritual transformation of the human society as the divinely ordained end, Sri Aurobindo could not subscribe to the doctrine of blind and organic nationalism.[9] As a person who like Rabindranath

7. Michael Bakunin (1814-76), the famous Russian anarchist and a contemporary of Marx was a permanent exile from his homeland. His work *God and the State* contains, perhaps, the fiercest attack on the institutions of church and state.

8. *Evolution of the Political Philosophy of Gandhi* (Chapter 10) by B. Bhattacharya, Calcutta Book House, 1969, is a fair introduction to the Gandhian concept of State. See also V.P. Varma, *The Political Philosophy of Mahatma Gandhi and Sarvodya,* Lakshmi Narayan Agarwal, Agra, 1959. See Joan. V. Bondurant, *Conquest of Violence: The Gandhian Philosophy of Conflict*, OUP (India), 1956, for a more advanced study of Gandhian idea of politics.

9. Organic nationalism is an extreme form of nationalism which demands total submission on the part of the individual to the Nation as a mystic and organic unity. It measures the value of the individual, who is supposed to derive relevance and sustenance from the Nation, in terms of his contribution to the state-organism. Nationalism of Fascist variety can be characterized as organic nationalism.

was committed to the ideal of human unity, he could not accept the State as the ultimate unit of global human society. He was convinced that the State would be transcended by some association more unifying, something greater than itself after all its possibilities are exhausted and all its potentialities actualized. This is the perspective on which his critique of the State is based.

Though this perspective was developed and given final shape by the post-political *yogī* Aurobindo, on his way to become *ṛṣi* Aurobindo, its embryonic presence may be felt even in his early political writings. A fiercely nationalist Aurobindo Ghosh, who denounced the British rule and moderate Congress leadership alike during the days of *Bande Mātaram* and *Karmayogin* never hesitated to strike a different note in his speeches and writings.

As early as 1894, Aurobindo hinted at the spiritual nature of political development. Life, he observed, is an affirmation of one's self. Hence any aggregate mass of humanity must inevitably strive to emerge and affirm its own essence. It must, "by the law of its own nature aspire towards life, aspire towards expansion, aspire towards perfecting of its potential strength in the free air of political recognition and the full light of political predominance."[10]

In the final paragraph of his article "Morality of Boycott" (seized by the Police and made an exhibit in the Alipur Conspiracy Case), Aurobindo pointed out that Man is of less terrestrial mould than is usually thought.

He has an element of the divine which the politician ignores. He misses what lies beyond material vision. He leaves out the divine, the incalculable in man.[11]

---

10. *New Lamps for the Old* (Indu Prakash, February, 1894), *Bande Mātaram,* Sri Aurobindo Ashram, Pondicherry, 1972.

11. Morality of Boycott was first published in 1948 and included as a supplement to *The Doctrine of Passive Resistance.*

It was not only a warning to the politicians in general; it also hinted at what Sri Aurobindo of later days thought to be one of the prime weaknesses of the State: its tendency to control the divinely inspired creativity of man. Sri Aurobindo, as pointed out earlier, rejected the Hegelian idea of State as the end of human development. He looked beyond the nation-state. For him, transcending the ethical life lies the goal of divine life. Political struggle, the will and efforts for the State, must lead to spiritual transformation. Thus in his article in *Bande Mātaram* dated 28th March, 1908, Aurobindo asserted that spirituality would become the dominant note of the coming era, and the movement (i.e. the Indian National Movement) of which the first outbreak was political would end in a spiritual consummation.[12]

If Sri Aurobindo's spiritual approach refuses to see the State in purely utilitarian light, his democratic temperament could hardly welcome its elitist character. Elitism in any form was anathema to him. One of his charges against the Indian National Congress was its elitist character, its being a "great middle class machine. . . ."[13] One of his claims for "Passive Resistance" was that only in this form of struggle everyone could participate equally and would suffer privation equally.[14] That is to say, a struggle waged by a minority can be materially successful, but not spiritually elevating. It may bring about political development, but not human development. Such observations reveal the set of values which Sri Aurobindo applied to his evaluation of the State.

---

12. *Spirituality and Nationalism.*
13. *New Lamps for Old* (Indu Prakash, 28.08.1894).
14. Doctrine of Passive Resistance (Chapter III), *Bande Mātaram*, Sri Aurobindo Ashram, Pondicherry (1972).

IV

If Gandhi's critique of State was based on his philosophy of non-violence, then Sri Aurobindo's was based on a democratic ethos rooted in his spiritual outlook on life. While Gandhi denounced the State as "organized violence," Aurobindo, while somewhat tolerant of its coercive nature, was very critical of the elitist character of the State in general. The State represents collective egoism. But who has the decision-making power with regard to collective aims? "It is a group of ruling persons," separated from the mass. The group may be large (a parliament) or small (a cabinet), popularly elected or a coterie of military junta, but it is always an oligarchy that rules. Whatever be the procedure or method of their recruitment, there is no guarantee that the best brains or noblest souls would be represented in the ruling body. This, according to Sri Aurobindo, is the main problem with the State. In theory, it is a community whose collective wisdom and force is organized for general good. In practice, it is the structure and form of the State that determines whose intellect and whose power are harnessed for its service. What Sri Aurobindo is suggesting here is significant: the social base of power always tends to be narrow in practice. Earlier in another major work of his *The Human Cycle* also (Chapter XX) he pointed out that ". . . government by organized State must mean always government by a number of individuals . . . it is always the reason and will of a comparatively few effective men that rules and regulates things with the consent of the half-hypnotized mass." A keen observer of politics around the globe in his days, Sri Aurobindo laments that the members of the political class hardly represent the soul of a people or its aspirations. They are usually petty, selfish and ego-centric. It is a matter of great regret that the State is, for all practical purposes, an agency constituted by them and it is to their hands that the good of all has to be entrusted. Things would improve only marginally even if recruitment of better elements is arranged. For, in Sri Aurobindo's opinion, the very structure of the State acts as a strainer and would prevent the major portion of available intellect and talent to reach the surface.

We should bear in mind that this critique of State was written when the First Great War was raging and even the most democratic states were using draconian powers to suppress dissent and regulate freedom. The First World War gave a lesson in what the State hailed by Hegel as the actualization of freedom could do to suppress freedom.[15] A democrat by temperament and a champion of individual initiative in matters both material and spiritual, Sri Aurobindo could hardly remain untouched. He saw in this phenomenon a new version of perpetual opposition between "state idea" and the "human idea." His critique shows whose side he was on in this conflict.[16] The State, Sri Aurobindo further writes, does not generally have the wisdom or courage to be innovative. Its collective conservatism leaves many things undone. It is the talent, initiative and imaginative efforts at individual level that pull the world forward. It is the creative energy of the individual which is "the really effective agent of collective progress." But the increasing power of the organized state marginalizes the individual.

There is remarkable similarity of views between the three great contemporaries — Sri Aurobindo, Mahatma Gandhi and Rabindranath — on this point. All three were equally critical of and anxious about the increasing helplessness of the individual *vis-à-vis* the Leviathan. Aurobindo wrote in *The Ideal of Human Unity* that a huge increase in organized power will "either eliminate free individual effort altogether or leave it dwarfed and cowed into helplessness." In *The Human Cycle*

15. See L.T. Hobhouse, *The Metaphysical Theory of State* (1918) for a critical evaluation of Hegel's theory of State, to which Hobhouse traces the ideological roots of the First Great War.

16. *The Ideal of Human Unity* (Chapter III).

(Chapter XX) also he observes that obedience to a mechanized government and rule is not part of human perfection.

Gandhi sounded a similar warning: "I look upon every increase in the power of State with the greatest fear, because . . . it does the greatest harm to mankind by destroying individuality which lies at the root of all progress."

Rabindranath, too, writes in an identical vein that Nation (i.e. nation-state) insists on strength and efficiency. This drive drains man's energy from his higher nature — from his self-sacrificing and creative nature. Submission to State diverts individual efforts from moral to mechanical objects. Man, Rabindranath believes, is the fairest creation of God. But he is transformed into a puppet by the national manufactory.

It is this negative impact of the State upon individuality that worried Sri Aurobindo most. He rejected the claim of the State that it could absorb all free individual activities. For that would result in a check upon human progress and in a "comfortably organized stagnancy." If the highest ideals transcend the political, then the State cannot demand self-immolation at its altar from the individual. The State can be a convenient instrument for social co-operation, harmony and common development. But it cannot train man to fulfil himself in the fulfilment of mankind. Man may be regulated by the State; but he lives in the Community. The former can never be a substitute for the latter.

Sri Aurobindo here appears to come very close to what is known as the pluralistic perspective on state-sovereignty. The pluralists deny the very claim of the State to undivided loyalty. They claim that non-state voluntary associations of society play no less significant a part in an individual's life as the State. It is through them that the individual is able to satisfy his creative urge. State cannot claim supremacy solely because it enjoys legitimate coercive power. MacIver observes that power is exercised only when relations are abnormal. Sri

Aurobindo appears to support the pluralist viewpoint when he writes in *The Human Cycle* (Chapter XX) that the group-soul works out its tendencies through diversities ". . . vitality of group-life depends upon the working of this diversity, its continuity and its richness."[17]

Sri Aurobindo, like Gandhi and Rabindranath, was equally critical of the mechanical character of the State. Rabindranath branded the nation-state as a power-machine and a wealth-producing machine. . . . [18] Gandhi described the State as a "soulless machine" which owes its existence to violence and which can never be weaned from violence. Sri Aurobindo, too, asserts that the State is not an organism like the community. It is a machinery. It works like a machine. It has no soul or only a rudimentary one. It tries to manufacture, for example, a national culture, a national religion or a national education. It thereby thwarts the growth of human creativity. The State always tends to uniformity. Natural variation does not go well with its mechanical nature.

Not only that, efforts towards uniformity on the part of the State interfere with the growth of human solidarity (organic solidarity as different from mechanical)[19] on the one side, and on the other, with the growth of individual freedom of thought and conscience. There is, Sri Aurobindo points out, a fundamental opposition between the dynamism of the

---

17. See R.M. MacIver, *The Modern State*, OUP, 1955 and H.J. Laski, *Grammar of Politics for the Pluralist Perspective on State-Sovereignty.*
18. Rabindranath Tagore, *Nationalism*, 1917 (Reprint, Macmillan, Madras, 1985).
19. Organic solidarity is supposed to be the outcome of differentiation and specialization, and a network of voluntary associations leading to interdependence; mechanical solidarity follows from homogeneity, i.e. from lack of social diversity. This idea was first developed by one of the pioneers of modern Sociology, Emille Durkheim (1858-1917) in his *Division of Labour in Society* (1893).

individual and the status-quoist ethos of the State as a mechanical collectivity. The former seeks growth and expansion; the latter seeks security in its established order.

Writing at the time of "breaking of nations," Sri Aurobindo drew attention to another danger that is inherent in the very nature of State. It is least hampered by internal scruples or external checks. It is more a force than an intellectual or ethical being. Consequently driven by a "sacred egoism," the more powerful ones tend to act as beast of prey *vis-à-vis* weaker states. The rudimentary growth of International Law, accompanied by growing economic dependence among nations, may appear to be emergent checks on the external behaviour of the States. But Sri Aurobindo feels that they have created "only a greater difficulty in devouring." The predatory nature of the State remains unchanged in spite of them.[20]

V

The man whose ambition, or call it mission, has been to lift man from the valley of death to the bliss of immortality was, however, an out and out optimist. He was not given to poetic disillusionment so poignantly voiced by Rabindranath in his *Sabhyatār Saṅkaṭ*. Armed with a firm belief in the ultimate spiritual destiny of Man, Sri Aurobindo finds in the very shortcomings of State the motor behind the movement towards the next higher stage. If humanity could conceive and develop the State to move beyond the imperfections of past aggregates, there is no reason why it should despairingly accept the State as a finality. Sri Aurobindo wrote — even before the end of First World War — that the inevitable trend of the working of the nature in human society made for larger and yet larger aggregations. This "cannot fail to arrive at a total aggregation of mankind in a closer international system."

20. *The Ideal of Human Unity,* (Chapter IV).

He pinned his firm hope on two factors: (a) the increasing closeness of common interests, making divisions and conflicts more and more ruinous; (b) common uniting sentiments that fashioned nation-states and federal unions out of separate aggregates. When we look at the European Union or at the North American Continent, we are led to believe that Sri Aurobindo was no romantic utopian as far as the trend towards global integration is concerned; he was a political Seer, whose vision was based on a cool appreciation of reality.

He was also aware of the fact that such future developments, though removing a great many material obstacles to the realization of human unity, would still be just quantitative changes. They would have to be supplemented by a qualitative transformation of the human psyche. That transformation is contingent upon man's learning to "live from his soul and not from his ego," learning to recognize inner spiritual unity of mankind. Nothing else can provide a truly enduring basis for human brotherhood.[21]

This brings us to the final point of difference between Gandhi and Sri Aurobindo with regard to their stand on the alternative to State. The Gandhian view of State is situated within the framework of his thoroughgoing critique of the West. Hence he goes back to India's past for his model of smallest possible autonomous and non-violent political unit. For Sri Aurobindo, West is a part of the human world; its history is a part of human history. His critique of State is based on values derived from the West, but supplemented and refined by the spiritual tradition of the East. He does not turn his back on the present; he looks beyond the present and into the future. He does not look for micro-divisions of the past; he looks for future macro-unions.

---

21. *The Ideal of Human Unity*, Chapter, XXXIV.

Part VII
On Yoga and Psychology

18

Relevance of Sri Aurobindo in Modern India

Kittu Reddy

THE forerunner of Jadavpur University was the Bengal National College and Sri Aurobindo was its first principal. In addition to Sri Aurobindo, there were other eminent personalities on the teaching staff of the College such as Raja Subodh Chandra Mallik, Brajendra Kishore Roychowdhury, Ras Behari Ghosh, and Rabindranath Tagore to name just a few.

Sri Aurobindo who was the first principal of the Bengal National College left the post after a short stint as he was preoccupied with political work. The *Swadeśī* movement was in full swing at that time and the intense spiritual patriotism of Sri Aurobindo was permeating the whole of the Bengali society. I quote a portion of his speech on the occasion of his leaving the College:

> The only piece of advice that I can give you now is — carry on the work, the mission, for which this college was created. I have no doubt that all of you have realized by this time what this mission means. When we established this college and left other occupations, other chances of life, to devote our lives to this institution, we did so because we hoped to see in it the foundation, the nucleus of a nation, of the new India which is to begin its career after this night of sorrow and trouble, on that day of glory and greatness when India

> will work for the world. What we want here is not merely to give you a little information, not merely to open to you careers for earning a livelihood, but to build up sons for the Motherland to work and to suffer for her. That is why we started this college and that is the work to which I want you to devote yourselves in future.
>
> What has been insufficiently and imperfectly begun by us, it is for you to complete and lead to perfection. When I come back I wish to see some of you becoming rich, rich not for yourselves but that you may enrich the Mother with your riches. I wish to see some of you becoming great, great not for your own sakes, not that you may satisfy your own vanity, but great for her, to make India great, to enable her to stand up with head erect among the nations of the earth, as she did in days of yore when the world looked up to her for light. Even those who will remain poor and obscure, I want to see their very poverty and obscurity devoted to the Motherland. There are times in a nation's history when Providence places before it one work, one aim, to which everything else, however high and noble in itself, is to be sacrificed. Such a time has now arrived for our Motherland when nothing is dearer than her service, when everything else is to be directed to that end. If you will study, study for her sake; train yourselves, body and mind and soul for her service. You will earn your living that you may live for her sake. You will go abroad to foreign lands that you may bring back knowledge with which you may do service to her. Work that she may prosper. Suffer that she may rejoice. All is contained in that one single advice.[1]

This is indeed a beautiful illustration of the spiritual patriotism of Sri Aurobindo. In this talk, I shall touch upon some aspects of Sri Aurobindo's political philosophy and its relevance to modern India. It will not be possible to analyse in any detail the political philosophy of Sri Aurobindo in one article. I shall,

---

1. Sri Aurobindo Birth centenary Library (SABCL), vol. 1, *Bandemataram*, p. 516.

therefore, just highlight some distinctive points of his philosophy which have immediate relevance today in the political situation of India and the world. The points that I am going to touch upon are:

1. His concept of the nation as a psychological entity,
2. the unification of India and Pakistan,
3. the communal problem and more generally the conflict of religions,
4. the concepts of Democracy and Socialism — their true meaning,
5. the role of the State, and
6. the political system in India today with reference to Parliamentary Democracy.

The Real and the Political Unit

One of the unique contributions of Sri Aurobindo to political thought is the distinction he makes between two types of collective units, the real unit and the political unit. In the modern world this concept is especially applicable to nations and other large groupings. The understanding of this concept is of great importance and has major political consequences. However, in this presentation, I shall illustrate this concept with the nation and the empire.

When we look at world history, we note that empires have existed from the most ancient times and in the words of Sri Aurobindo they have all been only political units and not real units. These empires or political units were created by force, in most cases by conquest and military force and in some cases by economic force. They exist, as political units and not real units; they have no life from within and owe their continuance to a force imposed on their constituent elements or else to a political conveniene felt or acquiesced in by the constituents and favoured by the world outside. If the political convenience of an empire of this kind ceases, if the constituent elements no longer acquiesce and are drawn more powerfully by a centrifugal force, if at the same time the world outside no longer favours the combination, then force alone remains as the one agent of an artificial unity.

On the other hand, real units are formed and held together by a cultural, spiritual and psychological bond. It is this psychological force that is the cementing force and keeps the unit intact through all the most turbulent and difficult periods of their history. Even when they cannot convert this psychological unity into a political unity, the unit survives through these difficult periods of internal conflict and external aggression. The nation is such a unit. This truth of a real unity is so strong that even nations which never in the past realized an outward unification, to which Fate and circumstance and their own selves have been adverse, nations which have been full of centrifugal forces and easily overpowered by foreign intrusions, have yet always developed a centripetal force as well and arrived inevitably after however a long time at organized oneness. It is a distinct group-soul which is driven by inward necessity and uses outward circumstances to constitute for itself an organized body. This is exemplified typically in the history of India. In the words of Sri Aurobindo:

> And the most striking example in history is the evolution of India. In no other country have the centrifugal forces been so strong, numerous, complex, obstinate. The mere time taken by the evolution has been prodigious; the disastrous vicissitudes through which it has had to work itself out have been appalling. And yet through it all the inevitable tendency has worked constantly, pertinaciously, with the dull, obscure, indomitable, relentless obstinacy of Nature when she is opposed in her instinctive purposes by man, and finally, after a struggle enduring through millenniums, has triumphed. And, as usually happens when she is thus

> opposed by her own mental and human material, it is the most adverse circumstances that the subconscious worker has turned into her most successful instruments. The political history of India is the story of a succession of empires, indigenous and foreign, each of them destroyed by centrifugal forces, but each bringing the centripetal tendency nearer to its triumphant emergence. And it is a significant circumstance that the more foreign the rule, the greater has been its force for the unification of the subject people. This is always a sure sign that the essential nation-unit is already there and that there is an indissoluble national vitality necessitating the inevitable emergence of the organized nation. In this instance, we see that the conversion of the psychological unity on which nationhood is based into the external organized unity by which it is perfectly realized, has taken a period of more than two thousand years and is not yet complete.[2]

And it must also be remembered that England, France, Germany, and modern Italy took each a thousand or two thousand years to become a well formed political unit. We may thus say that the nation is a persistent psychological unit which Nature has been busy developing throughout the world in the most various forms and educating into physical and political unity. Political unity is not the essential factor; it may not yet be realized and yet the nation persists and moves inevitably towards its realization; it may be destroyed and yet the nation persists and travails and suffers but refuses to be annihilated.

THE INDIAN NATION

The Indian nation has been such a psychological unit; it has been held together by a cultural and spiritual unity; as a result it has developed a distinct identity of its own and has a destiny which it has to fulfil. In the words of Sri Aurobindo:

2. SABCL, vol. 15, *Social and Political Thought*, pp. 288-89.

> Each nation is a Shakti or power of the evolving spirit in humanity and lives by the principle, which it embodies. India is the Bharata Shakti, the living energy of a great spiritual conception, and fidelity to it is the very principle of her existence. For by its virtue alone she has been one of the immortal nations; this alone has been the secret of her amazing persistence and perpetual force of survival and revival.[3]

Once we comprehend this properly, we will be in a position to understand the message that Sri Aurobindo gave on August 15, 1947. For in that message he had spoken of the five dreams that had been the basis of his life, and one of the dreams was the unity of India and the annulment of partition.

This is what he wrote:

> The first of these dreams was a revolutionary movement which would create a free and united India. India today is free but she has not achieved unity. The old communal division into Hindus and Muslims seems now to have hardened into a permanent political division of the country. It is to be hoped that this settled fact will not be accepted as settled forever or as anything more than a temporary expedient. For if it lasts, India may be seriously weakened, even crippled: civil strife may remain always possible, possibly even a new invasion and foreign conquest. India's internal development and prosperity may be impeded, her position among the nations weakened, her destiny impaired or even frustrated. This must not be; the partition must go. Let us hope that that may come about naturally, by an increasing recognition of the necessity not only of peace and concord but of common action, by the practice of common action and the creation of means for that purpose. . . . But by whatever means, in whatever way, the division must go; unity must and will be achieved, for it is necessary for the greatness of India's future.[4]

---

3. SABCL, vol. 14, *Foundations of Indian Culture*, p. 4.
4. SABCL, vol. 26, *On Himself*, pp. 401-02.

The fundamental reason and justification for annulling partition and bring about a unity is that Pakistan is not a real unit; rather it is a political unit held together by the force of its Army and sustained from outside by some big powers to suit their political convenience.

It is the very same concept that has been reiterated by the Mother when she sent a message to Shri Lal Bahadur Shastri, in 1965 during the Indo-Pak war. This is what she wrote:

> It is for the sake and the triumph of truth that India is fighting and must fight until India and Pakistan have once more become *One* because that is the truth of their being.[5]

This then is the first point in Sri Aurobindo's political thought that there are nations which are real units and some others that are political units created by artificial methods and accidents of history; these units will inevitably disintegrate in due course of time.

Religion and Secularism

I shall now move on to the second aspect of Sri Aurobindo's political thinking with regard to religion, secularism and spirituality. Even though on the surface, they do not seem to be connected with political thought, it should be evident that a proper understanding of these terms is of great political importance especially in the modern world. For all the nations in the world are facing problems arising from the interpretations of secularism and religion. As examples, in the United States it is the problem of abortion and gay marriages, in France, it is the display of religious symbols and in India it has taken huge proportions that is disturbing the whole polity. Since India is home to all the religions in the world, it will be a great boon and blessing to the world if India can find a harmonious solution to this vexing problem which the world

---

5. *White Roses* p. 279.

is facing today. One of the major consequences of this religious conflict has been the Partition of India in 1947.

THE PARTITION OF INDIA

It is evident that the Partition of India was due to the inability of the Indian leadership to solve the communal problem and more particularly the Hindu-Muslim problem. It is also evident that this problem can only be solved when the Hindu-Muslim problem is solved. I shall not go into the historical details as to why and how the Partition took place; it is no use in indulging in the blame game, rather it would be more useful to look into the future and see how the problem can be solved on a higher plane leading to stability in the political field and to a harmonious society.

As early as in 1906, immediately after the partition of Bengal, Sri Aurobindo had warned that this problem cannot be solved by political methods or by reservations; in this context he wrote:

> The question of separate representation for the Mohammedan community is one of those momentous issues raised in haste by a statesman unable to appreciate the forces with which he is dealing, which bear fruit no man expected and least of all the ill-advised Frankenstein who was responsible for its creation. . . . Our own attitude is clear. We will have no part or lot in reforms, which give no popular majority, no substantive control, no opportunity for Indian capacity and statesmanship, no seed for Indian democratic expansion. We will not for a moment accept separate electorates or separate representation, not because we are opposed to a large Mohammedan influence in popular assemblies when they come but because we will be no party to a distinction which recognizes Hindu and Mohammedan as permanently separate political units and thus precludes the growth of single and indivisible Indian nation. We oppose any such attempt at division whether it comes from an embarrassed Government seeking for political support

> or from an embittered Hindu community allowing the passions of the moment to obscure their vision of the future.[6]

In another article, he suggested that we have to go deeper down in the heart and mind to find the solution to the problem. Here is what he wrote:

> Of one thing we may be certain, that Hindu-Muslim unity cannot be affected by political adjustments or Congress flatteries. It must be sought deeper down in the heart and in the mind, for where the causes of disunion are there the remedies must be sought. We shall do well in trying to solve the problem to remember that misunderstanding is the most fruitful cause of our differences, that love compels love and that strength conciliates the strong. We must strive to remove the causes of misunderstanding by a better mutual knowledge and sympathy; we must extend the unfaltering love of the patriot to our Mussulman brother, remembering always that in him too Narayana dwells and to him too our Mother has given a permanent place in her bosom; but we must cease to approach him falsely or flatter out of a selfish weakness and cowardice. We believe this to be the only practical way of dealing with the difficulty. As a political question the Hindu-Muslim problem does not interest us at all, as a national problem it is of supreme importance. We shall make it a main part of our work to place Mohammed and Islam in a new light before our readers to spread juster views of Mohammedan history and civilization, to appreciate the Musulman's place in our national development and the means of harmonizing his communal life with our own, not ignoring the difficulties that stand in the way of the possibilities of brotherhood and mutual understanding. Intellectual sympathy can only draw together; the sympathy of the heart can alone unite. But the one is a good preparation for the other.[7]

---

6. SABCL, vol. 2, *Karmayogin,* pp. 245-46.
7. SABCL, vol. 2, *Karmayogin,* p. 24.

When we take a close look at these statements, the following points come out clearly. They are:

1. We must become Indians first and foremost and all religious or other affiliations are secondary.
2. Hindu-Muslim unity cannot be brought about by political means; it has to come by making a deep and sincere study of the religions which will lead to a greater understanding and harmony.
3. To fulfil this purpose, institutions could be set up which will study all the religions and bring about a deeper harmony among them. In fact, this university could institute a chair for this very purpose. In any case the message is clear — we have ultimately to move from religion to spirituality.

Much later, in Pondicherry he wrote:

> Each religion has helped mankind. Paganism increased in man the light of beauty, the largeness and heights of his life, his aim at a many-sided perfection. Christianity gave him some vision of Divine love and charity. Buddhism has shown him a noble way to be wiser, gentler and purer: Judaism and Islam, how to be religiously faithful in action and zealously devoted to God; Hinduism has opened to him the largest and profoundest spiritual possibilities. A great thing would be done if all these God-visions could embrace and cast themselves into each other; but intellectual dogma and cult-egoism stand in the way.
>
> All religions have saved a number of souls, but none yet has been able to spiritualize mankind. For that there is needed not cult and creed, but a sustained and all-comprehending effort at spiritual self-evolution.[8]

---

8. SABCL, vol. 16, *The Supramental Manifestation*, p. 394.

The message is clear, we have to go beyond narrow religion and graduate into spirituality.

Democracy and Socialism

I shall now take up the great political ideals of the modern world. These ideals are Democracy and Socialism. These ideals are the driving forces in the modern world and all governments are committed to them in practice. As we are all well aware, the French Revolution threw up the great ideals of Liberty, Equality and Fraternity. Sri Aurobindo wholly supported these ideals and regarded them as signposts for the future political evolution of humanity.

It would be relevant and of great importance to see how Sri Aurobindo interpreted these ideals. He believed that Democracy was an ideal that gave respect and dignity to the individual, and the reason was that he looked on the individual not merely as a body, a life and a mind but as a soul. Regarding the democratic ideal, he wrote: "there is this deeper truth which individualism has discovered, that the individual is not merely a social unit; his existence, his right and claim to live and grow are not founded solely on his social work and function. He is not merely a member of a human pack, hive or ant-hill; he is something in himself, a soul, a being, who has to fulfil his own individual truth and law as well as his natural or his assigned part in the truth and law of the existence. This is the basis of the democratic tendency of the world."[9]

In the same way he believed in the ideal of Socialism which he interpreted as the trend towards equality. In the words of Sri Aurobindo:

> The final aim of Nature in human life cannot be the exploitation of the many by the few or even of the few by the many, can never be the perfection of some at the cost of the

9. SABCL, vol. 15, *Social and Political Thought*, p. 20.

> abject submergence and ignorant subjection of the bulk of humanity; these can only be transient devices. Absolute equality is surely neither intended nor possible, just as absolute uniformity is both impossible and utterly undesirable; but a fundamental equality which will render the play of true superiority and difference inoffensive, is essential to any conceivable perfectibility of the human race.
>
> It is no longer possible that we should accept as an ideal any arrangement by which certain classes of society should arrogate development and full social fruition to themselves while assigning a bare and barren function of service alone to others. It is now fixed that social development and well-being mean the development and well-being of all the individuals in the society and not merely a flourishing of the community in the mass which resolves itself really into the splendour and power of one or two classes. This conception has been accepted in full by all progressive nations and is the basis of the present socialistic tendency of the world.[10]

The question was how to bring about this equality. What were the means that Socialism adopted to bring about equality?

> To eliminate poverty, not by the crude idea of equal distribution but by the holding of all property in common and its management through the organized State, to equalise opportunity and capacity as far as possible through universal education and training, again by means of the organized State, is the fundamental idea of modern Socialism. It implies an abrogation or at least a rigorous diminution of all individual liberty.[11]

A compromise between these two ideals seems to be the way most governments have taken.

---

10. SABCL, vol. 15, *Social and Political Thought,* p. 269.
11. SABCL, vol. 15, *Social and Political Thought,* p. 325.

> Democratic Socialism still clings indeed to the nineteenth-century ideal of political freedom; it insists on the equal right of all in the State to choose, judge and change their own governors, but all other liberty it is ready to sacrifice to its own central idea.[12]

Sri Aurobindo says that these two ideas have a master potency and no reaction can eliminate them. They have become permanent features of the future growth of humanity. And to these two ideals has been added a third one, Communism.

Communism which was born as a result of the Russian Revolution has also greatly contributed to the political ideals of humanity. Regarding Communism, Sri Aurobindo wrote:

> The communistic principle of society is intrinsically as superior to the individualistic as is brotherhood to jealousy and mutual slaughter; but all the practical schemes of Socialism invented in Europe are a yoke, tyranny and a prison.[13]

However, in actual practice these ideals have nowhere been able to do what they pretended or claimed to do. Yet despite these shortcomings in practice, they have certainly contributed to human society.

DEMOCRACY IN ACTUAL PRACTICE

When we look at the practical results of democracy we see that it has not been able to give the individual the freedom and dignity that is the goal of democracy. As a matter of fact, the sole democratic elements in today's polity are: public opinion, periodical elections and the power of the people to refuse re-election to those who have displeased it. Despite all democratic professions, the government is really in the hands of the bourgeoisie, the professional and businessmen, the

---

12. SABCL, vol. 15, *Social and Political Thought*, pp. 325-26.
13. SABCL, vol. 17, *Thoughts and Aphorisms*.

landholders, — where such a class still exists, — strengthened by the trade unions and the working-class; and unfortunately these classes very soon assimilate themselves to the political temperament and ideas of the governing classes.

SOCIALISM IN PRACTICE

Similarly, when we look at the practice of Socialism, we see that it lays great stress on the organized State and puts complete power in the hands of the State. However, Sri Aurobindo has reservations about the State. This is what he says:

> Whatever may be the perfection of the organized State, the suppression or oppression of individual freedom by the will of the majority or of a minority would still be there as a cardinal defect vitiating its very principle.[14]

Now Sri Aurobindo is of the view that neither of these two ideals, Democracy and Socialism can fulfil themselves unless they bring in the ideal of Fraternity, the third word of the French Revolution. And this brotherhood has to base itself not on mere association but on a deeper spiritual brotherhood and oneness. I shall deal with this later in the talk.

The role of the State

As we have previously mentioned, Sri Aurobindo did not believe in the supremacy of the State. In fact, he believed that the State must not take too much power into itself. He was clear that the State had a limited role to play. In the words of Sri Aurobindo:

> The business of the State, so long as it continues to be a necessary element in human life and growth, is to provide all possible facilities for cooperative action, to remove obstacles, to prevent all really harmful waste and friction,

---

14. SABCL, vol. 15, *Social and Political Thought*, p. 200.

> and, removing avoidable injustice, to secure for every individual a just and equal chance of self-development and satisfaction to the extent of his powers and in the line of his nature. So far the aim in modern socialism is right and good. But all unnecessary interference with the freedom of man's growth is or can be harmful. Even co-operative action is injurious if, instead of seeking the good of all compatibly with the necessities of individual growth — and without individual growth there can be no real and permanent good of all — it immolates the individual to a communal egoism and prevents so much free room and initiative as is necessary for the flowering of a more perfectly developed humanity.[15]

Similarly, in another reference to the role of the State, Sri Aurobindo has this to stay:

> I have no faith in government controls, because I believe in a certain amount of freedom — freedom to find out things for oneself in one's own way, even freedom to commit blunders. Nature leads us through various errors and mistakes; when Nature created the human being with all his possibilities for good and ill she knew very well what she was about. Freedom for experiment in human life is a great thing. Without the freedom to take risks and commit mistakes there can be no progress.[16]

And finally in a warning regarding the complete take-over of the economic life by the State, he says:

> It is better not to destroy the capitalist class as the Socialists want to: they are the source of national wealth. They should be encouraged to spend for the nation. Taxing is all right, but you must increase production, start new industries, and also raise the standard of living; without that if you increase the taxes there will be a state of depression.[17]

---

15. SABCL, vol. 15, *Social and Political Thought*, p. 283.
16. *India's Rebirth*, p. 205.
17. *India's Rebirth*, pp. 212-13.

The Political System in India

Lastly, we shall make a brief reference to the political system practised in India at the present moment. The last few years and in particular the last few days have shown the political parties and the political system in a very poor light. The political system has become one of the greatest obstacles to the growth and development of India.

In the early decades of the twentieth century, Sri Aurobindo wrote extensively about the renaissance taking place in India; he noted that it was particularly strong and vibrant in most of the fields of culture. The only exception was in the political field.

He remarked that this presented a serious danger to the soul of India. For a political Westernization of India would be followed by a social turn of the same kind and bring a cultural and spiritual death in its train. It is indispensable therefore that in the political field there has to be a true renaissance based on the genuine Indian political temperament and culture. One cannot ignore or minimize this danger as one sees that even today we are still hypnotized by the Western model in the field of politics, either by the Parliamentary type of democracy or by the Communist model.

It should be evident to all intelligent observers of Indian politics that the country has become very badly divided and this is the biggest obstacle to the development and growth of the Indian nation. The solution to this state of affairs lies in creating a national government, a government where the national interest is paramount, and the party interest must be relegated to a secondary position. India will have thus to find out its own political system. This needs a serious debate and consultation. The time has come to start this process.

In this article, I am suggesting some lines on which a debate can take place in the light of Sri Aurobindo's political thought.

Sri Aurobindo wrote in the beginning of the twentieth century:

> Spirituality is India's only politics . . . I have no doubt we shall have to go through our Parliamentary period in order to get rid of the notion of Western democracy by seeing in practice how helpless it is to make nations blessed. India is passing really through the first stages of a sort of national Yoga.[18]

In another context he said:

> Nowadays people want the modern type of democracy — the parliamentary form of government. The parliamentary system is doomed. [In India] one should begin with the old Panchayat system in the villages and then work up to the top. The Panchayat system and the guilds are more representative and they have a living contact with people; they are part of the people's ideas. On the contrary, the parliamentary system with local bodies — the municipal councils — is not workable: these councils have no living contact with the people; the councillors make only platform speeches and nobody knows what they do for three or four years; at the end they reshuffle and rearrange the whole thing, making their own pile during their period of power.[19]

The solution lies probably in the line of action as proposed in the following message by the Mother of Sri Aurobindo Ashram to the Prime Minister of India, Mrs. Indira Gandhi, in 1969:

> Let India work for the future and take the lead. Thus she will recover her true place in the world.
>
> Since long it was the habit to govern through division and opposition. The time has come to govern through union, mutual understanding and collaboration.

---

18. *India's Rebirth,* p. 18.
19. *India's Rebirth,* p. 213.

> To choose a collaborator, the value of the man is more important than the party to which he belongs.
>
> The greatness of a country does not depend on the victory of a party, but on the union of all parties.[20]

It has become imperative that a serious discussion among political parties and intellectuals is started to end this divisive politics on the lines suggested above.

To conclude, I shall finish with a passage from Sri Aurobindo which outlines the future direction in which the national life and the political system must take.

> But though these aims are of great importance in their own field, they are not the central thing; they can only be secure when founded upon a change of the inner human nature and inner way of living; they are themselves of importance only as means for giving a greater scope and a better field for man's development towards that change and, when it is once achieved, as an outward expression of the larger inward life. Freedom, equality, brotherhood are three godheads of the soul; they cannot be really achieved through the external machinery of society or by man so long as he lives only in the individual and the communal ego. When the ego claims liberty, it arrives at competitive individualism. When it asserts equality, it arrives first at strife, then at an attempt to ignore the variations of Nature, and, as the sole way of doing that successfully, it constructs an artificial and machine-made society. A society that pursues liberty as its ideal is unable to achieve equality; a society that aims at equality will be obliged to sacrifice liberty. For the ego to speak of fraternity is for it to speak of something contrary to its nature. All that it knows is association for the pursuit of common egoistic ends and the utmost that it can arrive at is a closer organization for the equal distribution of labour, production, consumption and enjoyment.

---

20. Message of the Mother to Mrs. Indira Gandhi in 1969.

Yet is brotherhood the real key to the triple gospel of the idea of humanity. The union of liberty and equality can only be achieved by the power of human brotherhood and it cannot be founded on anything else. But brotherhood exists only in the soul and by the soul; it can exist by nothing else. For this brotherhood is not a matter either of physical kinship or of vital association or of intellectual agreement. When the soul claims freedom, it is the freedom of its self-development, the self-development of the divine in man in all his being. When it claims equality, what it is claiming is that freedom equally for all and the recognition of the same soul, the same godhead in all human beings. When it strives for brotherhood, it is founding that equal freedom of self-development on a common aim, common life, a unity of mind and feeling founded upon the recognition of this inner spiritual unity. These three things are in fact the nature of the soul; for freedom, equality, unity are the eternal attributes of the Spirit. It is the practical recognition of this truth, it is the awakening of the soul in man and the attempt to get him to live from his soul and not from his ego which is the inner meaning of religion, and it is that to which the religion of humanity also must arrive before it can fulfil itself in the life of the race.[21]

21. SABCL, vol. 15, *Social and Political Thought,* p. 546.

19

Sri Aurobindo's Conception of Integral Yoga

V.N. Sheshagiri Rao

I

THE goal of evolution according to Sri Aurobindo consists in the attainment of divine life. It is Sri Aurobindo's firm conviction that such a state is bound to come sooner or later. But how to bring it on earth? How to expedite it? Sri Aurobindo's answer is: through *yoga* and through spiritual activities.

What is Sri Aurobindo's *yoga* in its full details? It is really difficult to explain because of its vastness and because of its intimate connection with Tantra. However, a glimpse of Sri Aurobindo's *yoga* may be outlined.

II

Sri Aurobindo's *yoga* may be called *integral,* as it attempts to give a synthesis of the main *yogas* and their philosophies. It tries to integrate into one system, their valuable points. In the view of Sri Aurobindo, *yoga* is the art of harmonious and creative living. It is something to be practised and it has nothing to do with speculative thinking. *Yoga* is a widening process of consciousness out of the limits of ego and the body. The practice of it results in the dawn of the descent of the supramental divine through transformation of the mind, life and body. It consists in the inner identification of the self with the divine. In a sense, life process itself is a *yoga*. In the words of Sri Aurobindo: "Life is the field of divine manifestation not yet completed. Here in life we have to unveil Godhead."[1] Through *yoga* one directly awakens oneself to the Universal truth.

Yoga, it may be said, is the practical path that should go with a close understanding of the process of evolution. According to Sri Aurobindo, evolution is both cosmic and individual. Evolution is nothing but a preparation for a leap into the spiritual. *Yoga* is needed to expedite this leap. Sri Aurobindo is very emphatic in this: "*Yoga* means union with the divine, a union either transcendental (above the universe) or cosmic (universal) or individual, or as in our *yoga*, all the three together."[2] *Yoga* is a process of divine *śakti* returning to itself. It is divine activity. It is individual activity in consonance with the divine activity. That is, by surrendering himself to God, the individual can be in consonance with God. So *yoga* means complete surrender to God. It is the way to the individual perfection by individual effort. In this process, the divine activity flows into the individuals. *Yoga* is individualistic in this sense.

But *yoga* could be cosmic also. Nature is itself performing *yoga*. Both go side by side. One is linked with the other. That is why Sri Aurobindo calls it Integral Yoga. Evolution viewed from the inner side is an ascent from a lower to a higher consciousness. It integrates the lower and higher consciousness. There is a transformation of lower consciousness into higher consciousness. In the words of Sri Aurobindo: "It (divine *śakti*) achieves the cosmic consciousness and extends itself to be commensurate with the universe."[3]

---

1. Sri Aurobindo, *The Synthesis of Yoga*, Pondicherry, 1988, p. 27.
2. Sri Aurobindo, *Lights on Yoga*.
3. Sri Aurobindo, *The synthesis of Yoga*, p. 27.

Yoga thus means the integration of our surface consciousness with the subliminal consciousness. It consists in removing the veil which hides our inner being. By practising *yoga*, the whole of our life, mind and matter is flooded with light. *Yoga* thus means integration of the whole personality.

That Sri Aurobindo's *yoga* is integral, can also be explained in another way. Integral Yoga lays stress on the balanced unity of meditation and action. It is bent on harmonizing the introverted tendencies of consciousness of the individual and nature. Only by striking a balance between the two that an individual self can attain self-perfection and self-fulfilment. What is the role played by meditation? Through meditation, one realizes more and more one's true self as a free centre of self-expression of the dynamic consciousness-force. Through meditation one explores the inner regions of the unconscious, removes the internal conflict and tensions and acquires profound spiritual insights. What is the place of action in Integral Yoga? Very profound. Through action, one more and more relates oneself to other fellow beings in love and constructive endeavour and contributes his mite towards the establishment of the divine society. Further, through action one keeps a firm hold on the concrete realities of the physical world.

III

Sri Aurobindo refers to the traditional *yoga*s put forward for self-realization, and appreciates their merits. The concern of *haṭha-yoga* is with the gross body. The chief processes of *haṭha-yoga* are *āsana*s and *prāṇāyāma*. Increased vitality, prolonged youth, health, longevity are the benefits of *haṭha-yoga*.

Rāja-yoga is concerned with the subtle body. It aims at the liberation and perfection of the mental being. Its eye is on *citta*, the stuff of mental Consciousness. It tranquillises the mind. It results in the cultivation of good habits of mind.

Jñāna-yoga proceeds by the method of intellectual reflection and discrimination. It distinguishes between different elements of phenomenal being and rejects them on the yardstick of the spiritual. Its goal is to arrive at the identification of the pure and unique self.

Bhakti-yoga proceeds to enjoy the supreme love and bliss of God. Here God is looked upon as a person who loves the universe. The world is a play of the Lord. The *bhakti-yoga* uses all human emotion and sentiments in its search for God.

Karma-yoga teaches man to dedicate every human activity to the supreme will. The results of actions are surrendered to God. *Karma-yoga* is renunciation in action and not renunciation of action.

IV

The aim of all kinds of *yoga*, according to Sri Aurobindo is the realization of divine unity. *Haṭha-yoga*, though emphasizes on longevity, never seems to rise above the physical body. The emphasis of other *yoga*s is on individual liberation. Some have negative attitude to life. Some are not within easy reach. In them the idea of integration is wanting. The straight jump to the heart of the divine is easy to conceive but difficult to perform. "The flight of the Alone to Alone" is attractive but socially inchoate and uninspiring. Here the soul has no real contact with the body, no contact with other souls. So to say the soul flies away from the body and world. Egoism continues to persist. The other *yoga*s are quietistic, individualistic and one-sided. Their aim seems to be total liberation from Nature.

But in Sri Aurobindo's *yoga*, material nature is not rejected. The physical, the vital and the mental are to be transformed into effective channels of expression of universal love, peace and all-unifying truth. In the view of Sri Aurobindo, *yoga* is a new birth; it is not a dissolution, not an absorption, not a swoon into a higher reality. To quote his words: "All *yoga* in its nature is a new birth; it is a birth out of the ordinary, the mentalized material life of man into a higher spiritual consciousness and a greater and diviner being."[4] *Yoga* thus is a new birth, a new life, a life non-different from mentalized material life; the individual rises to a greater divine existence, with a body, life, soul and mind. In this new birth body, life, mind and soul will be completely transformed and transmuted. Divinity, here, dominates over the mind. In such a life, the divine principle rules. The divine *avatāra* himself takes birth. This divine *avatāra* proves the divinity of man. In his *Essays on the Gītā,* Sri Aurobindo says that, birth of the *avatāra* in a human form means the rebirth of a man into the Godhead. This *avatāra* is the highest form of Divine existence.

V

The integral *yogī* touches the centre of all. His is a life of knowledge and virtue. He transmits divine vision. All that belongs to the individual are retained in Integral Yoga. The integral *yogī* carries the world with him. He makes the world enlightened and enabled. He is the divinized man of the divinized world. He realizes the divinity here on earth in the bodily state. The earth, the body, etc. continue to exist even after realization. They will not be annulled. There is no annihilation of the lower consciousness. There is the fullest development of body, mind and consciousness. In Sri Aurobindo's view, God in Himself is not alone; He is with man and the world. Normal consciousness of man becomes the consciousness of God. It removes all barriers that separate man from God. In the words of Sri Aurobindo: "Our mental, physical vital existence need not be destroyed by our self-exceeding nor are they lessened and impaired by being spiritualized. They can and do become much richer, greater, more powerful and more perfect."

---

4. Sri Aurobindo, *The synthesis of Yoga,* p. 21.

20

The Mother's Prayers and Meditations
Another Manifesto of Sri Aurobindo's Yoga

Goutam Ghosal

SRI Aurobindo's major prose works speak of the same theme in different styles. There is yet another style of expressing the essence of the new *yoga*, which is a mapless pilgrimage ("It is impossible for the mind to forecast in detail what the supramental change must be . . . " — Aurobindo: 1970:19:965). It comes from a woman with all the typical feminine sensitivity and force, through a poetry, which creates a sense of happening or action. By and large, the Mother's *Prayers and Meditations* (Prières et Méditations) is *The Life Divine* in a free poetic mode. It tells all about Sri Aurobindo and even anticipates his last great prose pieces on the destiny of the human body (Aurobindo: 1971:16:5-40). The great Aurobindonian period began in August 1914, when *The Life Divine* and *The Synthesis of Yoga* started coming out serially in *The Arya*. But, the Mother had recorded the basics, and quite often the details, of the new *yoga* at least two years before. The earliest evidence before us is her diary-prayer of 2 November 1912, which had been written a little less than seventeen months before the historic meeting between her and Sri Aurobindo on 29 March 1914. Just a clause may be cited to show her foreknowledge of Sri Aurobindo's integral philosophy:

> . . . for I have now a precise perception of the universal unity determining an absolute interdependence of all actions.
>
> — 2 November 1912.

She had already learnt to observe this "interdependence of all actions" from a secret observatory, stepping back from the vortex of action while remaining yet in the midst of overcrowding assignments. The book is another manifesto of Sri Aurobindo's Integral Yoga, a clarified manifesto except for a few complicated entries.

It was a strange thing happening at the start of the second decade of the last century. Two people living in two different parts of the planet were almost simultaneously engaged in shaping out the system of the new *yoga*, which embraces all life and promises the arrival of a new species beyond man. It was the *yoga* of love and death, of sacrifice and surrender, of giving and getting. It was the *yoga* of a new creation, the art of hastening towards a new species with the help of the existing leader — man — in a continuously evolving planet.

What is the basic theme of *Prayers and Meditations*? One may well ask for the principles, which link the text with *The Life Divine, The Synthesis of Yoga* and *Essays on the Gītā*. It is simply the simplest kind of love or the simplest kind of death, although it is not easy to achieve that simplicity of loving and dying, disappearing and reappearing as a new creation. Death means the exit of the old self and the entry of a new consciousness. Only love can initiate this supreme death of the old self. The Selfish Giant must break the walls of the ego, His Majesty Ego, which refuses to abdicate. Only then the supreme child of love will have a gatepass to his vacant self. Love and ego cannot co-exist. She aspires thus for an integral death, which means to give all and to get all. The integral death is an integral surrender, which initiates a growth into the true life or a growth into the real instrument, which mirrors the Divine. Life then becomes an exquisite piece of art. From the deepest depths of silence the Mother hears the voice.

> Never hast thou known how to die integrally. Always something in thee has wanted to know, to witness, to understand. Surrender completely, learn how to disappear, break the last barrier that separates thee from me; accomplish unreservedly thy act of Surrender. — 7 April 1914.

Both Sri Aurobindo and the Mother speak on or hint at the expectation of "return," offering as if an additional note to the *Gītā*'s famous gospel *mā phaleṣu kadācana*. Sri Aurobindo has drawn our notice to the point of expectation of a return glory in *The Synthesis of Yoga*. The relevant passage runs as follows:

> Our sacrifice is not a giving without any return or any fruitful acceptance from the other side; it is an interchange between the embodied soul and conscious Nature in us and the eternal Spirit. For even though no return is demanded, yet there is the knowledge deep within us that a marvellous return is inevitable. The soul knows that it does not give itself to God in vain; claiming nothing, it yet receives the infinite riches of the divine Power and Presence.
>
> — Aurobindo 1972:20:101.

Death of the old self is coveted, for only death can win the priceless gift. There is not just the rhetoric of a flaming love but also the quiet gesture of the incense, which burns unnoticed; it is to be noticed by just One whose reward is too precious. She wishes her beloved to set her aflame with a white fire of love. Only that can rescue her from "the dead wood of egoism" and "the black coals of ignorance" (16 December 1913).

Love creeps in smoothly in the noiseless self; its conditions are peace, serenity and equality. Tension is destructive; peace creative. We must know how to live and work from within with the help of an integral choice of Truth, an absolutely one-pointed surrender or unadulterous love, for which the Mother uses certain key words and phrases like "quiet incense," "a steady flame" and "a burning brazier." "By this law of love, Thy law I want to live more and more integrally; to it unreservedly I give myself" (23 July 1913). There are repeated deaths and repeated rebirths in one life. "Each time I find Thee anew, my communion with Thee grows more integral, more complete, more definitive" (13 January 1914).

While the Mother subjectivises in her prayers the awakened psychic being, pressing for the higher degrees of Truth, Sri Aurobindo presents for us his experiential theory of sacrifice in *The Synthesis of Yoga*: a sacrifice of works, a sacrifice of love and adoration and a sacrifice of knowledge (Aurobindo 1972:20:125), which are being led by the psychic being. "All depends on the psychic awakening in us, the completeness of our response to her and our growing surrender" (Ibid.: 173). But that is not the end part. The complete transformation can come only by the ascent of the sacrifice to its farthest heights and its action upon life with the power of the supermind Gnosis. "For then alone all the forces that are divided and express themselves imperfectly in life and its works are raised to their original unity, harmony, single truth, authentic absoluteness and entire significance" (Ibid.: 173).

In *Prayers and Meditations*, we see an individual working out the theory in practice. The author practises Integral Yoga leaving behind her footprints showing us the track to the life divine. The central theme of love and sacrifice has been surrounded by the allied themes of renewal and rebirth, cosmic consciousness and Oneness, strange speeches from her *Thou* and the evolution of love through counter movements.

> My love for Thee compressed so long, has leaped forth again, powerful, sovereign, irresistible — increased tenfold by the ordeal it has undergone. It has found strength in its seclusion, the strength to emerge to the surface of the being, impose itself as master on the entire consciousness, absorb everything in its overflowing stream. . . .
>
> — 25 November 1917.

Love is the central force behind this integral awareness and poetry images the nature of Integral Yoga. Never was there in the history of love-lyrics so much of refinement. The clamour of the flesh and the vital has made room for an immortal fire. Even the body has learnt to say "yes" to her love in a new way.

> My body smiles to Thee
> with happiness as before
> my soul smiled to Thee
>
> — 3 September 1919

In prayer after prayer, the inward turning speaks of a true universality (see *The Life Divine,* p. 1029). And like Sri Aurobindo, the author of the prayers harps on the images of a virgin and unpredictable path. The old *yogas* had a preview of things. The new *yoga* is a planless waiting for the Supernature to shape things out. The Mother's diary contains the whole of it, the whole of Sri Aurobindo's concept of *yoga* including the destiny of the body (17 March 1914) and man's role in the creation of a new species (29 August 1914). "Man is the link between what must be and what is" and this is another way of uttering Sri Aurobindo's words: "Man's greatness is not in what he is, but in what he makes possible" (Aurobindo, 1972:17:9). And she too knows about the Force that mediates between man and the Divine. Thus in quite a few prayers, she comes down to the lower level of the common individual and prays to herself, the Mother of the higher nature. As Sri Aurobindo explains: "It is the Mother in the lower nature addressing the Mother in the higher nature, the Mother herself carrying in the *Sādhanā* of the earth-consciousness for the transformation, praying to herself above from whom the forces of transformation come" (*Prayers* 1985: Appendix: 421). The Mother's diary is thus a practical handbook of Sri Aurobindo's *yoga*.

References

The Mother (1985), *Prayers and Meditations*, Sri Aurobindo Ashram, Pondicherry.

Sri Aurobindo (1971), Sri Aurobindo Birth Centenary Library, vol. 16 *(The Supramental Manifestation and other Writings)*, Sri Aurobindo Ashram, Pondicherry.

———, (1972), Sri Aurobindo Birth Centenary Library, vol. 20 (*The Synthesis of Yoga*), Sri Aurobindo Ashram, Pondicherry.

———, (1970), Sri Aurobindo Birth Centenary Library, vol. 19 (*The Life Divine*), Sri Aurobindo Ashram, Pondicherry.

———, (1972), Sri Aurobindo Birth Centenary Library, vol. 17 (*The Hour of God*), Sri Aurobindo Ashram, Pondicherry.

Goutam Ghosal (1997), *Notes on Prayers and Meditations*, Sri Mira Trust, Pondicherry.

21

Sri Aurobindo's Views on Psychology
Can it offer a better Therapeutic Model than Psychoanalysis?

Soumitra Basu

SRI Aurobindo and Sigmund Freud are contemporaries. Naturally while writing about human psychology Sri Aurobindo could not remain indifferent regarding Freudian views. In fact, there are striking similarities in their views regarding the nature and functioning of our mind. Both of them claim that mind is not coextensive with consciousness and thus both are free from the Cartesian dogma. Like Freud Sri Aurobindo also has emphasized the role of unconscious mind in building our personality and in the production of mental distress. Notwithstanding their similarities Sri Aurobindo expressed his reservations about Freudian psychology and criticized it. The aim of this article is to see, against the backdrop of Sri Aurobindo's critique of Freudian psychoanalysis, whether Sri Aurobindo's psychological views can offer a better model for alleviating psychological distress.

It is held in Freudian psychoanalytic method of treatment that to get cured of a mental ailment one needs to develop insight into the contents of the unconscious mind that are responsible for the suffering. Since these contents consist of basically aggressive and sexual desires the defence mechanism of the ego keeps them away from the level of conscious mind.

Till these contents are kept out of the reach of the conscious part of the ego it remains difficult for the ego to handle them. So for the proper management of these desires and wishes insight into their identity is a necessary prerequisite. Psychoanalytic method is designed to enable the client (sufferer) to develop the insight at proper time and in the proper way. But Sri Aurobindo expresses his skepticism regarding this intended propriety. Since psychoanalysis is least concerned with the analysis and significance of the conscious mind Sri Aurobindo apprehends that a disclosure of the unconscious is likely to be improper and harmful for the individual. He writes, "the psychoanalysis of Freud . . . takes up a certain part, the dark, the most perilous, the unhealthiest part of the nature . . . isolates some of its morbid phenomena and attributes to it and them an action out of proportion to its true role in nature. . . . To raise it up prematurely or improperly for experience is to risk suffering the conscious parts also with its dark and dirty stuff and thus poisoning the whole. . . ."[1]

Sri Aurobindo further observes, and observes correctly, that all the materials of the unconscious may not be harmful for the individuals.[2] I hold this observation to be correct on the ground that the possibility of sublimation entails its correctness. The phenomenon of sublimation shows that the unconscious contents can be used for constructive purposes. It is not possible for the client to know in advance which desire would be sublimated in due course and which not. But once an unconscious content becomes conscious through psychoanalysis it becomes weaker and gets placed in the remote part of the unconscious thus losing its power to yield constructive outcome.

---

1. Sri Aurobindo, "Letters on Yoga," in *Complete Works of Sri Aurobindo,* (CW), Centenary Edition, 1972, vol. 24, pp. 1606-08.

2. Satprem has developed this argument from the cues given by Sri Aurobindo. See *Sri Aurobindo or The Adventure of Consciousness*, The Mother's Institute of Research, Delhi, 1970, p. 236.

In his third argument against the theory of psychoanalysis Sri Aurobindo maintains that in holding that the unconscious determines our future structure of personality Freud underestimates the role of the future in forming our personality. Sri Aurobindo is of the opinion that human beings are no less forward-moving than they are determined by the past events. Since psychoanalysis neglects this fact it tends to "look from down up and explain the higher lights by the lower obscurities." But just as "the significance of the lotus is not to be found by analysing the secrets of the mud from which it grows,"[3] similarly the lower region of our psychological being does not explain (nor do they determine) what is going to take place in the higher region in future.

Without entering into the questions regarding the validity of these arguments (since that is not important for the purposes of this article) let us expect that Sri Aurobindo's system would be free from these pitfalls. To see how he may proceed to do it let us present in brief the main tenets of his psychology.

In Sri Aurobindo's opinion, "psychology is the science of consciousness and its states and operations in Nature."[4] It needs to be mentioned here that Sri Aurobindo uses the term "consciousness" both in psychological and metaphysical senses. My concern in this article will be confined to the psychologically relevant aspect of consciousness and I here shall not challenge the metaphysical presuppositions associated with his notion of consciousness. To come back to our discussion on psychology, though Sri Aurobindo claims that "psychology is a science of consciousness" he does not intend to take the expression "consciousness" in the sense of only that consciousness which is accessible to introspection. Sri Aurobindo is aware that he will be criticized by the proponents of "scientific" psychology

3. "Letters on Yoga," *CW*, vol. 24, p. 1608.
4. *CW*, vol. 17, p. 21.

for admitting consciousness as the subject matter of psychology and also for proposing that psychology may be concerned with that type of consciousness which is not given in introspection. Responding to this type of criticism Sri Aurobindo points out that it stems from undue physicalistic or behaviouristic bias: a bias which is grounded in assumed and unjustifiable similarities between human mind and animal mind. In this context Sri Aurobindo claims that a safe guide leading to the nature of mind cannot be found in ". . . a scientific psychology with a materialistic basis which assumes that the body and the biological and physiological factors of our nature are not only the starting point but the whole real foundation and regards human mind as only a subtle development from the life and the body. That may be the actual truth of the animal side of human nature and of the human mind in so far as it is limited and conditioned by the physical part of our being. But the whole difference between man and the animal is that the animal mind, as we know it, cannot get for one moment away from its origins, cannot break out from the covering, the close chrysalis which the bodily life has spun round the soul, and become something greater than its present self, a more free, magnificent and noble being, but in man mind reveals itself as a greater energy escaping from the restrictions of the vital and physical formula of being."[5] As a matter of fact Sri Aurobindo would point out a number of other potentialities of human mind that marks it off from animal mind and consequently he would be in favour of adopting different methodologies for the study of human mind and that of animal mind. Reacting against the proposal that psychology should not include anything beyond surface consciousness as its object of study, Sri Aurobindo says that this proposal itself goes against scientific spirit of enquiry. He observes: ". . . psychological enquiry in Europe . . . is only

---

5. "Synthesis of Yoga," *CW*, vol. 21, pp. 597-98.

beginning and has not gone very far, and what has reigned in men's minds up to now is a superficial statement of the superficial appearances of our consciousness as they look to us at first view and nothing more. But knowledge only begins when we get away from the surface phenomena and look behind them for their true operations and causes. To the superficial view of the outer mind and senses the sun is a little fiery ball circling in mid air round the earth and the stars twinkling little things stuck in the sky for our benefit at night. Scientific enquiry comes and knocks this infantile first view to pieces. . . . All sciences are like that, a contradiction of the sense-view or superficial appearances of things and an assertion of truths which are unguessed by the common and uninstructed reason. The same process has to be followed in psychology if we are really to know what our consciousness is, how it is built and made and what is the secret of its functionings or the way out of its disorders."[6]

Sri Aurobindo accordingly maintains that to limit psychology to the study of this surface consciousness would be to make the science too superficial: on this point also a parallel can be found in Freudian view. Freud claims that psychology would be "too narrow" if it be restricted to the study of introspectible consciousness alone. While appreciating the advent of this new trend in psychology which is prepared to admit subconscious or unconscious levels of consciousness Sri Aurobindo apprehends that any such attempt to extend the field of psychology would not be an easy task due to various errors that have been committed while developing the science of psychology in general. Referring to these errors Sri Aurobindo writes: "The new psychology seeks indeed to penetrate behind superficial appearances, but it is encumbered by the initial errors which prevent a profounder knowledge — the materialistic error which bases the study of mind upon the study of the body, the sceptical error which

6. "Letters on Yoga," *CW*, vol. 22, p. 321.

prevents any bold and clear-eyed investigation of the hidden profundities of our subjective existence, the error of conservative distrust and recoil which regards any subjective state or experience that departs from the ordinary operations of our mental and psychical nature as a morbidity or a hallucination — just as the Middle Ages regarded all new sciences as magic and a diabolical departure from the sane and right limits of human capacity; finally, the error of objectivity which leads the psychologist to study others from outside instead of seeing his true field of knowledge and laboratory of experiment in himself. Psychology is necessarily a subjective science and one must proceed in it from the knowledge of oneself to the knowledge of others."[7]

On Sri Aurobindo's view, it would be preposterous to claim that there can be no consciousness beyond our surface consciousness. He writes: "Consciousness is usually identified with mind, but mental consciousness is only the human range which no more exhausts all the possible ranges of consciousness than human sight exhausts all the gradations of colour, or human hearing all the gradations of sound."[8] Accordingly Sri Aurobindo goes on to speak about a spectrum of consciousness which ranges from Inconscient to superconscient. While, according to Sri Aurobindo, Inconscient is the nether-most level of consciousness — a level from which Matter is produced, superconscient is the zenith of consciousness which can "transform" everything in this world if it is brought down through human beings. But these levels of consciousness are generally beyond the reach of ordinary human beings and do not affect our day-to-day life. Accordingly for our purposes in this article I would restrict myself to the imports of those levels of consciousness that are between the two aforesaid extremes.

---

7. "The Supramental Manifestation and other writings," *CW*, vol. 16, p. 258.

8. "Letters on Yoga," *CW*, vol. 22, p. 234.

Viewed in the top-down direction first comes the level of surface consciousness. It is the level which is admitted in traditional psychology as the level of the mind. In this level the contents of consciousness are within the reach of awareness enabling us to communicate their presence if required. This level actually includes Freudian conscious and pre-conscious states. Our surface self-image is generally constituted and identified in terms of this level of consciousness. The subconscient on the other hand lies below the conscious mind, life and body. This level is unobserved by the mind and it covers the life or vital and the body or physical to a large extent. Sri Aurobindo says:

> We know now or we rediscover the truth that the conscious operation of mind is only a surface action. There is a much vaster and more potent subconscious mind which loses nothing of what the senses bring to it, it keeps all its wealth in an inexhaustible store of memory. . . . The surface mind may pay no attention, still the subconscious mind attends, receives, treasures up with an infallible accuracy. . . .[9]

The contents of the subconscient are dynamic: they can get them expressed through certain forms of thought and actions and events. Another important characteristic of subconscient contents is that they resist change and it is this characteristic that makes change of character of individuals a difficult job. The subliminal consciousness is different from both surface consciousness and subconscient. It is beyond the reach of surface consciousness but it has greater amount of consciousness than the waking mind. It is there behind the surface consciousness. It is a consciousness which is more luminous than the surface consciousness: it can know its objects directly and thus capable of much surer experience and action.

9. "The Upaniṣads," *CW*, vol. 12, p. 192.

This subliminal level brings in a sort of infinitude in the contents of the mind. Speaking about this Sri Aurobindo maintains:

> The Upaniṣads declare that the mind in us is infinite, it knows not only what has been seen but what has not been seen, not only what has been heard but what has not been heard, not only what has been discriminated by the thought but what has not been discriminated by the thought. Let us say, then, in the tongue of our modern knowledge that the surface man in us is limited by his physical experiences, he knows only what his nervous life in the body brings to his embodied mind, and even of those bringings he knows, he can retain and utilize so much as his surface mind-sense attends to and consciously remembers, but there is a larger subliminal consciousness within him which is not thus limited. That consciousness senses what has not been sensed by the surface mind and its organs and knows what the surface mind has not learned by its acquisitive thought."[10]

According to Sri Aurobindo this subliminal consciousness is the source of our art, poetry, philosophy, religious aspirations and so on.

The outer being of an individual is constituted by three elements which Sri Aurobindo calls physical, vital, and mental. Thus a man has a physical realm, a vital realm and a mental realm. Each of these realms has surface consciousness as well as subconscient parts. In other words each of these realms has consciousness. Citing reason for admitting consciousness in the realms of vital and physical Sri Aurobindo notes that these realms exhibit purposeful and intelligent activity, and since purposeful and intelligent actions are marks of consciousness, they must involve consciousness.

It is important to note that each of the above-mentioned elements has specific aspects that demarcate one element from

---

10. "The Upaniṣads," *CW*, vol. 12, pp. 192-93.

the other, and the consciousness associated to each has distinctive features too. Thus while body serves the purpose of survival, sensation, and movement, vital is the seat of energy, impulse, feeling and desires among others; and mind is concerned with the cognitive activity in general. Mind deals with idea, memory, thought, reasoning, etc. Let us bring out some important features of the mind in Sri Aurobindo's own words. He writes:

> Mind in its essence is a consciousness which measures, limits, cuts out forms of things from the indivisible whole and contains them as if each were a separate integer. Even with what exists only as obvious parts and fractions, Mind establishes this fiction of ordinary commerce that they are things with which it can deal separately and not merely as aspects of a whole. For, even when it knows that they are not things in themselves, it is obliged to deal with them as if they were things in themselves, otherwise it could not subject them to its own characteristic activity. It is this essential characteristic of Mind which conditions the workings of all its operative powers, whether conception, perception, sensation or the dealings of creative thought. . . . All its actions and enjoyments deal thus with wholes that form part of a greater whole, and these subordinate wholes again are broken up into parts which are also treated as wholes for the particular purposes they serve.[11]

The above-mentioned description of mind may lead one to think that mind is basically a seat of errors only. But Sri Aurobindo believes that despite its limitations mind can serve a greater purpose in evolution if it is properly groomed. He thus claims ". . . mind is not in its very nature an inventor of errors, a father of lies bound down to a capacity of falsehood, wedded to its own mistakes and the leader of a stumbling life as it too largely is at present owing to our human

---

11. "The Life Divine," *CW*, vol. 18, p. 162.

shortcomings: it is in its origin a principle of light, an instrument put forth from the supermind and, though set to work within limits or even set to create limits, yet the limits are luminous borders for a special working, voluntary and purposive bounds, a service of the finite ever-extending itself under the eye of infinity."[12] This dual nature of the mind, viz. its capacity to create and remove errors (though removal of errors at times depends on the contribution of higher levels of consciousness) can be shown to have an important role in all mental problems: mental consciousness contributes both to the causation and the alleviation of mental problems. The characteristic of mental consciousness includes rationality, objectivity, and consistency. The vital consciousness is characterized by energy, action and passion among others. The marks of physical consciousness are inertia, obscurity, repetitiveness and so forth.

The innermost being of the individual is constituted by an element which Sri Aurobindo calls "the psychic being." This psychic being accounts for our individuality. It is through this psychic being that a harmonious integration of the different aspects of the individual becomes possible. Activation of the subliminal level of consciousness is required to enable the psychic being to come to the forefront and guide the individual's life.

Now let us go back to our original project and try to see whether a model of psychotherapy can be developed in the light of Sri Aurobindo's psychological thought that would be free from the shortcomings of psychoanalysis.

While psychoanalysis explains the origin of psychological disorders in terms of intrapsychic conflict, Sri Aurobindo tends to explain it with the help of the notion of identification. Identification consists in "being one with something else" or "taking something to be one's indispensable part overlooking

---

12. *The Supramental Manifestation and other Writers,* pp. 53-54.

that it is an accidental association only. "It is held in Sri Aurobindo's system that in the states of strong emotions we become so much closely attached to the state that we fail to see that "my emotion" is different from "me." The Mother in this context says, "you identify yourself with a movement of anger and your whole being becomes one angry vibration, blind and precipitate, oblivious of everything else."[13] To be identified with some state is thus to become absorbed in that state. A psychologically unwell person gets so much absorbed in or preoccupied with his symptoms that his functionality gets affected. In Sri Aurobindo's view psychological distresses are produced when the individual identifies with some state of mind, life or body and fails to detach him at will.

Consequently regarding the procedure of the resolution of psychological problem also Sri Aurobindo's system would differ from the Freudian one. In Freudian psychoanalysis the resolution of conflict and thus that of the problem comes through the knowledge that the unconscious experiences are not harmful for the self-image. I would claim that in Sri Aurobindo's system it comes through two insights of the sufferer or client:

(a) "This state is not my integral part — it is coming from outside though it is associated with me." This insight reduces the strength of the identification.

(b) "Its presence is not catastrophic for the prospect of my future development."

To enable the client or the sufferer to get the aforesaid insights the methodology which will get the approval of the system of psychology of Sri Aurobindo would have the following features:

---

13. The Mother, *Collected works of the Mother*, vol. 3, Sri Aurobindo Ashram, 1978, p. 167.

(i) It will emphasize on starting from the conscious. The client should be helped to develop a clear idea about why he behaves in certain ways than in others. The method which is used to educate the different faculties can be used here. Thus the client can be helped to "observe himself: to note his reactions and impulses and their causes, to become a clear-sighted witness of his desires, his movements of violence and passion,"[14] and so on. The client may be asked to notice his thoughts to discover whether there is any pattern in his thinking. The aim of this emphasis on the conscious is not only to make the client aware about thought and reaction patterns but also to enable him to realize that he can change some of these reaction patterns or thought patterns if he feels the need to alter.

(ii) On the basis of one's knowledge regarding the conscious states this methodology will help the individual to develop insights regarding what is unique in him and what sort of a person he may become by using his positive conscious resources. If one becomes confident about one's resources, he would be able to accept the deficits if any in the unconscious level of his personality. In other words if a person can have a glimpse as to what he is and what he can become despite various divergences in his being he will be able to adjust himself with other divergences if any such thing surfaces in the future.

(iii) Sri Aurbindo's psychology will emphasize on the practice of silencing the mind to enable the client to realize that the things with which he consciously identifies himself are not really his part. In this context

---

14. These were said by the Mother in the context of educating the vital, *Sri Aurobindo and the Mother on Education*, Sri Aurobindo Ashram, Pondicherry, 1997.

> Sri Aurobindo emphatically observes that "Much more than half our thoughts and feelings are not our own in the sense that they take form out of ourselves, or hardly can it be said that it is truly original to our nature. A large part comes to us from others or from the environment, whether as raw material or as manufactured imports: but still more largely they come from universal Nature here or from other worlds and planes and their beings and powers and influences. . . . "[15] By silencing the mind the client will understand that the contents of his experience with which he identifies himself are coming from outside and not from within. This practice would activate the subliminal consciousness more than before and allow one to have a glimpse of the psychic being through this consciousness. This does not mean that the person would become an expert *yogī* or a liberated soul. In the context of therapy what is required is widening of the consciousness: if the subliminal comes more in touch with the surface-consciousness it would empower the latter to be strong enough to encounter the subconscient aspects of his being, to discern what is good and what is evil in the subconscient, and thus to utilize the good things from it while keeping the bad elements intact without getting negatively affected by them.

It is notable in this context that along with the process of silencing the mental Sri Aurobindo's system can make room for other psychological processes of self-analysis and self-observation. Sri Aurobindo does not deny the efficiency of these psychological processes in producing detachment. He maintains that the separation of thinking and thinker though a difficult task yet it is possible: as a matter of fact in all cases

---

15.. "Synthesis of Yoga," *CW*, pp. 69-70.

of self-observation we at times carry out this separating quite spontaneously, and this skill can further be developed through practice. Speaking about how this separation can be brought about by someone Sri Aurobindo says: ". . . it is not usually at the time of or in the very act of thinking that he can observe or review his thoughts — he has to do that in retrospect and with the aid of memory or by a critical pause of corrective judgement before he proceeds further . . ."[16] Sri Aurobindo is of the opinion that the processes of self-analysis and self-observation may produce in us a self-knowledge of such a type that may enable us to come out of our confusions that lead to attachment and consequent mental problems. Sri Aurobindo observes that "such analysis and such observation are, like the process of right thought, of immense value and practically indispensable. They may even, if rightly pursued, lead to a right thought of considerable power and effectivity. Like intellectual discrimination by the process of meditative thought they will have an effect of purification, they will lead to self-knowledge of a certain kind and to the setting right of the disorders of the soul and the heart and even of the disorders of the understanding."[17] It will not be inappropriate to note here that for developing detachment modification or purification of mental consciousness is not always adequate: What may further be required is modification in other planes like vital and physical. Sri Aurobindo would perhaps consider psychological management of the vital to be the most difficult task if not impossible. Thus about the vital he says, "it must be dealt with not by the mind but directly by the supramental power."[18] But the Mother has shown some way as to how mind can be used in this sphere also. She maintains that for dealing with the vital "one must gain a full knowledge of one's

16. "The Life Divine," *CW*, p. 526.
17. "Synthesis of Yoga," *CW*, p. 289.
18. "Letters on Yoga," *CW*, vol. 24, p. 1321.

character and then acquire control over one's movements so that one may achieve perfect mastery and transformation of all the elements that have to be transformed."[19]

The above-mentioned stages thereby will enable the individual to develop the required detachment and thus to come out of the grip of identification that caused the psychological distress. What sort of role on the part of the therapist would be approved by Sri Aurobindo's system becomes obvious from the sort of role he assigns to the teachers. Like the teacher the therapist also would not impose anything on the client. Unlike psychoanalysis here the therapist will not give any suggestion or interpretation regarding the validity of the client's experiences or regarding any moral stand. The emphasis would totally be on self-education. The therapist would just be with the client: encouraging his individuality and enhancing his will to come out of his present predicament.

Coming to the question of evaluation of this model I would express a mixed response. As regards the theoretical aspect its comparative strength lies in the fact that it can offer a much cogent view about what constitutes "cure by psychotherapy" than one presented in psychoanalysis. On psychoanalytical view cure consists in developing insight into the contents of the unconscious and making them acceptable to the ego by showing that they are not damaging for the self-image and thus making the super-ego non-reactive to these unconscious impulses. This view of cure presupposes the possibility of altering the reactions of the super-ego by means of reasons. But super-ego being as impulsive as the id is, it cannot be appeased by arguing "why" the unconscious contents should be allowed gratification. So this notion of cure is not quite acceptable. In Sri Aurobindo's model cure consists in getting oneself free from undesirable identification and it does not

19. *Sri Aurobindo and the Mother on Education*, p. 113.

involve either the idea of appeasing any third component like the super-ego or any sort of self-stultifying implication.

But the theoretical deficit that I find in Sri Aurobindo's model centres around the view regarding how a disorder is produced. Sri Aurobindo, as I have already mentioned, does not accept the conflict-model of disease formation but considers identification to be the root cause. I find this idea disquieting because in Sri Aurobindo's view in every mundane experience the consciousness identifies itself to its object, and if identification alone is the cause of psychological distress then none of us are free from it. In fact, from metaphysical standpoint this conclusion would be supported by Sri Aurobindo. The Mother has explicitly mentioned it. But from psychological viewpoint some of us are in a state of ailment and some not. How to explain it? Sri Aurobindo does not admit any third entity like the super-ego and so he can't hold that where there is identification along with a conflict with our moral sense the ailment sets in. Since moreover Sri Aurobindo places morality in the realm of mental and believes that moral sense cannot penetrate beyond the mental he can hardly explain how identification leads to distress. In fact, Sri Aurobindo was aware of this limitation and that may be the reason why he admits something like "adverse forces" which possess the being and make him distressed when the individual gets weaker due to undesirable identifications. My submission is that the admission of the adverse forces is avoidable (since this admission is not desirable in any scientific pursuit) by admitting conflict between the self-image constituted on the basis of experience and self-image unconsciously subscribed.

As regards the strength of this theory in its practical or applied aspect it may be claimed that it can make "emotional acceptance" easier than the Freudian system can. It may be mentioned here that for helping a person to come out of his ailment it is not sufficient to make him rationally understand that the unconscious thoughts are not damaging. One needs to be helped to accept it from the core of his feeling. But that is a very difficult job as evidenced by the cases of psychoanalysis. What is required for accepting something emotionally is not merely a rational insight into what is good or detrimental, but to have some alternative emotion deeply satisfied. This requires detachment from one emotion and conscious identification with some other emotion which can appropriately satisfy the person. The process suggested in Sri Aurobindo's psychology is potent enough to attain this goal in a much easier way compared to psychoanalysis.

The difficult part in Sri Aurobindo's model however consists in "silencing of the mind." Though this process can be viewed (as it is in fact viewed nowadays) as a process of relaxation and thus manuals can be prepared to make the process more user-friendly, it is possible that many clients would find it too difficult a task even to initiate it. The minds of the psychologically distressed persons are often tormented with so many thoughts and anxieties that to ask them to try to stop thinking may seem as absurd a proposal as expecting the sea to stop raising its waves. But this mental state is not very difficult to attain if one practises it when one is in his normal or cool state of mind. So even if as a therapeutic model it has its acceptability in selected cases, as a model for forming positive mental health it is definitely a precise and effective one.

Part VIII
Sri Aurobindo — A Century in Perspective

22

Sri Aurobindo
A Century in Perspective

Aster Patel

A 100 years have elapsed since the National College was founded, with Sri Aurobindo as it first Principal. And the years that followed saw the publication of his major works. Among the many perspectives that command the focus of our attention, there is one that stands out . . . which we wish to share on this occasion.

This perspective has three distinct markings as it unfolds itself:

1. The first of these was the period of time after the publication of the works of Sri Aurobindo. In the 1940s and 1950s, this new firmament — of thought and experience — lit the Indian skies with its brightness and newness. There were deep dialogues among the great philosophers of the time and earnest were their attempts to arrive at an understanding of this work in the light of the Indian tradition. Questions were raised, debated upon and an integration of the two was sought in a line of continuity . . . and of a growing fullness in our seeking for Truth and spiritual realizations. The Indian Philosophical Congress held a symposium in 1950 on the theme: "Has Sri Aurobindo

Refuted Māyāvāda?" . . . and the proceedings were subsequently published.

Sri Aurobindo's work had 'disturbed' the placid flow of the mighty Indian tradition, and great and intense was the effort made to assimilate the fresh findings of the spirit in man in the sweep of our history! Reverence was in the air before something so stupendous — but difficulties were also there to be encountered!

Towards the latter part of this period, as a young student of philosophy, one tried to sense this mighty activity that was taking place in India — in all the seats of learning in the country. There was a great upheaval in terms of both thought and the experience that gave it body.

Since then, the gradual process of its assimilation into the 'consciousness of the people' has taken place and the generation of today shows unmistakable signs of that silent absorption.

2. But today, at the turn of the third millennium, it is another world in which our contemporary consciousness places us. In calling it 'contemporary,' we imbue it with a framework of time and give it a form which has its own distinctive contours of specificity and a pressing need of what Sri Aurobindo offers us.

What are these distinctive contours of our consciousness as contemporary beings — and what is the nature of these pressing needs which seek their fulfilment?

The first phase was one of integration of this experience into the Indian tradition. Now we are in an advancing phase, which is taking rapid strides into the Future. In this perspective, a fresh look by India at the work of Sri Aurobindo is called for — so that she can seize the importance of truths that she may have been only partially alive to earlier and thus move forward with assurance. With the new findings at the frontier areas of scientific research, unprecedented tracks have been blazoned forth and much that was overlooked in the past finds its rightful place and significance only now.

For, Sri Aurobindo is the Future! A strong statement — but as we look at his work today — which had its beginnings about a 100 years ago, there is no other way to speak about it. A Future that recedes so far into unknown horizons, that the word itself escapes all definition and compass of time.

What is it that strikes us the most as we look at the work of Sri Aurobindo in the perspective of our contemporary consciousness? Can we identify some specificities which are singularly his?

3. For Sri Aurobindo . . .

   - The world is intensely real. And all man's effort at knowledge, at growth, at a many-sided self-perfection is significant.
   - The seeking for Bliss, Truth and a sense of secret Immortality is innate in him — and life itself is both the field and process for a progressive realization of this seeking.
   - This progressive realization takes place through the curve of 'evolution' in a wider, universal dimension of existence — which can be accelerated by the practice of a *yoga* aiming at similar results, by an individual effort and a collective seeking.
   - The upward curve of evolution describes the fullness of a cycle in which the descending movement of the 'involution' of the Spirit in Matter,

holding latent in it the powers of life and mind, is implicit.

The movement of evolution makes manifest — by the twin dynamism of forces that is operative therein — these powers, and others, of the conscious Being that pervades all Existence.

- Man is moving towards a point in the fullness of this circle where the descending and ascending movements of involution and evolution are leading to their 'integration' by the emergence of a power and range of Conscious Being, the Supermind, which holds the two ends of Existence as One. The wholeness of Spirit and Matter as a manifested reality — with Matter revealing not only the powers of Life and Mind embedded in its very matrix, but the puissance of Totality, which makes it the '*substance*' of Spirit itself.
- It is this scaling to the height of 'integration' that marks a critical point in the entire cycle of evolution, leading to an unprecedented acceleration of the pace in which all events and movements take place and change their very nature and quality. This anticipates a greater possibility in the offing which throws all else, so far achieved and realized, into a gear where all established moorings are shaken and pulled out . . . and a seeming state of chaos prevails, with an absence of known orders.
- This creates, in the life of man, a crisis of 'being' itself, which beckons to Sri Aurobindo as his field of action . . .

— What is this 'action,' a mighty action?

— What are its tools, its processes and forms?

— How to make this 'action' understood by man? By his reason? And in terms of a concrete experience which he can consciously make?

— By man in his individual self? And as an entity in the collective being of himself?

These are some of the mounting questions before us that scale a peak and to which we must address ourselves if we wish to find points of entry into the total body of the work of Sri Aurobindo. To see the specific areas in terms of a new form of philosophical method and articulation is certainly a possibility. But there are equally others — such as a new form of the practice of *yoga*; an entire structure of the psychology of man; a fuller understanding of his social being and organization; other modes of a political and economic re-shaping; a new pattern of education, following specific processes leading to a goal and result put before us by the process of evolution itself; of creating art and literature and the many forms in which civilizations seek to fulfil themselves . . . and culture grows in its own stature towards a greater perfection.

All this is possible if we wish to break up the Whole into parts! But to see the Whole in its qualitative form and structure is to see far more than when we try to look solely for the 'parts,' in their own specificity.

If we thus turn to the work of Sri Aurobindo, what are the questions foremost in our consciousness as they are thrown up by the present findings at the frontiers areas of scientific research?

We can identify three principal areas which give rise to these questions:

(a) The exploration into the nature of Matter and the functioning of the material universe by sciences, such as physics and biology, have yielded results that have led to a reversal of all previous findings. 'Wholes' are found to be primary — that are organic and dynamic in their energy and functioning — and 'parts' are patterns of interlinking within the structure of the 'Whole,' It is the 'Whole' that gives to the 'parts' their nature and function.

No reversal of knowledge could have been more total or irreversible in its results. The present-day technology and the rapid pace of its growth follows from these truths.

(b) The reductionist method, which had been so successfully pursued by science in the last four centuries, stands at a crossroad in front of the present findings. But in leading to them, the question arises, can it proceed further to seize dynamic and organic 'wholes'? A method structured to break up into 'parts' and to deal with the specificity of 'parts,' can it be made to serve an altogether other function?

There is today an implicit seeking for a new possibility of method, for another framework of epistemology which can relate to the existence of 'wholes' and their qualitative functioning.

This question is of the utmost importance for our times and marks a turn, of a radical kind, in our very quest for knowledge and the possibility of another cycle of evolution of man.

(c) A sense of 'transformation' of man sweeps the earth, and the very air vibrates with it. 'Transformative practices' of all shades and hues abound! Practices that peer closely into 'cellular structures' of life and question 'death' itself. Is 'immortality' ingrained in the fundamental structures of life? The questions of our times are vertiginous in their mounting scale — and work on the ground proceeds apace.

> Is 'matter' itself — of which all is made — undergoing a change of its density, its porosity? Is it re-covering some essential truth of itself? Is it becoming 'self-conscious?' Conscious of itself as 'substance' of Being?

These are the questions of our times at the frontier areas of our lives. This is the stuff of which our contemporary consciousness is made, and such is the matrix of our being. It is thus that we seek to look afresh at the work of Sri Aurobindo.

We wish to offer two points in conclusion:

1. The question of method is of the utmost importance. A new epistemological framework is in the air — one which seeks its answers in the work of Sri Aurobindo and through it in the Indian tradition as a whole. This quest relates itself directly to the body of work known as:
    - Integral Psychology.
    - Integral Education.
    - Integral Yoga.
2. India, excelling as she does, in scientific research and taking hold once again of matter, and life-in-matter, needs a new body of experience, its formulation in thought-forms, and a way of practice, to serve as its solid foundation and provide the needed philosophical structure — complete with metaphysics, epistemology, logic, psychology and *yoga* — on which to take her firm stand as she proceeds with this work. If her scientific work has to yield results different from those that arise from other premises and foundations of knowledge and method, she must discover her roots — those on which she can build with assurance and which can lead to fresh creativity.

> Sri Aurobindo offers to India such a basis. Not only to India but to a world looking beyond its persent frontiers in these fields — to fields yet unknown and existing only on a distant horizon.

Sri Aurobindo came here to found the National College — for an India young, free and new. India is young, with 75 per cent of her population below 35 years of age, she is free, and can lead to a new future — for herself and for the world.

It is given perhaps to Jadavpur University to take the lead, as it was a century ago.

Appendix

We take the liberty to suggest a few lines of research and exploration which could be undertaken —

1. A great epistemological truth is contained in Sri Aurobindo's words: "Our ways of knowing must be appropriate to that which is to be known." In the context of the contemporary situation regarding questions of 'method,' it could be extremely valuable to work out the implications of this statement — as in an 'ascending' framework of methodology.
2. It is in this line of possibility that Sri Aurobindo presents 'the Logic of the Infinite.' In the light of this, it will be fruitful to draw out the implications of present-day explorations in the field of logic.
3. A nascent trend in other parts of the world is termed 'Applied Philosophy.' How is this to be seen in the lineage of the Indian tradition of philosophy as *darśana* and *yoga*?
4. In our times, the 'Integral Yoga' is a new creation of practice by Sri Aurobindo and The Mother — which has now a cumulative experience, in terms of both the individual and collective dimensions, of a 100 years.

In many parts of the world, there is a growing attraction to its pursuit — as way of practice, with the processes that it holds, and the sense of the goal that it sets before us — the 'transformation of Matter' leading to the possibility of a 'life divine on earth' for mankind.

In this context, it would be of great value to look at the 'Integral Yoga' in the perspective of all the *yoga*s that have a millennial history in India's tradition.

5. What have come to be known as 'transformative practices,' abound in the world today. These take a great diversity of forms and processes — from meditation to psychological practices and therapies, attitudinal changes, nutrition, physical exercises, varying ecological lifestyles — the list is long. A study of them in the light of 'Integral Yoga' would lead to clarity regarding the goal being pursued and the path leading to it.

6. 'Matter' and the deeper unravelling of its secrets is the preoccupation of our times. The scientist continues his exploration by the reductionist method — and Sri Aurobindo and The Mother do so by the method of a 'conscious identity' with it — in its 'inner' composition and outer form. At this moment, nothing is as fascinating for us as to see how these two approaches converge to a piercing of the wall between the 'objective' and the 'subjective' till the two cease to exist in their separate boundaries. An 'expanse' of whatever there is . . . extends before us and in us. Such a possibility of integration marks our times and calls for a sustained study.

7. The importance of the human body as a 'vehicle of change'— as a means for 'effecting' the transformation of Matter, which Nature in her further evolution offers

us — is brought home to us along many paths of research and varied life-patterns.

The body itself works out the 'will' in Nature to become more and more conscious — and to be re-made in a 'substance' that is conscious of itself, of a matter that has recovered its secret sense of the spirit.

Between the work done on the body by Sri Aurobindo and The Mother and that which has been done in the past in India — and the attempts being made in the world all over — there is need to put many things together and arrive at a fuller perspective of possibilities that lie ahead.

8. Do the cellular structures in the body themselves contain the secret of these far-reaching achievements? Is 'transformation of Matter' built into the very function of these cells?

There is work being done in these areas today — and the two approaches as represented by the work of the scientist and by Sri Aurobindo and The Mother need to be seen as being necessary to one another for a greater completeness. Shall we say that because the latter has been pursued in terms of consciousness that the former has become possible!

We are reminded of the last testimony of the physicist, Dr D.S. Kothari, that "Matter cannot be known unless we know Consciousness."

This line of exploration is the edge we tread on. And India has much to say on this subject given all her past experience and present on-going one. This is her time to say it!

The Contributors

Arabinda Basu is Editor, *Gaveṣaṇa, Review of Philosophy and Yoga*, Sri Aurobindo International Centre of Education. He was earlier Professor with Banaras Hindu University. He served as a Lecturer in Indian Philosophy and Religion, University of Durham, England. He had been a Visiting Professor/Lecturer at the Universities in Jerusalem (Israel); Dubuque (Iowa, USA); Celigny (Switzerland); Claremont Colleges CA (USA); and the Punjabi University Patiala (Punjab). His publications include *Chariot of Jagannatha* (English translation of Sri Aurobindo's Bengali book); *A Preface to the Study of Bhāgavata Purāṇa*; *Brahman and Ishwara in the Philosophies of Shankara and Sri Aurobindo*, besides various articles have been published in India and abroad. Arabinda Basu has been the Editor of various English and Bengali books. He has been on the Editorial Board of Sri Aurobindo, a Centenary Tribute, set up by the Government of India. He is also connected with the Institute of Philosophic and Humanistic Studies, Paris (supported by UNESCO) [**address:** Sri Aurobindo Asharm, Pondicherry – 605 002].

Aster Patel has been teaching for the last several years at the Sri Aurobindo International Centre of Education. For over three decades, she has been attached to the Bharat Nivas, Auroville, at the Centre of Indian Studies setting up research programmes and organising conferences. She is presently a member of the Governing Board of the Auroville Foundation. Since early childhood, she lived in the Sri Aurobindo Ashram, Pondicherry and studied at the Sri Aurobindo International Centre of Education till the "Higher Courses" in Philosophy and Internal Psychology. She later studied at the

University of Paris (Sarboune) and received a Ph.D in Comparative Philosophy. She also held the Sri Aurobindo Chair of Philosophy at the Banaras Hindu University. Meera Patel has participated in several conferences and has lectured within India and in the USA, and at the UNESCO, in Paris and at the United Nations in New York. Her articles have been published in various publications and a recent one is a collection under the title: "The Presence of Time." She has been awarded the Sri Aurobindo Puraskar for 2005 [**address**: Bharat Nivas, Auroville – 605 101, Tamil Nadu, **e-mail**: <asterpatel@auroville.org.in>].

Dasharathi Sengupta, formerly Asst. Professor of Political Science in West Bengal Education Service, taught in a number of Goverment Colleges including Presidency College, Kolkata. Two books *Focus India* (vol. 2) and *Theme India* have been published under his editorship. He has written several articles on the divisive ingredients of Indian politics. His main field of interest, however, happens to be Political Thought both Western and Indian [**address**: 240, Khagrajole Road, Chinsurah, Hooghly – 712 101, West Bengal, **e-mail**: <dasharathi.sengupta@gmail.com>].

Dilip Kumar Roy (b. 1939–) was in West Bengal Educational Service and taught Philosophy in Presidency College, Kolkata, for a long period. His noteworthy publications include *The Philosophy of George Santayana, The Comparative Study of Religions, The Dynamic Absolute — A Preface of Sri Aurobindo's Integral Advaita and Upaniṣad Prasange Sri Aurobindo*. He is at present the Secretary of Sri Aurobindo Institute of Education, Salt Lake, Kolkata [**address**: "Banabithi," KB 6, Flat-2, Sector III, Salt Lake City, Kolkata – 700 098, **e-mail**: <diluroy@yahoo.com>].

Goutam Ghosal is Professor of English, Viśva-Bhāratī, Santiniketan, India. He is a leading interpreter of Sri Aurobindo's philosophy and Literature. Ghosal is at present Editor-in-Chief of the *Viśva-Bhāratī Quarterly*. His major books include *Sri Aurobindo and World Literature;*

Sri Aurobindo's Prose Style; and *Notes on the Mother's Prayers and Meditations* [**address**: 7 Sevapalli, Santiniketan - 731 235, Distt. Birbhum, West Bengal, **e-mail**: goutamji@sancharnet.in].

INDRANI SANYAL is Professor at the Department of Philosophy, Centre of Advanced Study in Philosophy, Jadavpur University, Kolkata. Prof. Sanyal is also the Director, Centre for Sri Aurobindo Studies, Department of Philosophy, Jadavpur University. She is an Alumni of Jadavpur University who did her both M.A. and PhD from this University. Her areas of specialisation include Ethics, especially Indian Ethics and its application to various issues of life, Philosophy of Logic and Language, Metaphysics, both Western and Indian and Philosophy of Sri Aurobindo. Under the Indo-French Exchange Programme in Humanities and Social Sciences, she visited universities and research institutes in Paris. Her publications include *On Essentialist Claims,* Allied Publishers Private Ltd., New Delhi in collaboration with Jadavpur University, Kolkata (2002), *Wittgenstein: Jagat, Bhasa O Cintan,* (co-editor), Allied Publishers Private Ltd. and Jadavpur University, Kolkata, (2000). She has published many articles in various anthologies and journals of repute. [**address**: Chirag, 2nd Floor, 56/4, Ballygunge, Circular Road, Kolkata - 700 019, **e-mail:** <csas-ju@yahoo.com>].

KH. GOKULCHANDRA SINGH, M.A., PhD, teaches Philosophy at D.M. College of Arts, Manipur University, Imphal. His publication include a book titled, *A.J. Ayer's Theory of Perceptual Knowledge.* Some of his articles have been published in different journals and anthologies. He has served as General Secretary of Manipuri Sahitya Parishad. He was the Joint Editor *Sahitya*, published by the Parishad, and also of *Sahitya Leichal*, published by Manipuri Literary Society. He is Member of Editorial Board of various literary anthologies. He has also been a Joint Secretary of the Publication Committee, *Reflections*, a philosophical journal published by Philosophy Department of the Manipur University [**address**: Khurai Soibam Leikai, Imphal East – 795 001, Manipur, **e-mail**: <khgsingh@yahoo.com>].

Kireet Joshi (b.1931–) has studied Philosophy and Law at the University of Bombay. He was selected for the I.A.S. in 1955 but resigned immediately the next year in order to devote himself at Pondicherry to the study and practice of the integral *yoga* of Sri Aurobindo and The Mother. He taught Philosophy and Psychology at the Sri Aurobindo International Centre of Education at Pondicherry and participated in numerous educational experiments under the direct guidance of The Mother. In 1976, the Goverment of India invited him to be Educational Adviser in the Union Ministry of Education. In 1983, he was appointed Special Secretary to the Government of India, and he held this post until 1988. He was Founder-Member Secretary of Indian Council of Philosophical Research and of the Rashtriya Veda Vidya Pratisthan. He was Vice-Chairman of the UNESCO Institute of Education, Hamburg from 1988 to 1990. He was Chairman of Indian Council of Philosophical Research from 2000 to 2006 and also Chairman of Auroville Foundation from 1999 to 2005. He was Vice-Chairman of the Rashtriya Veda Vidya Pratisthan from 1999 to 2005. His published works include *Sri Aurobindo and The Mother; Integral Yoga and Sri Aurobindo; Education for Character Development; A National Agenda for Education; Education for Tomorrow;* and *An Education at Cross-roads.* He has also edited a number of books including *The Aim of Life; The Good Teacher and the Pupil; The Mystery and Excellence of the Human Body;* and *The Philosophy of Supermind* [**address:** 192, Sukhdev Vihar, New Delhi – 110 025, **e-mail**: <mothersinstitute@hotmail.com>].

Kittu Reddy, born in the Anantapur district of Andhra Pradesh in 1936, is the nephew of Late Sanjiva Reddy, the former President of India. He had all his education at the Sri Aurobindo International Centre of Education from where he graduated in 1957. In 1958, he started teaching at the same Centre, his subjects being: Indian Culture, Political and Social Science, besides History. In 1987, he came in contact with the Indian Army and has been working closely with them on Motivation and Leadership. In 1994, at the request of

General B.C. Joshi who was then the Chief of Army Staff appointed him as Adviser to the Army Welfare Education Society. He has written a book for the Army entitled *Bravest of the Brave* and two monographs *Kargil — The Manifestation of a Deeper Problem* and *Secularism, Religion and Spirituality*. He has also written two other books titled *History of India — A New Approach* and *A Vision of United India — Problems and Solutions* [**address**: Sri Aurobindo International Centre of Education, Pondicherry - 605 002].

KRISHNA ROY has recently retired from the Department of Philosophy, Jadavpur University, Kolkata. Her areas of interest include Phenomenology, Existentialism, Hermeneutics, Social and Political Philosophy, etc. Her several articles have been published on subjects like Hermeneutics: East and West (Allied Publishers, 1993). She has edited a book *Fusion of Horizons: Socio-Spiritual Heritage of India* (Allied Publishers, 2000). She has also co-edited three anthologies: *Language, Knowledge and Ontology* (ICPR, 1988); *Essays in Social and Political Philosophy* (Allied/ICPR, 1989); and *Theory and Practice* (Allied Publishers, 2003). She had been earlier a member of Indian Council of Philosophical Research, New Delhi [**address**: 18 Jatin Bagchi Road, Kolkata - 700 029].

PABITRAKUMAR ROY, presently Fellow of Indian Institute of Advanced Study, Shimla, was till recently Senior Fellow of Indian Council of Philosophical Research, New Delhi. Roy taught Philosophy for over three decades at Visva-Bharati, Santiniketan and the University of North Bengal. He had been Visiting Faculty at various Indian Universities and British Council Scholar at King's College Cambridge and University of Reading. Roy has authored scores of papers and some of his works are *David Hume; Rabindranath Tagore; Hume and Kant: A Study in Linkages, Man and Technology*. The areas of his interest lie in Moral Psychology and Aesthetics [**address**: Fellow, Indian Institute of Advanced Study, Rashtrapati Nivas, Summerhill, Shimla - 171 005].

PRIYA M. VAIDYA has done Doctorate in Philosophy from the University of Mumbai on the theme "Philosophy of Education According to Swami Vivekananda and Sri Aurobindo" under the guidance of Prof. Dr Shubhada Joshi, Dept. of Philosophy, University of Mumbai. Currently she is Senior Lecturer at Guru Nanak College of Arts, Science and Commerce, Mumbai, besides being a Visiting Faculty at the Dept. of Philosophy, University of Mumbai [**address:** 8/113, Sardar Nagar no. 4, Sion Koliwada, Mumbai – 400 037, **e-mail**: <preeya26@yahoo.com>].

RASHMI SETHI, presently taking B. Ed. classes for the last 10 years at the Department of Education (C.I.E), University of Delhi, did her M.Sc. (Endocrinology), B.Ed, M.Ed. and Ph.D, all from Delhi University and secured First Division throughout with distinctions in B.Ed and M.Ed. She completed her Ph.D thesis entitled "A Study of the Facets of Integral Philosophy of Sri Aurobindo and their Educational Ramification." She was awarded the All-round Best Student Prize in Masters in Education, besides Junior and Senior Research Fellowships in Education and the Short-term Fellowship from ICPR. She presented papers at Hemvati Nandan Bahuguna University, Garhwal and with the Dept. of Philosophy, Jadavpur University, Kolkata. She contributed an article in the NCTE-UNESCO project on Peace Education [**address**: D-887, New Friends Colony, New Delhi – 110 065].

SARNATH BASU is a retired Professor of Philosophy from Burdwan University. He had been teaching at the Jogamaya Devi College, Kolkata and also at the University of North Bengal. The Nyāya-Vaiśeṣika, Advaita Vedānta and Philosophy of Sri Aurobindo are his special areas of study. He was a Sectional President of the 62nd session of the Indian Philosophical Congress held at the University of Kashmir in 1987. He had delivered Maharshi Devendranath Thakur Memorial Lecture at Visva-Bharati, Santiniketan in 2004 [**address:** 123, D.D. Tewari Road, Kotalhat, Burdwan – 713 102, West Bengal].

Soumitra Basu is a Reader in the Department of Philosophy, Jadavpur University. His areas of specialization include Philosophy of Psychology, Philosophy of Language, Contemporary Indian Philosophy and Applied Philosophy. He is a trained Psychological Counsellor and has a wide experience in this field. Along with several research projects in Philosophy, he is associated with research projects of the Cognitive Science Programme of Jadavpur University. A number of articles of Dr Basu have been published. This includes, among others, the "Alienation, Exploitation and Beyond: An Exposition of the Views of Vivekananda," "On Redundancy of Ethical Theories," and "Scientific Psychology and Betterment of Society" [**address**: Department of Philosophy, Jadavpur University, Kolkata – 700 032].

Supriyo Bhattacharya has been on the teaching faculty of the Department of Economics, University of Kalyani, since 1984. First class M.A. in Economics from Calcutta University, he worked as Assistant Secretary in the Bengal National Chamber of Commerce and Industries, Kolkata. He is engaged in research on Sri Aurobindo and has been connected with Research work that is being done at Kolkata Sri Aurobindo Bhavan and at Pondicherry. Prof. Bhattacharya has been editing for 12 years *Srinvantu* (a monthy Bengali journal and a biannual English journal). He received in 2006 "Sri Aurobindo Puroskar" (Sri Aurobindo Award) from the Governor of West Bengal. [**address:** Praity, HB Town, 1st Road, (Opposite Mother Dairy), 3rd Floor, P.O. Sodepur, North 24 Parganas, Kolkata – 700 110, West Bengal].

Susmita Bhattacharya is an Assistant Teacher in Philosophy at the Patha-Bhavan School, Kolkata. She worked as a Research Fellow in the Asiatic Society on the topics of Existential Philosophy and Sri Aurobindo's Philosophy from 2001 to 2005. She has got published a few research papers in different journals. Ms. Bhattacharya served as a Guest Lecturer in Bethune College, Surendranath College, East Calcutta Girls College, Kolkata and Hooghly Mohsin College,

Hooghly. [**address:** Praity, HB Town, 1st Road, (Opposite Mother Dairy,) 2nd Floor, P.O. Sodepur, North 24 Parganas, Kolkata – 700 110, West Bengal].

SUSHMITA BHOWMIK passed M.A. in the year 2003 from Jadavpur University. She is Lecturer in Philosophy, Budge Budge College, Kolkata, since August 2006. She is also doing research under Jadavpur University on "Regeneration of Values: A Comparison Between Mahatma Gandhi and Sri Aurobindo" [**address**: 23A/4 R.K. Sarani, Vivekananda Palli, Behala, Kolkata – 700 060].

U.C.DUBEY, currently Professor, is teaching in the Department of Philosophy and Religion, Banaras Hindu University, since 1977. Prof. Dubey is also former Head of the Department and Coordinator of UGC-DSA Programme and UGC- Infrastructure Strengthening Programme in Humanities and Social Sciences in the Department of Philosophy and Religion, Banaras Hindu University, Varanasi. He is the recipient of Swami Pranavanand Darshan Award (1993) presented by the Akhil Bharatiya Darshan Parishad for his book *Sri Aurobindo's Philosophy of Culture* (in Hindi) [**address:** N-1/30, A-3-4, Nagwa, Lanka, Varanasi – 221 005, Uttar Pradesh, **e-mail**: <ucd_1@rediffmail.com>].

VIRAPASAMUDRA NARASINGA RAO SHESHAGIRI obtained his Master's Degree in Philosophy (1974) and Ph.D (1981) from the University of Mysore. He worked for his Ph.D on the Philosophy of Vācaspati Mishra, which has been published (1984). He is specialized in Comparative Philosophy and has contributed a good number of Research articles published in many journals. He wields his pen, with equal felicity, both in English and Kannada. He is on the staff of Philosophy Department of Mysore University since 1974. His publications include: *Vācaspati's Contribution to Advaita* (1984); *Samakaleena Bhārateeya Tattva Shastra* (published by Mysore University, 1985); *Western Philosophical Thought* (*Pāschatya Tāttvika Chintane,* published by Mysore University, 1985); and *Sārvapalli*

Radhakrishnan — Baduku Baraha Mattu Tattva Jñāna (published by Karnataka Government, 1992). He has successfully guided over a dozen candidates for their Ph.D. At present, Prof. Rao is the Head of the Department of Philosophy, Mysore University [**address**: LIG 112, "Bhāmati", II Cross, Gangotri HUDCO Layout, Saraswatipuram, Mysore – 570 009, **e-mail**: <rao.sheshagiri@rediffmail.com>].

Vladimir Yatsenko is a Sanskrit teacher in Auroville since 1993, working at Savitri Bhavan. He graduated in Sanskrit and General Linguistics from St. Petersburg University in Russia and studied Sanskrit Grammar in Poona University during 1991-92. He is a life-member of Bhandarkar Oriental Reasearch Institute in Poona. For the last three years he is doing research on "Vedic Imagery in Sri Aurobindo's Savitri" [**address**: Prarthana, Auroville – 605 101, Tamil Nadu, **e-mail**: <vlad@auroville.org.in>].

Index